Peripheral Visions

Images of Nationhood in Contemporary British Fiction

edited by

IAN A. BELL

UNIVERSITY OF WALES PRESS

CARDIFF

1995

Learning Resources
Centre

© The Contributors, 1995

British Library Cataloguing-in-Publication Data

A catalogue record for this book is available from the British Library.

ISBN 0-7083-1260-8

Cover design by John Garland, Pentan Partnership, Cardiff
Typeset at the University of Wales Press
Printed in Great Britain by Bookcraft, Midsomer Norton, Avon

9.7.96

Contents

Contents

The Contributors

Ian A. Bell is Professor of English at the University of Wales, Swansea.

Tony Bianchi is Literature Director at the Arts Council of Wales.

A. L. Kennedy is a novelist and short-story writer, resident in Glasgow.

Alan M. Kent is a novelist, based in Cornwall.

Stephen Knight is Professor of English at the University of Wales, Cardiff.

Dorothy McMillan is a Lecturer in English at the University of Glasgow.

Eve Patten, formerly of Queen's University in Belfast, now works for the British Council in Bucharest.

Glenn Patterson is a novelist, currently based in Belfast.

Wiliam Owen Roberts is a Welsh-language novelist and writer, based in Cardiff.

Penny Smith is a Lecturer in the School of Critical and Historical Studies in the University of Northumbria at Newcastle.

Ella Westland works in the Department of Continuing and Adult Education at the University of Exeter.

Margaret Wilkinson is a writer, now living in Newcastle.

Ken Worpole has been involved in teaching, under the auspices of the Workers' Educational Association, for many years. He has also been active in the Federation of Worker Writers, and in the Comedia Publishing House project.

George Wotton teaches literature in the School of Humanities and Education at the University of Hertfordshire.

1

Introduction:
the politics of place and writing

IAN A. BELL

Groups of nations put together artificially will not have sufficient identity to stay together, and they will collapse.
(Margaret Thatcher, 16 November 1991)

Like all cultural activity worthy of serious attention, contemporary British writing addresses and mediates questions of race, class and gender, the most complex and urgent questions of personal identity and citizenship. The printed page in all its many manifestations is still a reasonably accessible forum in which the vital consideration of who 'we' are can be reassessed, problematized and perhaps even transformed. Through the traditionally venerated forms of fiction, poetry and drama, writers may consolidate or contest the restricted range of images available to them, offering heightened and stylized versions of themselves and ourselves which we may unconsciously internalize or actively resist. In much recent writing, the ideological fabrication of 'Britishness' – that prime cultural site in which race, class and gender can sometimes be made to coalesce – has been subjected to repeated examinations, exposing the inherent cracks and fissures within it, bringing into greater prominence voices and issues kept silent or subservient for so long in the authorized version of a 'united kingdom'.

But while there is evidence that such an examination can be carried out with success, it must be remembered that the possibilities of writing confidently from within a particular non-metropolitan identity in the UK are not available with equal ease in all kinds of writing. In poetry, the heroic persistence of small-scale local publishing and the co-existence of strong independent regional traditions has allowed for multivocality and a proper attention to the heteroglot

1

constituents of the 'Yookay', be they the distinctive sonorities of British West Indian writers or the dialect voices of Tony Harrison's 'Loiners' or even the Gaelic verse of Sorley MacLean. In the theatre, too, the hegemonic centrality of London and an authorized version of 'Englishness' has been contested in a number of alternative practices and venues, with localized indigenous forms of performance still persisting elsewhere. Denotatively, the National Theatre may be the name of a particular (and carbuncular) building in London, but its connotative meaning would have to include not only more explicitly regional theatre companies like 7:84 or Brith Gof but also a range of informal performance practices ranging from eisteddfodau in Wales to working-men's clubs in the north of England, all of which are addressed to local and recognizable audiences and deal with specifically non-metropolitan issues.

Seen alongside these small-scale and self-consciously provincial enterprises, the more discursive and metropolitan form of the novel at once offers the largest and most challenging tapestry on which to represent (or re-present) the national community. By means of its extensive testimony to lived experience, the novel seems to offer the possibility of exploring local communities and marginalized identities in the most elaborate ways. However, that expressive freedom does not come cheaply, and any writer seeking to exploit it has to engage in dialogue with the received images made available to him or her through previous writing and through other forms of cultural production. Furthermore, by its very metropolitanism, and as a result of the material circumstances of publishing and the cosmopolitan nature of the audience, the British novel inevitably conglomerates around London, and its exploration of the remainder of Britain in the post-war period has been at best patchy and 'touristy', conducted almost entirely through the official vernacular of Standard English. No matter how strongly novelists feel their sense of dissidence from the authorized version of our culture and no matter how deeply run their local affiliations, the novel – by its very form – often implicitly reproduces the hegemonic gaze.

Maybe that last statement looks too pessimistic. After all, from the middle of the nineteenth century onwards, the novel has sought to offer us scenes from provincial life, with greater or lesser success, although almost invariably from and for the metropolitan perspective. And more recently there was a well-publicized brief period in the late 1950s and early 1960s when a seemingly concerted group of authors (Alan Sillitoe, John Braine, David Storey, Keith Waterhouse, Barry Hines, Stan Barstow) brought the specific structure of feeling of male working-class north of England writers of the time into prominence. Each of these novelists was writing from within a strong sense of local identity, but (and this point is vital) they were all inevitably writing to a metropolitan audience, satisfying that London-based audience's appetite for the full sordid details of life 'up North'. Instead of introducing and consolidating a challenging alternative voice, these novelists were unwittingly absorbed into the greater national consciousness, becoming a tokenist presence rather than a fully realized identity. The prevailing image of nationhood, paradoxically, was consolidated by the incorporation of these alternative voices, which then became the authorized way of imagining 'the North', impeding any attempts to write of the experience differently.

That brief period is now over, and no such concerted efforts can be readily seen in contemporary England. Today, such an assertive and confident decentralization of the novel seems to be found exclusively in Scotland, in the work of writers like James Kelman, Agnes Owens, Jeff Torrington, Irvine Welsh, A. L. Kennedy and Janice Galloway – the days when Glasgow could be thought of as under-imagined, as Alasdair Gray argued in *Lanark*, are now surely long gone. These writers seem to be actively contesting the status of London as the 'core' of British culture, and the corresponding sense that Scotland is part of the 'periphery', demanding the right to record the lives of Scottish figures in forms appropriate to these lives, explicitly contesting the patronizing and belittling assumptions lying behind much more conventional fiction. This is a brave and laudable project, also visible in a smaller way in Wales, Northern Ireland and various English regions, but perhaps it needs to be remembered in this particular case that from a different point of view such writers are simply relocating that 'core' in the central belt of urban Scotland, consigning other Scottish voices once again to the 'periphery', and, as Dorothy McMillan's article suggests, the question of audience remains deeply problematic.

Scotland is certainly the most public case of recent novelistic agitation, and there are only a few signs of it elsewhere. Or, at least, that is how it *seems* – there are other voices to be heard, if you listen closely enough, whispering their resistance in various parts of the British Isles. Despite the increasingly authoritarian and centralized control over cultural expression being exercised in the 1990s, British fiction is still in its own stealthy way actively making and remaking the UK, constructing and deconstructing the national characters. For one thing, the emergence of community publishing, women's groups and writing associations has led to a steady growth of self-consciously local and parochial literature, largely ignored by the 'national' press. These developments deserve further investigation, but they are not the only sign of local and provincial activism.

In both the literary and the popular novel, the questions of nationhood and the national character(s) remain at the forefront of discussion, deserving to be analysed in some detail, and the attempts to mount challenges to more privileged accounts of British life need to be brought into greater prominence. The aim of this collection of essays and statements is to investigate the ways in which contemporary writing disseminates a consciousness of local and national identity, and reveal the ways in which writers somehow manage to negotiate a space for their locality amidst the interference of the authorized versions of life in the so-called periphery. In terms of the multivocality of contemporary British writing, there are important questions to be asked. Is British fiction still trapped in the South-East of England, recognizing other patterns of life only as less important provincial activities? What price do writers have to pay for their desire or need to explore other structures of feeling? Given that so much privileged British writing seeks to stereotype its minority figures in infuriating and even humiliating ways, how can 'local' writers – especially novelists – combat such marginalization, and how can they reinvigorate their own sense of self?

The chosen procedure of this book is to create a space for collaboration between commentators and practitioners, mutual interest groups so often needlessly rendered adversarial. After two essays surveying the ways in which the nation has been anatomized in travel writing and crime fiction, each of the main geographically orientated sections involves an extensive commentary by an academic or critic, articulating connections and drawing more speculative conclusions, followed by a testimony from a writer describing what is involved in trying to renegotiate some sense of local allegiance in fiction. The essays and statements deal with the issues arising from trying to write as a Welsh novelist (Tony Bianchi and Wil Owen Roberts), a Scottish novelist (Dorothy McMillan and A. L. Kennedy), a Cornish novelist (Ella Westland and Alan Kent), or as a novelist from the North-East of England (Penny Smith and Margaret Wilkinson) or from Northern Ireland (Eve Patten and Glenn Patterson). In each case, the 'place' is attended by the sepulchral presence of its prior imaginings, and each writer has to choose whether to collaborate with this unwanted inheritance or to contest it.

After the geographical surveys, we return to London, with Ken Worpole's account of the recent alternative and underground ways of imagining the metropolis, and the book concludes with a speculative essay by George Wotton, describing the ways in which novels create their own internal communities, mediating the communities outside their pages. The overall aim of the collection, then, is to see how successfully the novel can be exploited by marginalized and overlooked British voices. When I started out, I was very pessimistic – I thought the publishing industry was so tightly controlled and so firmly wedded to a stifling set of assumptions about Britishness that there was very little room for alternatives. But as I have been working on this project, I have found more and more evidence that articulate resistance is possible and that the novel can be used to consolidate identities as well as to fabricate them. It is not easy to mount such a challenge to the powerful hegemony of the press, but it seems possible, and so this book is dedicated to all those writers who are engaged in that struggle, in Britain and beyond.

2

To see ourselves: travel narratives and national identity in contemporary Britain

IAN A. BELL

Travellers taxonomized

> Thus the whole circle of travellers may be reduced to the following *Heads*.
>
> > Idle Travellers,
> > Inquisitive Travellers,
> > Lying Travellers,
> > Proud Travellers,
> > Vain Travellers,
> > Splenetic Travellers.
>
> Then following the Travellers of Necessity.
>
> The delinquent and felonious Traveller,
> The unfortunate and innocent Traveller,
> The simple Traveller,
> and last of all (if you please) The Sentimental Traveller (meaning thereby myself) . . . [1]

Laurence Sterne's taxonomy of travellers, from *A Sentimental Journey through France and Italy* (1768), may now seem pleasantly antique, but at its self-consciously generous heart lies the perception that travel and travel writing have always been as much processes of selective interpretation and construction as they have been vehicles of innocent observation. Written under the guise of his sentimental *alter ego* 'Mr Yorick', Sterne's travelogue explicitly contested the acerbic and xenophobic account of a journey through the same countries five years earlier written by the splenetic valetudinarian Tobias Smollett –

caricatured in the later text as the vile 'Smelfungus' – offering the alternative possibility that the world might look altogether more stimulating to a benevolent and receptive sensibility. While each writer claimed the authority of bearing witness and personal testimony for his observations, their contending accounts were none the less imprinted with the marks of spleen or sentiment respectively. In short, even in 1768 Sterne recognized that what the travel writer sees and reports depends almost entirely on what he or she was looking for in the first place. Whereas Smollett's revelation of the unspeakable behaviour of foreigners sought to be the final word on the matter, Sterne introduced the notion of pluralism. He takes it for granted that the world will offer different sensations to different kinds of traveller – the reports of a 'Vain Traveller', for example, will inevitably differ from those of an 'Inquisitive Traveller' – and so the many accounts of travel published around this time can properly be seen as oblique (if unconscious) exercises in autobiography, direct or indirect projections of the self. As Sterne saw it, the discourse of travel writing did not enshrine a contest for truth-telling authority, but displayed instead a procession of differing views, each of which represented and articulated the dominant psychological perspective of the particular observer.

For more astute readers of such literature, the outward-going movement of the travel narrative should always be supported by an inward-looking enquiry, seeking to discover the more or less hidden agenda of the narrator. We may well ask: 'Who are these people who eat strange food, smell odd, and have such curious habits?' But we must also ask: 'And what kind of traveller is telling us about them?' In accounts of the behaviour of foreigners, the first question takes precedence. With greater or lesser authority, the travel writer is relaying news of unknown places, describing unknown peoples, reliant on the informative serendipity of unplanned meetings and episodes. The reader, in normal circumstances, has no immediate reason to doubt the reliability of the narrator, who is seen as a person much like him or herself, only distinguished by being more observant and articulate. However, the question of the nature of the traveller can never entirely be dismissed, and, as we shall see, there are particular circumstances in which it may well come to dominate.

Of course, there are different ways of answering that question. Sterne's account of the traveller's perspective is characteristically psychopathological in orientation – Smollett/Smelfungus writes as he does, and Sterne/Yorick writes as he does, because of their respective medical conditions, temperaments, and overall psychological dis-positions. Interestingly, Sterne does not see the differences between himself and Smollett as racial or national – the fact that one traveller is Irish and one Scottish does not gain prominence in either narrative.

Underlying Sterne's perception, we can see a covert essentialism, which at times begins to diminish the distance between observer and observed. The sentimental traveller is so eager to discover fellow-feeling in his subjects that he almost entirely surrenders the anthropological imperatives of Smollett and other more orthodox inquisitive travellers, replacing any indicators of cultural difference with swelling threnodies to the pleasures of shared human experience. Although the book may start, as some argue, with an expression of interest in the Continental habit of drinking toasts during and after meals – 'They order, said I, this matter better in France' – that concern with behavioural difference soon disappears. Once embarked, Yorick is considerably more concerned with the universal matters of the heart than with the cultural specificity of table manners.

In these cases, the travel writer was bringing back reports from afar, inviting the reader to compare habits and behaviours on both sides of what was even then called the 'English' Channel. Rather different priorities emerge when the traveller is on more familiar ground, replacing an account of the grand tour with more homely fare. As well as itemizing the peculiarities of foreigners, the travel writer may investigate the grand narrative of a more local culture, describing the habits of the nation of which the reader is assumed to be a citizen. Just as well-off young men were being conducted around Europe to further their education, other eighteenth-century travellers left the metropolis of London to explore the recently constituted nation of Great Britain, and as they did so, the presence of pressing ideological imperatives behind their writing became increasingly obvious.

The earliest schematic narrative accounts of Britain came from the Tudor topographers, intrepid figures like John Leland and William Camden, whose attempts to describe the farthest reaches of the kingdom are replete with antiquarian interests and asides about local customs. After the Act of Union in 1707, travellers were able to articulate greater concern with the underlying unity of the newly formed nation, and were eager to discover some sense of continuity throughout its regions. Many of those travellers were foreigners, writing for their home readership, whose descriptions were subsequently published in Britain for their curiosity value, like J. W. von Archenholz's *A Picture of England* (1789). However, a more interesting group comprised peripatetic British writers, offering accounts of Great Britain designed for an audience of fellow Britons. The most prominent among these early internal tourists was Daniel Defoe, whose *Tour Through the Whole Island of Great Britain* appeared in 1724. In the taxonomy of travellers, Defoe is clearly inquisitive (and no doubt acquisitive), but he is constantly at pains to avoid whimsy, and very earnest in his desire to demystify the landscape:

8

I shall sing you no songs here of the river in the first person of a water-nymph, a goddess, (and I know not what) according to the honour of the ancient poets. I shall talk nothing of the marriage of old Isis, the male river, with the beautiful Thame, the female river, a whimsy as simple as the subject was empty, but I shall speak of the river as occasion presents, as it really is made glorious by the splendour of its shores, gilded with noble palaces, strong fortifications, large hospitals, and public buildings; with the greatest bridge, and the greatest city in the world, made famous by the opulence of its merchants, the increase and extensiveness of its commerce; by its invincible navies, and by the innumerable ships sailing upon it, to and from all parts of the world.[2]

Defoe's anatomy of his country is addressed to its inhabitants, and yet his language denies all attempts at idealization or patriotic panegyric. However, it is obvious that rather than making the magic disappear entirely, he merely transfers it from wood-nymphs to waterways, from tree-gods to tradesmen. After assuring the reader that the Thames will be described 'as it really is', Defoe offers a passage of magical embellishment which would not seem entirely out of place in Italo Calvino's *Invisible Cities*. The recurrent theme in Defoe's progressivist account of the nation is of its recent and quickening development, its economic improvement and its mercantile growth. Entirely ignoring those picturesque evocations of scenery and historical relics which came to dominate many later accounts – his hostility to the unappealing 'barrenness' of the Lake District is especially telling – he concentrates instead upon the civic and urban, and above all upon the contemporary:

If novelty pleases, here is the present state of the country described, the improvement, as well in culture, as in commerce, the increase of people, and employment for them. Also here you have an account of the increase of buildings, as well in great cities and towns, as in the new seats and dwellings of the nobility and gentry; also the increase of wealth, in many eminent particulars . . .

(Tour, p. 43)

Even without wishing to see this as straightforward government propaganda (to which the writer was no stranger), it remains a highly interpretive account, consciously supportive of the recent Union and consolidating the political solidity of Great Britain. Detailed and persuasive though it is, Defoe's sense of persistent improvement is so flagrantly at odds with the apocalyptic cultural analysis of his contemporaries Alexander Pope and Jonathan Swift – in the first version of *The Dunciad* (1728) and in *Gulliver's Travels* (1726) which

9

are both rival accounts of journeys through the contemporary world, albeit imaginary – that there can be no reason now to shroud his words in the cloak of authority.

Yet nor can the differences between his account and theirs be seen simply in terms of temperament or psychology. After all, Defoe's optimistic tone is anticipated in the much chattier and more domestically orientated journeys of Celia Fiennes, who roamed around England between 1685 and 1703, remarking on how industrious the world was becoming and how splendidly its sanitation was coming along. Even more emphatically than Fiennes, Defoe wrote as an apologist for the developing mercantile economy within the newly created nation, eager to detect the green shoots of economic recovery wherever they might be. Although himself persistently an alienated and peripheral figure within his culture, his *Tour* can be read as an act of assertion and assimilation: it identifies and glorifies an emergent nation in which members of Defoe's class can at last claim their rightful cultural supremacy. Emphasizing the adjective, the 'whole island' (ignoring Ireland) is subjected to a totalizing vision which neglects the adumbration of minute local behavioural differences in favour of assembling a coherent fabric of increasing prosperity within a national market economy. The small-scale feudal or subsistence economy of the past has at last been left behind, communications have been improved, and in the modern world each part of the island can make its particular contribution to the overall improvement of the interdependent nation under emergent capitalism.

Thus, despite Defoe's avowed disparagement of 'whimsy', his presentation of Britain in the 1720s is an imaginative construction, dominated by a set of ideological demands, designed to test the Whiggish hypothesis of economic improvement. Only seventeen years after the invention of 'Great' Britain, Defoe drew on all his earlier experiences of travel to put his peregrination at the service of that renewed greatness, producing a version of the island which itemized its nuances in passing, but eventually made it speak with the one voice of trade. For Defoe, the map of Great Britain in 1724 was an economic chart rather than a demographic or ethnographic one, the constituent parts of the island to be differentiated from each other by the nature of their local trading activities. By means of a travel narrative, Defoe sought to turn the geographical phenomenon of an island into the political phenomenon of a nation, and the sense of national identity conferred upon citizens was wholly identified with their role in the successful management of a cohesive market economy.

Between the acts

A full account of internal tourism in Britain would have to include those important eighteenth- and nineteenth-century writers who invented and idealized the picturesque, as well as those who continued Defoe's work on analysing an integrated economy. Yet the very different versions of their journeys given by William Gilpin and George Borrow on the one hand and William Cobbett or Arthur Young on the other all operate within the boundaries of a nation perceived to be more or less intact. Although their accounts differ radically in emphasis, none of these writers sought to challenge the overall integrity of Great Britain, preferring on the whole to rescue a rural sensibility (variously defined) in an increasingly urban world.

With the great social and economic crises of the late 1920s and 1930s, however, a more profound and disturbing national introspection became necessary. Many contemporary commentators saw the dramatic upheavals of the time as not only undermining the intricate workings of the capitalist economy, but also as endangering the very fabric of the nation. As the future Prime Minister Harold Macmillan saw it:

> Now, after 1931, many of us felt that the disease was more deep-rooted. It had become evident that the structure of capitalist society in its old form had broken down, not only in Britain, but all over Europe and even in the United States. The whole system had to be reassessed. Perhaps it could not survive at all; it certainly could not survive without radical change . . . Something like a revolutionary situation had developed, not only at home but overseas.[3]

To investigate this malaise, and see whether there really was a 'revolutionary situation', many artists became concerned with the condition of England once again, and several highly individualistic writers set off on journeys around Britain to record their impressions of different parts of the nation in its moment of crisis. One of the most significant explorations of the national character in the late 1920s is H. V. Morton's very popular *In Search of England* (1927), 'the record of a motor-car journey round England'. Morton's itinerary is deliberately inconsequential, following in the footsteps (or wheel-ruts) of earlier travellers, without any strong sense of urgency or any pronounced agenda of intellectual enquiry. Describing his book, he says:

> I will see what lies off the beaten track. I will, as the mood takes me, go into famous towns and unknown hamlets. I will shake up the dust of kings and abbots; I will bring the knights and the cavaliers back to

11

the roads, and, once in a while, I will hear the thunder of old quarrels at earthwork and church door. If I become weary of dream and legend I will just sit and watch the ducks on the village pond, or take the horses to water. I will talk with lords and cottagers, tramps, gipsies, and dogs; I will, in fact, do anything that comes into my head as suddenly and light-heartedly as I will accept anything, and everything, that comes in my way in rain or sun along the road.[4]

Morton's initial celebration of the freedom of the highway makes the book seem like an account of a prolonged touring holiday, with the gentleman-traveller having the leisure to stop wherever he pleases and linger awhile untroubled – more reminiscent of the dreamy tone of Jerome K. Jerome's *Three Men in a Boat* than of any urgent investigative project. But not far beneath this casual surface there lies a real sense of anxiety, and a strong sense of very pressing questions needing to be asked. As we quickly see, the journey is valetudinarian. The book opens with a dramatic account of the narrator in Palestine, feverish and thinking himself near death, yearning for an idyllic England about which he knows too little. On recovery, Morton goes looking for that England, although knowing it to be a fantasy:

> This village that symbolizes England sleeps in the sub-consciousness of many a townsman. A little London factory hand whom I met during the war confessed to me when pressed, and after great mental difficulty, that he visualized the England he was fighting for – the England of the 'England wants YOU' poster – as not London, not his own street, but as Epping Forest, the green place where he had spent Bank Holidays. And I think most of us did. The village and the English country-side are the germs of all we are and all we have become: our manufacturing cities belong to the last century and a half; our villages stand with their roots in the Heptarchy. (p.2)

Behind the façade of the lazy ramble lies nothing less than an interrogation of what the troops in the trenches had been fighting and dying for, and a Rupert Brooke-style investigation of the state of the 'real' England after the war. In the relaxed days of peace after victory – 'the Great War was the war that ended wars, wasn't it?' (p.73) – Morton searches for an England which he fears may have physically vanished (if it ever existed at all) but which remains at the ideological and spiritual heart of Englishness, and thus – it is assumed, if never explicitly stated – at the core of any sense of Britishness. The talismanic England of the country village is not to be summoned up at will, only to be happened upon by the contingency of undirected travel. So for all its modernity the book is sustained by a curious version of the quest motif, with Morton in pursuit of a particularly

English grail, beset by the false glitter of the urban experience and the ever-present dangers of despondency, the traveller combining the innocent purity of an Arthurian knight with the robust single-mindedness of Bunyan's Christian. To Morton's relief, the lineaments of the heroic past remain easily discernible wherever he roams, and the present maintains its continuity with the great days of Olde England in a way the traveller finds deeply replenishing.

Morton then represents the traveller as pilgrim, and his journey reaches an appropriate conclusion in a moment of sublime apotheosis in an Anglican church. Although dominated by this sense of a spiritual continuum, the book does acknowledge the damage inflicted by the Great War, and the sense of immediate crisis generated by the General Strike of the preceding year. The latter is referred to in passing by a Cornish rustic as 'that bit of a strike you had up in Lunnon' (p.83), which he had heard about on his new-fangled wireless. It is thus a phenomenon restricted to inauthentic cosmopolitan experience, quickly dismissed by the 'real' Englishman of the rural periphery, who knows his place, and is content to remain within it. Such passing acknowledgements of the contemporary political situation do no more than contribute to the traveller's 'vague mental toothache' (p.46), and the main function of the narrative is to piece together a damaged fabric, not by the statistical enumerations of Defoe, but by the encompassing vision of a therapeutic community of past and present. By the end of the book, the essential image of an intact and essentially continuous 'England' has been reinstalled in Morton's imagination, just as he has been reintegrated within it. Eventually, it is as though the Great War was only a dream and the General Strike but a momentary aberration.

Also drawing on the deepening sense of post-war and (pre-war) crises and depression, but with a much less confident vision of recuperative wholeness, is J. B. Priestley's *English Journey: Being a Rambling but Truthful Account of What One Man Saw and Heard and Felt and Thought During a Journey Through England During the Autumn of the Year 1933* (1934). Like Morton, Priestley more or less haphazardly roams the country assessing the state of the nation – understood once again in an entirely Anglocentric way – searching for moments of continuity and discontinuity with the past. Early on, as he buses through Hampshire, he briefly feels in intimate contact with a glorious pre-Norman past:

> Together we rolled along over the pleasant empty countryside of Hampshire, which, once your eyes have left the road, has a timeless quality. The Saxons, wandering over their Wessex, must have seen much of what we saw that morning.[5]

But these moments of continuity with a remote past are infrequent, and the no-nonsense Yorkshire sensibility of Priestley never entertains Morton's magical ruralism or his regenerative faith in the lasting virtues of the English peasantry. In casual conversation with 'an ex-officer of the Regular Army' who believes in some kind of return to the land, Priestley puts forward a much less starry-eyed view of the life of the agricultural labourer than the one offered by the valetudinarian motorist:

> . . . on the few occasions I had come into contact with peasants I had not greatly liked them . . . A peasant on paper, a romantic literary man's peasant, I hinted, was all very well, but always seemed a very different sort of creature from the actual ignorant, stupid, mean peasant of reality. (p.49)

In fact, as Priestley begins to investigate the conditions of contemporary urban England, he finds no sustaining myth of integrity or wholesomeness, and the nation turns instead into a complex and challenging problem requiring the most urgent action. At one point, he describes the living conditions of the inhabitants of Birmingham, taking them as symptomatic of 'our urban and industrial civilisation':

> It was so many miles of ugliness, squalor, and the wrong kind of vulgarity, the decayed anaemic kind . . . I loathed the whole long array of shops, with their nasty bits of meat, their cough mixtures, their *Racing Specials*, their sticky cheap furniture, their shoddy clothes, their fly-blown pastry, their coupons and lies and dreariness and ugliness . . . I think I caught a glimpse then of what may seem to future historians one of the dreadful ironies of this time of ours, when there were never more men doing nothing and there never was before so much to be done. (pp.86–7)

A sense of dissatisfaction with the contemporary condition of England is intensified by the narrator's identification with these people of the abyss – 'I am too near them myself' (p.86). Yet apart from the closing recognition that there remains 'so much to be done', the traveller has no clear stance, no obvious programme of renewal, and his statement of allegiance is never more than gestural. Priestley may present himself as a man of the people, but he retains the right to be selective about which people he wishes to deal with.

Elsewhere, Priestley seems to rely on a Defoe-like (or Macmillan-like) campaign of capitalist reinvigoration of the economy, only very sketchily described, involving sacrifice for many, but justified by the unusual urgency of the situation:

. . . I am here, in a time of stress, to look at the face of England,
however blank or bleak that face may chance to appear, and to
report truthfully what I see there. I know there is deep distress in the
country. I have seen some of it, just had a glimpse of it, already, and
I know there is far, far more ahead of me. We need a rational
economic system, not altogether removed from austerity. Without
such a system, we shall soon perish. All hands must be on deck.
(pp.61–2)

The search for some cohesive and 'rational' economic system seems
like a return to Defoe's totalizing vision of the nation as an intact
mercantile community. But by looking at the actual human effects of
industry – glaring features of the landscape which Morton ignored –
Priestley becomes much less sanguine about the benignity of the
market economy, and the terrible distress it has created is more
obvious to him than any solution it might offer. His anxieties become
most pronounced when he visits Tyneside, where the obvious ravages
and the human cost of heavy industry dramatize the sense that such
activity need not be seen as either wholesome or collaborative. Lacking
a vision of transcendental 'Englishness' to obliterate the wretchedness
in front of him, he relies on his compassion and humanity. But in the
end, his confrontation with the unacceptable face of capitalism leaves
him only with a series of unanswerable questions:

England would not be the England we know if Tyneside were not the
Tyneside we know. Coal, millions of tons of it, had been poured out
down this channel; great ships had been built and repaired; engines
had been constructed and sent away by the thousand; there had
been enormous fortunes spent in wages and material, in profits and
dividends. But still I wondered, as I stood there, shivering a little,
whether it had all been worthwhile. Here was the pleasant green
estuary, blackened and ruined, it seemed, for ever. Here was a
warren of people living in wretched conditions, in a parody of either
rural or urban life, many of them now without work or wages or
hope, not half the men their peasant ancestors were . . . And the
fortunes, the piles of gold that the alchemy of industry had conjured
from this steam and filth and din, where were they? What great work,
I asked myself, owes its existence to those vast profits, those
mounting dividends? What sciences and arts had they nourished?
What new graces had they added to English life in return for what
they had taken away from here? (p.318)

The questions go unanswered, and it is clear that no positive response
is to be expected. Industry, it seems, no longer nourishes and
invigorates the nation, as Defoe believed. Instead, it only despoils and

disfigures it, impoverishing the lives of its main victims, the ordinary citizens of Britain.

Despite the grimness, Priestley is eager to conclude on a more positive note, and his final remarks pay tribute to English 'liberty' and the native distrust of demagogueries, but also to the affecting stoicism and resilience of the down-at-heel. Furthermore, his innate patriotism remains unshaken – 'I would rather spend a holiday in Tuscany than in the Black Country, but if I were compelled to choose between living in West Bromwich and Florence, I should make straight for West Bromwich' (p.416). Suburban West Brom presumably does not share metropolitan Birmingham's deplorable taste for cough mixtures, sticky cheap furniture and the wrong kind of vulgarity. England, for all its flaws, still seems enchanted and desirable, not least because it is not somewhere else, not foreign, a belief intensified by Priestley's persistent anti-Irish asides.

At the end of this journey, Priestley keeps the horrors of potential revolution at bay by the fabrication of a national identity called 'Englishness', whose components include liberty, stoicism, 'the natural kindness and courtesy of the ordinary English people', with some Milton and Shakespeare and a few cathedrals thrown in. Taken together, these icons provide 'that inner glowing tradition of the English spirit' (p.417), to be contrasted with worthless pastimes like the *Racing Special* with which the populace of the cities so foolishly fill up their hours. Eventually, despite an acquaintance with the awfulness of industrial capitalism, and despite the capacity to express outrage at the infliction of needless suffering on the impoverished, Priestley turns for comfort to a selective mysticism and ruralism similar to Morton's, and his journey ends with the narrator returning to the private domain by re-entering the warmth and comfort of a middle-class English home.

A more radical challenge to prevailing social circumstances and to the class-based assumptions of Morton and Priestley was mounted four years later by George Orwell, whose account of a 1936 journey to the north of England, *The Road to Wigan Pier* (1937) – undertaken thanks to a commission (and a handsome advance) from Victor Gollancz – sought to confront and articulate the inequities that Morton ignored and Priestley tried somehow to smooth over. In an earlier book, *Down and Out in Paris and London* (1933), Orwell had given his own personal testimony to the day-to-day indignities of life below the poverty line; but in this later text, he conducts a more ambitious investigative experiment, stimulated by his desire to test his beliefs against experience:

In the earlier chapters of this book I have given a rather fragmentary account of various things I saw in the coal areas of Lancashire and

Yorkshire. I went there partly because I wanted to see the most typical section of the English working class at close quarters. This was necessary to me as part of my approach to Socialism, for before you can be sure whether you are genuinely in favour of Socialism, you have got to decide whether things at present are tolerable or not tolerable, and you have got to take up a definite attitude on the terribly difficult issue of class . . .[6]

By adding the 'Socialist Traveller' to Sterne's taxonomy, Orwell makes the ideological imperatives behind his journey obvious. Like Engels or Mayhew exposing the poor, he concentrates on a documentary investigation of the lives of the industrial lower classes, to gauge thereby the state of the nation and assess the need for remedial action from above. Once again, however, the observation of others is conducted primarily as a means of helping the less well-integrated observer to define his own position and attitudes, particularly those concerning 'the terribly difficult issue of class', and the grand narrative he is testing is not so much nationhood as 'Socialism'.

Although his description of domestic life in Yorkshire and Lancashire is closer to Smelfungus than to Yorick (especially on the subject of hygiene), Orwell's account of poverty is grim and compelling, and his descriptions of the coal-mines still make chastening reading. But that account only takes up half the text, and the remainder offers a meditation upon the significance of what has been seen. The 'lower-upper-middle class' old-Etonian ex-colonel Orwell emphasizes his role as an outsider in these communities, looking in on the experience of others. In a famous passage, he describes the problems faced by a 'Southerner' like himself in trying to be taken as an ally by a 'Northerner':

There is nevertheless a real difference between North and South, and there is at least a tinge of truth in the picture of Southern England as one enormous Brighton inhabited by lounge-lizards. For climatic reasons the parasitic dividend-drawing class tend to settle in the South. In a Lancashire cotton-town you could probably go for months on end without hearing an 'educated' accent, whereas there can hardly be a town in the South of England where you could throw a brick without hitting the niece of a bishop. Consequently, with no petty gentry to set the pace, the bourgeoisification of the working class, though it is taking place in the North, is taking place more slowly. All the Northern accents, for instance, persist strongly, while the Southern ones are collapsing before the movies and the B.B.C. Hence your 'educated' accent stamps you rather as a foreigner than as a chunk of the petty gentry; and this is an immense advantage, for it makes it much easier to get into contact with the working class. (p.102)

A journey into the unknown territories of 'the North' is thus an opportunity to explore a different class, as though there were no workers and no poverty in the south. But the attempt at sympathetic affiliation is not without difficulties. While it is easier for Orwell to meet 'ordinary' people in northern mining areas, free from the interference of the despised petty gentry of the south, he remains sceptical about the depth and genuineness of that contact – 'But is it ever really possible to be really intimate with the working class?' (p.102). And as he points out, Orwell never found it as easy to get on equal terms with working people as he did with his fellow-outcasts, the tramps and indigents of *Down and Out in Paris and London*.

To some extent, Orwell in the north of England still retains vestiges of the colonial officer he was in Burma, and his journey is like a trip to a remote part of the British Empire. He feels affiliated to his subjects, linked to them by the contending grand narratives of socialism and nationhood, and yet more obviously to be estranged from them by his own class and origins. Always he remains on the outside, looking in, travelling through and past these regions, never belonging to them. Unable to partake fully of their communal pleasures, he is allowed privileged glimpses of their lives, but the journey continues, and he at least has places to move on to. In one very powerful passage, he looks through a train window, and experiences a kind of epiphany:

The train bore me away, through the monstrous scenery of slag-heaps, chimneys, piled scrap-iron, foul canals, paths of cindery mud criss-crossed by the prints of clogs . . . As we moved slowly, through the outskirts of the town we passed row after row of little grey slum houses running at right angles to the embankment. At the back of one of the houses a young woman was kneeling on the stones, poking a stick up the leaden waste-pipe which ran from the sink inside and which I suppose was blocked. I had time to see everything about her – her sacking apron, her clumsy clogs, her arms reddened by the cold. She looked up as the train passed, and I was almost near enough to catch her eye. She had a round pale face, the usual exhausted face of the slum girl who is twenty-five and looks forty, thanks to miscarriages and drudgery; and it wore, for the second in which I saw it, the most desolate, hopeless expression I have ever seen. It struck me then that we are mistaken when we say that 'It isn't the same for them as it would be for us,' and that people bred in the slums can imagine nothing but the slums. For what I saw in her face was not the ignorant suffering of an animal. She knew well enough what was happening to her – understood as well as I did how dreadful a destiny it was to be kneeling there in the bitter cold, on the slimy stones of a slum backyard, poking a stick up a foul drain-pipe. (pp.16–17)

Although granted no more than the briefest glimpse of this woman, Orwell seems to have discovered a great deal about her. From her state of mind to her gynaecological history, all is open to his inspection. His authority to comment on her life goes unquestioned, but he can do no more than that. There remains a barrier between them more impermeable than a train window, and there is no time for conversation or real contact – 'But quite soon the train drew away into open country.'

By the contingency of such brief encounters, Orwell confirms his ideology and reinforces his call for organized socialism as the only answer to the problems uncovered. His gestures of solidarity and affiliation, however, are deeply compromised by his perceived alienation and his lack of identity with his subjects, transforming the apparent open-mindedness of the travel narrative into an altogether more tendentious and self-referring account of a 'lower-upper-middle class' socialist's unsentimental education. The point to be made from all three of these journeys through crisis-torn England in the 1920s and 1930s is that rather than being a way of discovering the 'real' country beyond London, the narrative is primarily a way of reproducing a particular ideological frame of reference, into which the nation – be it England, Britain or the United Kingdom – is inserted. In each of these narratives the periphery of England is seen to carry different meanings for the traveller, meanings which may be regenerative or disconcerting, and which may integrate or alienate the metropolitan traveller.

Where Morton rediscovers the seamless continuity of past and present, the grand narrative of English tradition, and Priestley defends the middle-class common Englishman against his critics, Orwell sees a landscape scarred by uncrossable class divides, where common humanity and any sense of national identity are disfigured by ignorance and hostility, just as they were in the Spain of his *Homage to Catalonia*, published the following year. Where Orwell's journey to Spain made him see the cracks in the grand fabric of socialism, his tour of the north of England exposed him to the challenges inherent in any totalizing vision of nationhood. The writer as domestic traveller may find the journey replenishing or disorientating, but in all these cases what he sees remains an ideological construction, begging those very questions he sought to answer.

Trains and boats and plain speaking

Having looked at how travel writing participated in the construction of the 'British' nation in the eighteenth century, and in its fragmentation during the inter-war crises, we may now turn to the subsequent bout of national navel-gazing conducted during the Thatcher years. Like the 1930s, the 1980s saw a radical reconsideration of the nature of Britishness, carried on under the forbidding and intolerant stare of the then prime minister, who so regularly and stridently articulated her own very fervent, yet very idiosyncratic, notion of what it meant to be British.

As the Conservative government enacted deeply divisive and disenfranchising social policies, beset once more by the complexities of the Irish presence in the United Kingdom and by the growing power of the European Community, its members became yet more firmly wedded to a cohesive ideology of Britishness, somehow mixing a sanitized 'heritage' sense of the past with more bellicose echoes of a dimly remembered imperialism and 'greatness'. The successful marketing of this curious Anglocentric ideological concoction was one of the key factors in Thatcher's dominance of British politics for so long, making her the custodian and representative of all things British, and turning disagreements with party policy into an unpatriotic activity, a new kind of petty treason.

In response to such a powerful attempt at creating hegemony, and in an attempt to analyse more carefully the contemporary mood and identity of the nation, British writing in the 1980s took on greater analytic responsibilities than previously, and many writers addressed themselves to the question of what (if anything) now constituted Britishness. Elsewhere in this volume, there are accounts of the ways the 'Yookay' (as Raymond Williams called it) was deconstructed from within as the periphery fought back. Some metropolitan writers used conventional novel forms to dramatize this analysis – Martin Amis's *London Fields* (1989) is often cited as a paradigm case, although Jonathan Raban's *Foreign Land* (1985) might better serve – but others used more explicitly documentary techniques. In Robert Chesshyre's *The Return of a Native Reporter* (1987), the author takes advantage of a four-year absence to detect changes in emphasis in his native land, and he describes a very rapid deterioration in behaviour, suggesting that the cohesiveness of Britain is under threat. Equally sombre, if at times ludicrously ill-informed, is Bill Buford's *Among the Thugs* (1990), which takes the peripatetic and often violent football fan as a symbol for the brutish Briton of the late 1980s. There are many similar exercises in journalistic sociology, cast in various forms, some more sensational than others, some more persuasive. However, of greater importance here are the numbers of writers who tried to analyse what it meant to be British nowadays by the familiar means of the round-Britain journey.

Some of these books were explicit rewritings of the texts from the 1930s, fifty years on, like Beryl Bainbridge's *English Journey* (1984), which deliberately retraced Priestley, only to end inconclusively, or Beatrix Campbell's *Wigan Pier Revisited* (1984), which reported on the continuing hardship of the north of England under Thatcher, deconstructing ideas of progress and recharging the imperatives of socialism. In Tom Vernon's *Fat Man on a Roman Road* (1983), the author reports on an indirect bicycle journey around Britain, following the Roman roads and so taking in village life. The predominantly English journey, including only a brief visit to Scotland, and none to Wales or Ireland, undertaken (like Bainbridge's) at the behest of the BBC, is designed to discover 'whether my own country and its people *were* lovable'.[7] Clearly, there is room for doubt, and Vernon seems to combine something of Morton's idealized ruralism with his own softened version of the class issue, all the time dimly aware of the distant thunder of the Falklands War, and the more local violence of IRA bomb attacks in London. In Devon, he takes pleasure in the tranquillity and parochialism of a little England redolent of Ealing comedies:

> While the rest of the world was killing people – this was also the time of the massacre in Beirut – in my two days in Devon I had seen no more sign of civil disorder than a vandalised telephone box, and was in hopes of coming upon a couple of minor graffiti to make me feel more at home – although in the policeman's column in the parish magazine, I saw that scarcely a month went by when there was not at least one act of minor law-breaking, and in the same issue a local councillor was calling for the reintroduction of the birch and capital punishment because some girls had taken a wicker gate off its hinges and 'badly damaged' it. (pp.29–30)

The comic postcard England of rural tranquillity, village bobbies and red-faced councillors seems curiously intact to the urban traveller, and its persistence is an ironized reminder of an alternative ideological fantasy, a version of the pastoral still identifiable in the remote periphery, one of Virgil's *Georgics* still available in the remote south-west of England. However, all is not as well as it seems, and the palliative image quickly begins to break up. In particular, the new development of the shopping precinct causes the narrator to despair:

> Exeter has not suffered anything approaching the municipal vandalism of many other city: it keeps a pleasant relaxed air among

gentle hills, but if Devon is the crown of England . . . and Exeter the jewel of that crown, it is in danger of getting rather loose in its setting . . . The thing that always worries me about development is that it has its heart in its wallet (usually), or its social conscience (occasionally), or anywhere but in the place where a heart ought to be. Much, much too often it makes people's lives colder when it ought to make them warmer. I couldn't see much warmth in the new parts of Exeter as I wandered round the shopping precinct . . . (p.38)

Nothing could be further from Defoe's tribute to the totalizing effect of trade than Vernon's view. As he sees it, the development of trade through the whole island has started to homogenize British life, without energizing it, and the loss of local identity has not been compensated for by any renewed sense of belonging to a truly national culture. There may still be local trades and manufacturing industries – like the Melton Mowbray pork pie he likes so much – but these are being phased out by inauthentic multinational consumerism, and the traditional skilled work-force is being moved into service industries. The contrast between the Roman roads and the modern world only serves to celebrate those few survivals of individuality and much-prized eccentricity in an increasingly impoverished culture.

Like Orwell, Vernon feels greater solidarity with the indigent travellers he meets than he does with those firmly installed in the system. Even so, time and again he encounters informants whose tales of British life are full of a sense of loss and decline. While Vernon's account tries to be upbeat and amusing, its overall register is elegiac, and deeply inconclusive about the question of nationhood. The final words of Beryl Bainbridge serve to provide the shrug-of-the-shoulders ending to both her book and his:

And I came to the conclusion, such as it is, that the English are a surprising people. How tolerant they are, how extremely eccentric, and how variously they live in the insular villages, the cosy cathedral towns, and brutal wastes of the northern cities. And I thought that was about it, one way and another.[8]

The oddest thing about both Vernon and Bainbridge is the way they lack any coherent picture at the end. The totalizing impulse of all the previous writers has been surrendered for an anecdotal and individualist style which replaces a concern with the state of the nation with an inconsequential series of chance meetings. There seems to be no sense of a 'whole island' in either book, and each traveller ends up with very little to report other than a series of unconnected interviews.

A very different approach is taken in Paul Theroux's *The Kingdom by the Sea* (1983), in which the evaluative perspective of the observer is made obvious right from the start:

> Britain was the most written-about country in the world. That was the problem, really. You read one book about China and you think you've got a good idea of the place; you read twenty books about Britain, even *English Traits* and *Rural Rides*, and you know you haven't got the slightest.[9]

In Theroux's view, Britain has been over-imagined, over-imposed upon by contending and contradictory images. In pursuit of an authentic version of Britain, Theroux – an American who at the time of his writing had spent eleven years in London – forsakes the metropolis for a tour of the coastline, heightening his awareness of 'Britishness' by searching for it in an unfamiliar context. In Theroux's text, an open-minded receptivity to experience fights it out with the most blinkered vision of what British people are really like:

> They wallpaper their ceilings! They put little knitted bobble-hats on their soft-boiled eggs to keep them warm! They don't give you bags in supermarkets! They say sorry when they step on your toes! . . . They smoke on buses! They drive on the left! They spy for the Russians! They say 'Nigger' and 'Jewboy' without flinching! They call their houses 'Holmleigh' and 'Sparrow View'! They sunbathe in their underwear! . . . (p.14)

The list continues, itemizing the ways the 'English' present themselves as quaint or offensive to the sensitivities of the traveller, and it serves throughout as a template within which the main travel narrative will be embraced. Rather than contesting this vision, Theroux's unusually joyless journey through England, Wales, Scotland and Northern Ireland encrusts it with further examples of oddity, and his eventual version of the national identity is as inconsequential as Vernon's or Bainbridge's. When he is asked to sum up the appealing features of a place, he produces a list of small, seemingly insignificant pleasures:

> But what I liked in Aberdeen was what I liked generally in Britain: the bread, the fish, the cheese, the flower gardens, the apples, the clouds, the newspapers, the beer, the woollen cloth, the radio programmes, the parks, the Indian restaurants and amateur dramatics, the postal service, the fresh vegetables, the trains, and the modesty and truthfulness of people. (p.299)

Apart from the final more grandiose item, the catalogue of the positive features of British life seems incidental, and no real sense of an all-embracing national identity seems to be discoverable. Yet, as Theroux travels, just such a sense is being promulgated by the dramatic representation of 'this Falklands business' (Theroux, p.21). His journey around Britain runs concurrently with the Falklands conflict, and it is used as a sounding device to test the sense of national solidarity felt by Theroux's informants. What emerges most strikingly from the narrative is the way no real unanimity is discovered. Just as the press stridently tries to orchestrate a climate of single-minded jingoism and xenophobia, rejoicing in the sinking of the *General Belgrano* and exulting in the triumph of arms, so the reactions of individual citizens vary. To some extent, the campaign succeeds, as Theroux discovers when he visits Butlin's:

> I scrutinized the Visitor's Book. It asked for nationality, and people listed 'Welsh' or 'Cornish' or 'English' or 'Scottish' next to their names. There was a scattering of Irish. But after the middle of April – after the Falklands war had begun – people had started to put 'British'. (p.145)

But this sense of a national identity and affiliation seems wholly gestural and insubstantial, and many of the author's encounters run directly contradictory to the official triumphalism. Elsewhere in the book, it is abundantly clear that British people generally pay much more attention to local allegiances than to national ones, and the culture that Theroux discovers is more factional, sectarian and even tribal than it is truly national.

A similar conclusion is reached in Jonathan Raban's *Coasting* (1986), which approaches England with caution, just skirting around the edges in a small boat. On this journey, too, it becomes apparent that national identity is a mirage, except in occasional moments of xenophobic insularity, temporarily inflamed by 'this Falklands business', which unleashes the darker side of the 'national subconscious'.[10] So while there may be unifying features of a British identity, they remain dormant most of the time, rarely interfering in the lives of most people. Instead, Raban's informants firmly believe that they belong to a local environment, in economic decline but still emotionally and culturally strong. It is their memory of belonging to a particular place which makes them what they are, even in a fragmented and post-modern culture, where despite all the efforts to standardize British culture the 'periphery' lives on and at times seems stronger than the 'core'.

Like Theroux, Raban encounters oddities aplenty on his voyage, but the sense of an encompassing national identity remains elusive. In its place, he discovers lingering loyalties to place and class, vividly dramatized in the miners' strike of 1984. At one point, Raban has joined some pickets, but as soon as he speaks, he gives away his origins and is treated with overt hostility:

It was the extraordinary speed of it which was so English. It wasn't my clothes . . . It was accent, and nothing but accent. *How far's Rossington* was enough to open the chasm of all the dirty and invidious distinctions of the English class set-up. It was like the boy scout trick of starting a fire with two sticks. In three words, you could spark off the whole miserable, loggerhead confrontation between state and private schools, owner-occupiers and council tenants, The North and The South, Chapel and Church, Labour and Tory, those with jobs and those without. It was no good pretending to be a coaster here; you don't coast in Doncaster, you sail with your class colours firmly nailed to the mast. (p.248)

The non-aligned 'coasting' traveller is here strongly challenged, and his pretence of objectivity is unmasked. To his discomfort, Raban is being implicated in the process which he only wishes to observe.

This last example from Jonathan Raban makes the most important point about recent travel writing very clearly. Where the writers have been in pursuit of what they saw as truth, a 'grand narrative' of nationhood, they discover only a conflict of various moods and attitudes. In Raymond Williams's terms, they·have been able to identify the dominant or hegemonic structure of feeling – Thatcherism and the valorization of the market economy – but they are also confronted by a competing range of residual and emergent ideologies. Some of these residual structures of feeling, like the importance of class in the miners' strike or of the remembrance of things past in Grimsby, are strengthening and empowering for their subjects, however disconcerting they may be to travel writers. Others, like the militarism of old buffers in a yachting club, look absurd. The emergent structures of feeling, typified for Raban by the insularity of tax-avoiders on the Isle of Man, are deeply unattractive. And all the time, the dominant ideology seeks to obliterate these memories and replace them with a sanitized notion of 'heritage'. Raban is consistently interested in the 'Masque of Britain' – developing the notion of urban life as theatre explored in his earlier book *Soft City* – but the concern has wider applications, and brings us to a rather depressing conclusion. What we see in Vernon, Bainbridge, Theroux, Raban and many others is the emergent conjunction between the travel writer and the tourist, and the corresponding transformation of Britain into a kind of theme park. After the mighty economic unity identified by Defoe, we have arrived at a nation which is held together only as a spectacle, its internal life restricted and diminished to little more than a peep-show of eccentric characters.

References

1 Laurence Sterne, *A Sentimental Journey Through France and Italy* (1768), ed. Ian Jack (Oxford, OUP, 1984), p.11.
2 Daniel Defoe, *A Tour Through the Whole Island of Great Britain* (1724), ed. Pat Rogers (Harmondsworth, Penguin, 1971), pp.181–2.
3 Harold Macmillan, *Winds of Change* (London, Macmillan, 1966), p.283.
4 H. V. Morton, *In Search of England* (London, Methuen, 1927), p.4.
5 J. B. Priestley, *English Journey* (London, Heinemann, 1934), p.9.
6 George Orwell, *The Road to Wigan Pier* (1937; reprinted Harmondsworth, Penguin, 1972), p.106.
7 Tom Vernon, *Fat Man on a Roman Road* (London, Michael Joseph, 1983), p.11.
8 Beryl Bainbridge, *English Journey* (London, Flamingo, 1984), p.158.
9 Paul Theroux, *The Kingdom by the Sea* (London, Hamish Hamilton, 1983), p.13.
10 Jonathan Raban, *Coasting* (London, Collins, 1986), pp.95–8.

3

Regional crime squads:
location and dislocation in the British mystery

STEPHEN KNIGHT

Place and displacement

At a distance, place seems securely located at the heart of the mystery. From Raymond Chandler's love–hate for southern California and Agatha Christie's minutely mapped village life, to the televisual impact of Simenon's Paris and Dexter's Oxford, setting appears to have more than contextual significance in the most widely successful forms of modern crime fiction.

A closer view finds the mapping less simple. In none of those cases does the location in fact have a central or directly formative role in the drama. Marlowe may suspect urban corruption, as if he were inside a Hammett novel, but all of Chandler's mysteries boil down to personal betrayal, invariably by a woman. The point of Miss Marple's context is to inform a transcendental moralism that can expose what Christie consciously regarded as sin. More devious, but just as individualistic, Simenon uses Paris as no more than a site for psychic crime, without any of the sense of a centre of class conflict that ran so strongly through the early crime stories of Eugène Sue and Emile Gaboriau. In the same idealized way Dexter writes Oxford as a sign for quirky cleverness, never attending to the genuine strains of that strangely double city, as suggested in Raymond Williams's *Second Generation*. These settings, that is, are addresses for personal correspondence, not sites for social analysis refracted through the prism of crime. The plot of the mysteries may not be a socio-economic chart.

But such elision of place can amount to displacement, a crucial mechanism in the way stories mean, as what is actually of major significance may be too important or too deeply buried to be treated as itself. Place may play a role of this elusive but ultimately central kind in the patterns of crime fiction, especially when it is self-consciously regional, that is not metropolitan, and so other forms of displacement are already on the agenda.

This chapter will concentrate on the structures to be identified around that issue in British crime fiction and especially on the representations of regionality in the form. That emphasis, it will appear, and fortunately so, is not a perverse anti-metropolitan concentration, but a way of going to the heart of the double articulation that dynamizes place in the mystery story: one movement is the interaction of setting and meaning, the way in which place is relocated within the narrative to generate and represent certain dynamic meanings. The second movement is the way in which a sense of region, especially provincial against metropolitan, interacts consistently to define the forces at work upon and through the people in the story – including the detective. Place and region as issues and as signs are deep-laid voices of meaning in crime fiction, especially (as readers of Sherlock Holmes will know) when they are apparently most silent.

Regions and origins

Location and relocation of various kinds are basic to the development of crime fiction as an identifiable genre, and a relatively modern one. An intellectualist false trail was laid by connoisseurs like Dorothy Sayers, who claimed that crime fiction could be traced back to classical acts of detection like Oedipus solving the riddle of the Sphinx or the attempted deception of Isaac. Such idealizing fancies claimed antiquity for a form that was in fact generated quite recently, when the growing complexity of social life in its physical reality made it improbable that a criminal could be easily detected by the social group against which he or she had sinned.

The development of mass living in the cities gave criminals the ability to escape, hide, exchange stolen goods for cash, assume a new identity; and at the same time it generated the need for a specially skilled and full-time professional to pursue the aberrant enemies of society. The changing patterns of response to crime are visible in the pages of *The Newgate Calendar*, where old-fashioned forms of crime control are shown both in hopeful operation, and also in actual failure.[1] In the classic crime stories, as in the cony-catching pamphlets of the seventeenth century, in sensational stories like *Moll Flanders* and its many avatars, the criminal is apprehended in the act, or known by reputation, or sometimes is simply stricken with guilt and led to confess.

Whether such systems of a past world's policing ever really worked or not is doubtful – the medieval rate of arrest was very low and conviction almost non-existent according to John Bellamy.[2] The process by which the community of God did the detecting was certainly not working by the mid-eighteenth century and the Bow Street Runners were one response, organized by a writer whose fictions included major aspects of both crime and personal relocation, Henry Fielding. Urban society and its publishing processes are the media for the development of the fictional detective, whether in maestro form like Eugène Vidocq, 'the French police spy' whose *Mémoires* appeared in 1828, or in humbler mode like the plodding police of the Bow Street Runner stories by 'Richmond' (1827) or the 'Detective Officer' stories by 'Waters' that first appeared in book form in 1856.

The recurrent mechanism of these stories is travel to resolve mysterious crimes: up the road to York, out to the towns of the Thames valley, in and around the swelling villages that were rapidly becoming London. Criminals are also on the move, and consistently assume new identities: farmers' sons masquerade as gentry, ladies' maids steal jewels to set their lovers up in shops. Social and geographic mobility are closely interwoven and the police detective – at this early stage there are no amateurs – moves as an agent of fictional protection through this bemusingly unstable new world, which is constructed by the process of capital and increasingly focused on the capital city itself.

Archetypal to the structure of a newly nervous mobility are two novels that stand at the start and end of the development of the new genre. *Moll Flanders* (1722) bespeaks many kinds of novelty and one of them is that Moll's mobility in place and social terms is the means by which her criminality is both exciting and successful. But there is also the question of detection: nobody can identify Moll's criminality except herself, because no one else could keep up with her dazzling résumé of personal, social and criminal mobility. No public narrator or inquirer could manage to identify the private guilt or innocence of this most elusive figure, so she speaks her own mysterious career. *Moll Flanders* breaks the mould of the old socially controlled crime story, but without generating the detective genre.

At the other end of the period of the high development of mercantile society, with all its facilities for anonymous crime, comes Wilkie Collins's *The Woman in White* (1860), a book still not adequately discussed in either generic or sociopolitical terms. Identity, regionality, gender and inheritance are thrown together in a complex of challenges to established practice. The woman in question first appears to a city worker walking home to the village that Hampstead no longer really was. In the broader structure of the novel London is the hub, but the action is crucially in Cumberland and Hampshire, on estates that are old, enfeebled and prone to criminal subversion. The revelations of such conservative crimes occur, however, through the most modern of media, the railway train with its crucial system of timetables to control motion, and in the brand-new conurbation that has grown beside Sir Percival Glyde's place of ancient deception; in the same inventive way, Collins provides detection not through the artisan class assistance of police specialists but through representatives of bourgeois social modernity – a professional artist and a prototype New Woman.

Crucially, Defoe and Collins link provincial areas (including in Moll's case America) with the metropolis in a dynamic form of conflict, but the books manage without the overweening simplicity of the brilliant detective, and both chart dramatically the deep interrelation between social mobility and crime in the formation of the genre.

That connection is at once more mechanical and more far-reaching than these novels indicate, though Collins characteristically provides the crucial hint. As Wolfgang Schivelbush has shown in a fine and undernoticed book called *The Railway Journey*,[3] people at first found train travel very disconcerting. In part they felt their minds would be deranged by travelling faster than human or animal agency had previously made possible, but it was not the power of the machine that really alarmed them and gave rise to a responding fictional genre. Rather, it was the enforced democracy of the new mode of travel. The British railway train's form was based on a model of road travel, and the railway car was essentially a series of stagecoach bodies on a flat-bed. As a result, each carriage was separate and no one could change compartments when the train was in motion. People felt very anxious locked up with mysterious strangers (unlike in America, where water travel was dominant, and the large riverboat-style saloon gave security in numbers). The railway murder itself became a part of the new genre that was selling very well on the station bookstalls which sprang up, carrying both the new yellowback novels and also the magazines that flourished after the reduction of stamp duty in 1836, almost all issues carrying at least one crime story.

Sir Arthur Conan Doyle especially capitalized on the context of motion. The success of Sherlock Holmes lies partly in Doyle's capacity to combine a dense plot with drily vivid writing, but central was an appeal to the new class of distance commuters who rode the trains in from the home counties and bought copies of *Strand* magazine on the bookstalls. Major forces for both plot and audience were mobility up and down society and across the face of south-east England. What the travellers read about was personal failure in the face of new circumstances: financial strain in the respectable suburbs and commuter districts led to robbery, deception, occasionally murder – all resolved by the kinds of individualist scientism that was an evaluative ideal of this new world. The West End of London was merely a base for the great detective's healing travels; they range widely through the extended metropolis as far as its playgrounds – a racing stable on Exmoor ('Silver Blaze') and boating on the upper Thames ('The Cardboard Box'), but mostly in the fine mansions of the home counties where the masters of mercantilism lived and the commuting reader aspired to reside – and where Doyle himself settled, on the basis of his success in mythicizing the period's relocational anxieties.

It is only the later 'heritage' reading of Holmes that drenches the stories in fogs and hansom cabs. In the original form he is the exorcizer of the evils of the newly developed system of London-centred business; a good fairy of mercantile capitalism. Like the amateur detectives of *The Woman in White*, like the pedestrian police of the 'Waters' stories, he moves through the country resolving problems of greed, deception, colonial misprision, distorted inheritance, a whole range of offences which represent the strains of living in a world where a region is no longer self-sufficient and its magistrates no longer deal with its local crimes through the unmediated brutality of stringing up a highwayman, putting a coiner in the pillory or burning a witch or a husband-murderer.

The weakening of the regions as self-sufficient sites in terms of their own legislative power and parochial confidence – the old formation that economic historians call local circulation – is the story of national mercantile and capital development; it is also a story that is retold, consciously or not, in the patterns of place in modern crime fiction – as should be the case, since the genre itself is a product of the forces that caused that rearrangement of national social and cultural structures in the first place.

Imaginary regionalism

Like travel, reading is often remembered with a difference. The image usually held of Agatha Christie's novels is static, a world that is self-contained, self-contented. The texts belie such simplicity, as when, in the opening of *The Mirror Crack'd from Side to Side*, Miss Marple muses about change:

> One had to face the fact: St Mary Mead was not the place it had been. In a sense, of course, nothing was what it had been. You could blame the war (or both the wars), or the younger generation, or women going out to work, or the atom bomb, or just the

31

Government – but what one really meant was the simple fact that one was growing old . . .

St Mary Mead, the old-world core of it, was still there. The Blue Boar was there, and the church and the vicarage and the little nest of Queen Anne and Georgian houses, of which hers was one . . .

But though the houses looked much as before, the same could hardly be said of the village street. When shops changed hands there, it was with a view to immediate and intemperate modernization . . . where Mr Toms had once had his basket shop stood a glittering new supermarket – anathema to the elderly ladies of St Mary Mead.

'Packets of things one's never heard of,' exclaimed Miss Hartnell. 'All those great packets of breakfast cereal instead of cooking a child a proper breakfast of bacon and eggs . . . And then a long queue waiting to pay as you go out. Most tiring. Of course, it's all very well for the people from the Development –'

At this point she stopped.

Because, as was now usual, the sentence came to an end there. The Development, Period, as they would say in modern terms. It had an entity of its own, and a capital letter.[4]

Christie sums up in 1960s terms the threat of regional invasion that has always been present in her work; Roger Ackroyd from 1926 was a manufacturer of waggon wheels, a figure of mobility in more ways than one. Miss Marple's St Mary Mead lament encapsulates, with perhaps surprising literary and intellectual force, what an author with a higher-flying intellectual reputation, Fredric Jameson, has called the logic of late capitalism. And who is to say what a doyen of clues like Christie meant by her last remark about Development having a *capital* letter?

After this opening statement about modern mobility, Christie as usual delves into hidden betrayals in the private domain; some are beginning to see remarkable sophistication, even aspects of proto-feminism, in these representations of social flaws seen in the personal glass.[5] There is certainly a strong element of symbolized politics embedded in the private violence and the conflicts of place are displaced, not elided. In *The Mirror Crack'd from Side to Side* a particularly strong form of internationalism – Hollywood itself – is shown unable to reproduce itself (in childbirth, and symbolically more widely than that) at the most intimate and local level in Marple's rural regime. Those who are part of what Christie calls 'immediate and intemperate modernization' pay a tragic price for importing Development into this fictionally defended domain. Mystery plot and regional theme are elegantly condensed, and that suggests there may well be structural roots for Christie's success.

In this deep-laid strength of design, as in the sharp-edged acuity of her plotting and the conservative conventionality of her characterization, Christie's pattern can stand as a strong form of a basic mode of the British mystery. Many other writers, household names only to those who live with library catalogues, consistently open their novels by sketching in an attractive imaginary regional setting. Soon they will indicate that change is an alarming feature, and then show that those who have internalized and tried to introduce modernization are the villains, those who represent virtues felt to be ancient and durable are both victims and survivors and – most important of all – detectives.

Any 'Selected Crime' section in any public library holds many versions of this formulaic mode. Two successful contemporary examples would be W. J. Burley, with his Cornwall-based 'Wycliffe' mysteries and Dorothy Simpson's plain-style puzzles set in Kent and featuring the topographically named Inspector Thanet. Their police detectives have a touched-in private life, a little troubled perhaps, but enriched with feeling and a sense of duty both private and public. While they nobly resist a sadly changing world and its incursive influences, the victims have toyed with modernization a little too much – a farmer has got into Eurodebt, a girl stayed too long at a village disco. But, through the miasmas of humdrum life, the thoughtful representatives of wishful stability will eventually trace the over-modernized person who has set off this chain reaction of innovative intervention. The region as it once was, as it is imagined to exist, acts throughout as an off-stage focus of value, a vanishing point for the wished-for convergence of heritage verities. To support this structure there will be occasional touchstones of an unpolluted past: a thatched roof or a beautiful beach will be offered as indices of what has been lost, icons that will intensify the sense of deprivation.

There is a touristic sense about these novels, and it is hardly surprising that they are easily enough produced by writers who are themselves not native to the culture like Martha Grimes and Elizabeth George, American novelists, whose research skills and narrative confidence give a special force to their technically sound, if slightly patronizing, crime stories; they tend to focus on suitably quaint corners of Britain where there are capacities for mildly gothic sensation as well as the requisite contemporary kinds of personal betrayal.

Some writers use a fuller kind of topographic fictionalization. Many are the imaginary worlds of mystery like Catherine Aird's Calleshire or Ruth Rendell's almost equally vague Kingsmarkham (in her Wexford series). Names and some descriptions are foregrounded at first, but the place itself soon blurs: these fictionalized settings never seem to have the weight and detail of Dickens's Coketown or Eliot's

Middlemarch. In this genre the Barsetshire approach tends to be escapist.

That is certainly the effect, if a disappointing one, of Colin Watson's creation of Flaxborough for his series. He shapes in considerable detail a town, area and populace and sets out to construct social interactions reflecting on the ways in which work, local position, the value attached to a house and a setting all act as part of human self-evaluation. As Jane Austen and Thomas Hardy showed, the best (and most libel-free) social fictions may well derive from the fabrication of a society capable of being analysed fully. Watson, himself an exposer of the political oversimplifications of classic crime fiction in his book *Snobbery with Violence* (1971), proves as a social critic to be stronger on the ridiculous than the revelatory; his account of East Anglian life is determinedly old-fashioned, making Flaxborough a model of an old-style market town that has been able to exist like a fly in antique urban amber. They may exist – Stamford in Lincolnshire is an example – but they do not provide dynamic or veridical fiction in terms of either nation or region.

That type of regionalism is conservative by default, setting out to be shrewd and insightful, but through the balm of irony arriving at little more than playful praise of English eccentricity. A more deliberately positive form of rural traditionality is found in Frank Parrish's intriguing novels which set rustic practices and values firmly, and even violently, against those who seek to renovate and, therefore, in this account, defile the true depths of England. Dan Mallet is the hero of *Fire in the Barley* (1977) and two other novels, set in an unidentified part of the south-west near a market town called Milchester – the implied location is somewhere west of Wessex. Dan is a poacher, deep in rural cunning and hatred of the hypocrites and tricksters who import citified ideas into his beloved countryside. But he has not exactly sprung from the soil. At his mother's wish he trained as a bank clerk, and wore a suit and tie before returning to his country fastness. He retains the skills of the enemy: in *Fire in the Barley*, crucial to his frustration of a complex extortion plot is a mastery of telephones and kinds of contemporary trickery that are far from the world of what Marx called rural idiocy. Irresistible to women, deadly to rabbits, Dan Mallet is a hero for the drop-out decade rather than a credible voice of regional self-sufficiency, and for all his entertaining anti-urban feeling and a lively flow of field and stream information, Parrish's pastures seem overfertilized with parochial sentiment.

Such ruralism seems especially static, even self-indulgent, when compared with the more searching, and also self-consciously controlled, use of what might be called critical regionalism. A fine example is P. D. James's long and acclaimed novel *Devices and Desires*;

she attacks the issues from the start, stating in an Author's Preface:

> This story is set on an imaginary headland on the north-east coast of
> Norfolk. Lovers of this remote and fascinating part of East Anglia
> will place it between Cromer and Great Yarmouth, but they must not
> expect to recognise its topography nor to find Larksoken Nuclear
> Power Station, Lydsett village or Larksoken Mill . . . In this novel
> only the past and the future are real; the present, like the people and
> the setting, exist only in the imagination of the writer and her
> readers.[6]

The complex plot is filled out with strong characterization as is usual
in James and others (like Patricia Highsmith, Margaret Millar, Pat
Flower and Ruth Rendell) in what is essentially the psycho-thriller
genre, whether they have police detection or not. *Devices and Desires*
dramatizes a range of conflicts in the present – within the family,
across generations, between sexes, and on into the politics of modern
science and sociology. But also into history: the person who apparently
did the central murder lived in the anciently resonant Martyr's
Cottage, and, as one of the survivors says, 'Terrible things have
happened in the past to people living on this headland'.[7]

What James does here is effectively reverse Christie's insistence
that time's changes are hostile to her most valued characters. James has
fully internalized place and its significance to make the imaginary
headland a palimpsest of personal tragedies through time, projections
of nothing more than the individualizing effect of historical and social
change. Region itself becomes no less – but also no more – than a
language for privacy and its dramas, just as she has made her police
detective a poet and lonely sufferer. Christie wants time to stop in the
same place; James sees both time and place merely as modes of private
being.

This novel, with its strongly developed form as a saga of
criminalities, is one of James's stations on her remarkable journey
through the possibilities of the genre – on the way she has also dealt
with and moved away from police detection in the Dalgleish series,
towards the pure psycho-thriller with *Innocent Blood* (1980) and the
potential of feminist thrillers – private eye mode – in *An Unsuitable Job
for a Woman* (1972) and even a female police procedural as half of *A
Taste for Death* (1987). Most of these, interestingly, deal with both
London and its deep hinterland. But if *Devices and Desires* as critical
regionalism has special weight from James's confidence and skill,
especially in its psychologization of place, it is not in fact a unique
form.

June Thomson, for example, is a relatively little-known exponent
of this psychically absorbed regionalism. Operating around the

Chelmsford area, her Inspector Jack Finch is another sensitive loner who deals with conflicts faced by people who are themselves often represented by Thomson through the use of landscape and setting as a screen on which to project their anxieties; this, like *Devices and Desires*, is not so much a regional fiction as a fictionalization of the region. In *The Dark Stream* (1986) the very detailed topography of a village charts the passionately constrained feelings of an overlooked wife; in *The Spoils of Time* (1989) a woman returns to the area where she shared a life with her dead artist husband and finds both recognizable conflict and the trace of a new life – back in London; in Thomson's first novel, *Not One of Us* (1972), a man gives up business in London for isolation and victimization in a carefully chartered semi-rural terrain of human miscomprehension. In none of these, however, is the crime fully integrated with the psychologization of landscape: Thomson lacks the condensation of plot and place central to James and Christie. Indeed, that art of uniting the threat of the crime and the strains of regionality is close to the centre of the most successful crime writing – Collins again is the model, with his journeys of deception and his landscapes of fear. This lack may explain, why Thomson has not been so well known, for all her effective work, and why, sadly, she now seems to be turning to more marketable and rootless modes like her recent Sherlock Holmes pastiches.

Regional realities

All of the writers discussed above show different ways of employing an imaginary setting in the overall pattern of the crime novel. There is, however, another way of writing through place, which is to insist on the reality of the setting and to relish it in certain overt ways. Here, too, there are differences in approach, intensity and success. Some authors make setting everything. It would be a rare reader who can remember who actually did it in Arthur Upfield's *Death of Lake* (1954) or *Wings Above the Diamantina* (1936) but hardly any will not recall the stark scenes of Lake Eyre drying up, or the strange space of the Queensland clay-pans, seen from the air. Indeed, so strong is the role of setting in Australian crime fiction that not infrequently the landscape becomes a character and vengeance is achieved through flood, fire or ferocious fauna. That amount of emphasis is rare in Britain, though Dorothy Sayers's *The Nine Tailors* (1934) enlists the fenland waters as the agent of justice, and a particularly strong use of setting is found in some of her other novels, especially the Galloway expressionism of *The Five Red Herrings* (1931) and the Oxford guidebook tone of *Gaudy Night* (1935).

In those two, however, it seems that setting is merely part of Sayers's constant wish to 'write up' the detective form into something more than a mere puzzle; the greater involvement of a largely real setting in the action of *The Nine Tailors* might be thought to derive from the fact that she herself grew up in those parts, but that might itself be an oversimplification, like much that has been thought about setting in the mystery. Writers who very effectively realize context through plot are in themselves usually not natives of the area. Chandler was raised in London; Doyle came from Edinburgh; Simenon was Belgian; Christie only wrote rarely of her native South-West. Sayers might in this respect, as well as in her early espousal of the thriller mode as of genuine value, be not unfairly called an exceptional pioneer. On the occasions when Sayers's factual localization is plot-involved that also makes her especially unusual in the genre; the normal pattern in the 'realistic setting' regional crime story is (as in the run-of-the-mill 'imaginary setting' novel) to touch in here and there the context, especially at the beginning, and then move on to a more or less internalized representation of regional types bad and good.

Realism of setting, however apparently combative against the metropolis, is not necessarily realistic in the long run. John Harvey, the Nottingham loyalist, is in his views remarkably close to the pattern exemplified above from Christie's *The Mirror Crack'd from Side to Side*, as in the scene-setting sequence from *Cutting Edge*:

> When Resnick had first been a beat copper, walking these streets in uniform, himself and Ben Riley, the winoes, the down-and-outers, the homeless, had looked away as they passed. A scattering of old men who sat around their bottles of cider. Now there were kids who hung around the soup kitchens, the shelters, young enough to have been Resnick's own. And these thrust out a hand, looked you in the eye.
>
> Eighteen to twenty six. Smack in the trap. Too many reasons for not living at home, too few jobs, precious little from the state: now they shared Slab Square with the pigeons, sprawled or hunched before the pillars of the Council House, the ornate mosaic of the city's coat of arms, the pair of polished limousines waiting to carry civic dignitaries to this important function or that.
>
> The more you descended Goose Gate, the less prestigious the shops became. Two sets of lights and you were in the wholesale market, broken crates and discarded dark blue tissues, and beyond that Sneinton, where gentrification was still a word best left to crosswords. Fourteen Across: A process of changing the character of the inner-city.[8]

The eye is sympathetic to those who suffer change and degradation; it is also a little irritated by the aggression of the degraded young, and that links with the character of the analysis, more humanist and affective than Christie's somewhat macro-economic account. Harvey's final comment about crosswords is revealing, and authentic to his place-escaping mode: it shifts the focus into the observer's own intellectualizing – and it may be trivializing – mind, and that is what happens to the process of localization in this book, which is characteristic of Harvey's work. After its cityscape start, the plot becomes concerned with personal violence, with a subdued strain of medical corruption, and the observed themes of poverty and displacement are themselves focused through Resnick's own dislocated personal life, even in the context-privileging, but in this case distinctly languorous, television form. Nottingham may be the official setting, but value is only found in Resnick's emotive sensitivity and his own love of jazz, a combination of the fully private and the supra-socially transcendent. Idealized culture validates the hero's intuition; regionality is transcended into a fully bourgeois plane of values, at once above the regional and below the social.

A more coloured version of the same pattern is found in Colin Dexter's series of Inspector Morse novels which touch on the touristic possibilities of the Oxford area and, in keeping with their greater emphasis on soft-core masculinism, have provided the more successful of the two television series. Resnick is more of a dissenter, and his sense of layers of conflict within the Nottingham area do at least relate to, if not actually explore, the city's intricate industrial history, whereas Dexter only touches the most superficial aspects of Oxford, donnish cleverness and youthful flesh.

Regionalization has less name but more inherent place in the well-known series by Reginald Hill. The plots usually have a Yorkshire setting, but it is not oppressively overt. No noble old mills or heart-stopping moorscapes overload the text. Instead, rather like James but without the operatic summaries, Hill archeologizes the structure of the region's society at varying levels. *Deadheads* (1983) represents a whole range of local conflict, in business at both management and labour levels, in the emergence of black police, in public and private education, and through endemic social competition that leads to murder in surprising ways. These might well seem national issues, but by interrelating forms of social mobility characteristic of the area Hill maps a specific district and its community in a particular time and with some conviction. *Underworld* (1988) focuses the same techniques and area differently: the lines of strain are explored between a mining village and the wider world of recent history, especially against the trauma of 1984, but also inspected are the fissures in village communality. Against these revelations of a region's forms of unrest, with effective subtlety Hill offers the values of two police detectives who represent varied Yorkshire virtues in the apparently brutish but actually subtle Dalziell and the well-educated but somewhat uncertain Pascoe, who relies heavily on his wife, herself a local academic of pronounced social mobility and insight. That Dalziell resembles an aging macho caricature seems not to trouble most readers, but may have led to greater stress on the Pascoes in recent novels.

By focusing strongly on a region as itself, Hill has dismissed the simple and querulous category of regionality as merely defined against the capital. The novels are regional in the *Middlemarch* sense, and achieve what Colin Watson promises but fails to provide – a rich and self-sufficient cross-section of a particular society. More interestingly, Hill has not fallen into the heritage consolations of Christie nor yet the existential angst of James. He and his police see crime as very hard to identify, or at least to punish, and as a result his novels have a solidity of concern, a sense that the region can stand alone and examine itself, which is quite unusual. There are some exceptions, where Pascoe in particular travels to a crime elsewhere, and the commentary tends to be reduced to a somewhat pasteboard satire, as in *An Advancement of Learning* (1971) or *A Killing Kindness* (1980), but in general Hill's novels are a model of a thorough and subtly articulated engagement with the life of an area.

This full style of a positive regionalism that needs not speak the name is also found in John Wainwright's police stories set in unnamed northern towns – *All on a Summers Day* (1981) is a good example. It represents the area of a place like Leeds as entirely self-sufficient as far as policing is concerned, and regarding with derision any need for help from the Met – by the later 1970s known as a police force compromised by corruption (in large part due to the operations of crime fiction itself in the hands of G. F. Newman's police corruption stories like *Sir You Bastard* (1970) and the less austere revelations of the writers of *The Sweeney*). Wainwright is in mode a police procedural writer, learning from 'Ed McBain' and J. J. Marric, metropolitan masters of the form, who fictionalize New York and London respectively, but he avoids their patriarchal patterns of authority in both police and plot. In its swift cutting and unsentimentality, *All on a Summers Day* seems closer to television quasi-documentary like *Z Cars* and is one of Wainwright's most austerely credible and multi-levelled novels in the sub-genre; like George V. Higgins with a Yorkshire accent he presents a Leeds-like region self-absorbed and not minding very much the fact that, as he notes towards the end, 'This wasn't the Met'.[9]

Local accent, self-fascination, a satisfied sense of otherness – on modern British crime fiction those features must soon enough imply little but Glasgow and McIlvanney. In addition to his novels which deal with aspects of Scottish life such as the historical working class (*Docherty*), urban crime (*The Big Man*) and university affairs (*Remedy is None*), he has produced three novels about a tough and wise Glasgow police inspector beginning with the eponymous *Laidlaw* (1977). It sets the tone:

> 'Over here a minute,' Laidlaw said.
> They were at Glasgow Cross. After waiting a little while, they managed to get across the street to the pedestrian area in front of Krazy House. Laidlaw stopped before the small grey building Harkness had always assumed was on the site of the old Tollbooth – a kind of midget tower with a small balustrade at the top and above that the figure of a unicorn.
> 'How about that ?' Laidlaw said.
> Harkness was puzzled.
> 'The inscription,' Laidlaw explained.
> Harkness read the words carved on the stone: '*Nemo me impune lacessit.*' He knew it was Latin but didn't know what it meant.
> 'No one assails me with impunity,' Laidlaw said. 'Wha daur meddle wi' me ? Did you know that was there ?'
> 'I like the civic honesty of that.' Laidlaw was smiling. 'That's the wee message carved on the heart of Glasgow. Visitors are advised not to be cheeky.'
> The message gained force as they went beyond the Cross. At that point the Trongate divides into two streets running east, the Gallowgate on the north, London Road on the south. The sense of a choice is illusory. Both lead to the same waste of slum tenements hopefully punctuated with redevelopments, like ornamental fountains in a desert.[10]

Like the other Laidlaw novels, and indeed all of McIlvanney's work, this passage hovers between sentimental Scottery and a cool eye on one of Europe's centres of industrial exploitation. Laidlaw's remarks can be read variously. Does he suggest that the Black Watch, whose motto is praised, went to the gallows by going down the road to London? Is it implied that urban development would be a fantasy in such a desensitized town? Is the underlying voice that of the detective or the author? Closer as he is to the tough fantasy of Dalziell than the new-man urgency of Pascoe, Laidlaw himself is a questionable voice. McIlvanney has said, in his introduction to the educational edition of *Laidlaw*, that he wrote the novel primarily about Glasgow itself (of which, by the way, he was not a native) and that 'What I feel in Glasgow is the accumulated weight of working-class experience'.[11] This, he makes it clear, includes being pressured into wrong-doing, and that is what Laidlaw both understands and exposes as the core of the region's meaning in the context of crime.

McIlvanney is claiming a double function, both regional and class-based, for his crime novel. It is a strong introduction, as fluent and also as limited as Chandler's famous self-justification in 'The Simple Art of Murder'. Whereas Chandler claimed he returned murder to real killers, McIlvanney asserts that we might all be of that criminal ilk. Regionalism serves two functions for McIlvanney: it is a way to feel both underprivileged against other and more southerly regions, and also proud of an enduring particularity. As is shown by McIlvanney's occasional slide into sentiment, even self-pity, this overt kind of regionalism can share the vices of nationalism. But local feeling is also penetrated, as it is in different ways by James, Christie and Hill, for a statement about general verities that is a good deal more powerful. Regionalism can be both a restricted horizon and a speaking position.

Whether it is marginal or overdone, elided or absorbed, invented or authentic – and those pairs of terms are not necessarily opposites – the impact of regionalism in the British crime novel is both complex and elusive. At the heart of the forming of the genre, capable of focusing a naïve sense of grievance over change, equally able to become a metaphor for the human anxieties that surround crime and social crisis of all kinds, regionality at its most fully effective exists to define a certain area for thorough investigation and to stratify in local authenticity the tensions in personal and social life that crime fiction can focus through the drama and mystery of a particular offence.

The metropolitan region

None of the patterns discussed, of course, is in theory incapable of being written in and about that other major region, London itself. If that suggests that finely imagined thrillers have been written about London areas, with a sense of human complexity symbolized through setting, it is patently true – Josephine Bell's *The Port of London Murders* (1938) and Christianna Brand's *London Particular* (1952) are two strong examples. But if to suggest that London too can be a region is just a way of dismissing the whole usefulness of regionality as a way of analysing British fiction, then the statement becomes only a bland assurance about the polymorphousness of crime fiction and so by extension a dismissal of the value of regionality as a concept. That negative use of the idea of London as a region must face two grounds for opposition, two ways of insisting that regionality is indeed a varied and dynamic force in British crime fiction, objections that emerge from considering the quasi-regional character of London writing.

The first point is that London writers do not in general see their characters' problems as being in some sense founded on the historical and social forces of metropolitan power against the rest of the country: in her 1970s psycho-thrillers Ruth Rendell made the streets of north London run with self-destructive menace, but there is no sense of national drama involved in those encounters. Julian Symons's suburban melodramas have held up a mirror to many Londoners concerned with status and self, but they are without any wider socio-geographic perspective. Because London's regionality is itself rooted in national tensions, these London-only novels strip the capital of its full historicity and the potential comprehension of its own making; crime fiction written in that setting is reduced to privatized angst.

The other, related, comment that rises from considering London as if it were a region is that those who have written most powerfully of London's setting as a way of figuring human strain are those who have made the city reach out to its hinterland and beyond – Rendell at times, especially when writing as Barbara Vine, James in some of her recent novels, and above all Collins and Doyle, progenitors of the crime-fiction form in its fully integrated localization, which included the new interrelation of regions in a dynamics of power. They operated across a wide enough area in plot and terrain to embrace in their treatment of metropolitan anxieties the topographical and historical mobilities which established in the first place the anxious metropolis, that force-field through which the patterns of crime fiction first and lastingly took their generic shape as explorations of the darker areas, regions even, of human and social anxiety.

Born when regions had to recognize the power of the metropolis to complicate the uncovering of crime, developed through the interrelationship of extra-regional power to both create and resolve local disorder, enfeebled by too great a reliance on regional naïvety, strengthened by a comprehension of the genuine structures of an area's forces, crime fiction as it has developed in this country is not merely a literary model of regional culture but, much more than that, it is also a living medium, at varying times strident and subtle, timid and courageous, of how people of many kinds have coped with the forces of modern society and their impact across the varying regions of Britain.

References

[1] See Stephen Knight, *Form and Ideology in Crime Fiction* (London, Macmillan, 1980), pp.11–15.
[2] John Bellamy, *Crime and Public Order in England in the Later Middle Ages* (London, Routledge, 1973), pp.4–5.

3 Wolfgang Schivelbush, *The Railway Journey* (Oxford, Blackwell, 1980).
4 Agatha Christie, *The Mirror Crack'd from Side to Side* (London, Collins, 1962).
5 Marion Shaw and Sabine Vanacker, *Reflecting on Miss Marple* (London, Routledge, 1991).
6 P. D. James, *Devices and Desires* (London, Faber, 1989).
7 Ibid., p.408.
8 John Harvey, *Cutting Edge* (London, Viking, 1991), pp.7–8.
9 John Wainwright, *All on a Summer's Day* (London, Macmillan, 1981), p.286.
10 William McIlvanney, *Laidlaw* (London, Hodder, 1977), p.92.
11 William McIlvanney, *Laidlaw* (London, Hodder, 1989), p.ix.

4

Aztecs in Troedrhiwgwair:
recent fictions in Wales

TONY BIANCHI

We supplemented our diet with tinned goods from the shops in Tredegar which had escaped looting before the town was abandoned during the main retreat into mid-Wales. There, in the empty heartlands of their nation, the Welsh believed themselves safe from further Aztec encroachment.[1]

Christopher Evans's *Aztec Century* (1993) projects a parallel universe in which Britain is colonized by Aztecs. Narrated, unreliably, by the self-styled Princess Catherine, daughter of the King of Britain, it employs Wales as her place of exile, as a last redoubt for the vanquished British, and as home for the 'true native, Bevan'. Most of the story, however, takes place elsewhere in Britain, in Russia and in the imperial capital, Mexico City. At the end of the novel, Catherine learns of the Aztec belief in 'countless existences, all occurring together but apart from one another, like multiple reflections in a mirror'. Passing through the 'doorway' of that mirror, she enters a different and more radical exile in our own Wales – 'lost not only to history but to memory itself' – and is left awaiting an apocalypse of 'gold and feathers and serpents of fire'. Much concerned with belonging, displacement, thresholds of identity and the 'fragile sense of self', the narrative parallels two possible worlds without finally ratifying either. Wales becomes either the only anchor of reality, or merely one of a number of possible worlds: the reader who demands realistic fidelity will choose one meaning, the less fettered reader another, although the unreliability of the narrator casts further doubt over both.

Aztec Century has not, to date, been reviewed or marketed as a 'Welsh' novel, as a novel about Wales, or as a work of any particular interest to Welsh readers. Its author, a native of Tredegar but living in

London, has nowhere been formally recognized as a Welsh writer.[2] Indeed, in any simple representational or referential sense, his novel has little to do with Welsh topography, people or history. And yet, although not an incisive work, it can be seen to articulate in an acute form many of the preoccupations of contemporary Welsh writers: preoccupations with boundaries of time, space and identity in a period of profound change; with the signs by which these boundaries are less and less adequately recognized; and with the dislocated subject seeking, through these uncertainties, a stable habitation.

For the writer, Wales has become a blind spot which will not let the narrative gaze settle centrally. Demographically volatile for over a century, it is now the most heterogeneous of the four 'home countries'.[3] Between 1976 and 1986 over one million people – 36 per cent of the population – moved in or out of Wales, and over large areas of the country only a bare majority of the population is Welsh-born. This process has both intensified traditional definitions of 'inside' and 'outside' and, at the same time, rendered them increasingly inadequate to reflect new patterns of diversity. In a society for which mass migration to and from English cities is a defining and formative feature, notions of borders and spatial identity have become ambiguous and confusing. Internally, changes in patterns of employment, linguistic behaviour and class relations have rendered traditional totalizing discourses progressively redundant. In Gwynedd, Welsh speakers are less well represented in high-status occupations than English-born immigrants, a situation which lends support to an internal colonial reading of social relations. In industrial south Wales, however, the Welsh-speaking minority is much better represented at this level than the native-born, English-speaking majority, provoking a quite different perception of ethnic privilege and power. At the same time, moving across and through these divisions is an increasingly privatized culture associated with the decline of traditional industries and the erosion of the communal ethos they generated: a culture of consumption and lifestyle enhancement in which indicators such as VCR ownership, DIY activity and clothing style have supplanted more collective arenas of cultural and political identification. Although a melodramatic formulation, it is easy to see the devolution referendum of 1979 and the miners' strike of 1984–5 as the historic moments of collapse of the two grand narratives of Welsh identity and continuity. In their wake, a Wales of new contradictions and paradoxes has emerged. Increasing institutional cohesion accompanies declining cultural and political homogeneity. The eclipse of faith in traditional icons is drowned out by their repackaging as saleable commodities. In a Wales which has 'become its own industry',[4] the crisis of recognition is seen most vividly as a crisis of semiotics.

It is, in particular, the new proliferation of consumer- and investor-targeted rhetorics against which the more muted vocabularies of fiction must be put into perspective. It is in the craft-shop and museum, the brochure insists, that 'the real Wales awaits your discovery':[5] a 'secret Wales' which, paradoxically, requires the tourist gaze to quicken it. Through reconstructing 'the spine-tingling land of spirits' and the 'fiery Denbigh Dragon', Rhyl's 'Knights Caverns' affect to reveal 'the nation's history with startling realism'.[6] At Llanberis's 'Power of Wales' exhibition, gobbets of historical discourse are synchronized with winking fibre-glass oak trees. The Development Board for Rural Wales markets its territory as 'the British Business Park',[7] hiring Smith and Jones to promote the 'New Wales Solution'[8] to the mobility-conscious international businessman. Aimed at the outsider, and serving the interests of discourses conducted and controlled elsewhere, these narratives nevertheless become potently self-constituting, concocting a Wales which is in fact neither old nor new, but a banal sloganization of perceived economic imperatives.

For the reader, there is a more specific problem of recognition, in that contemporary Welsh fiction is never in fact what it might academically be construed to be: constituting a community of readers is as difficult as constituting a shared Wales. Many of the works of writers discussed here, including Alun Richards and Ron Berry, are out of print. Most of those in Welsh are not available in translation. Others are issued by small publishers and are marginalized in the commercial book trade and only patchily reviewed in the press. In terms of market penetration, Iris Gower's nine million sales render virtually insignificant those of all other novelists who use Wales as their raw material. In terms of production, seventy-one of ninety-two novels published by Welsh writers between 1989 and 1992 were issued by non-Welsh publishers, who conform not to any indigenous agenda of cultural value or interest but to the commercial requirements of the metropolitan publishing industry. For most readers in Wales and outside, *How Green Was My Valley* (1939) remains ubiquitously visible as a contemporary novel while Wiliam Owen Roberts's *Pestilence* (1991) is already inaccessible. The real arena where contesting narratives of Wales meet is severely skewed, as it must always be, by the material circumstances of cultural production and consumption.

Nor, however, does that community of readers exist even in the reduced form of a coherent intelligentsia. There is no comprehensive taxonomy of Welsh fiction even in the most basic bibliographical and cataloguing senses, let alone a developed critical context in which the usual negotiations of canons and comparative readings can take place. In English, partial readings do exist: in D. Tecwyn Lloyd's critique of rural romance,[9] for example, and in the readings of working-class fiction provided by Raymond Williams and Dai Smith.[10] A wider critique, however, remains as elusive as 'The Great Welsh Novel' itself. In Welsh, the first book-length study of (predominantly) the twentieth-century novel appeared only in 1992.[11] Remarkably, although it invokes Eco, Brecht, Flaubert and Joyce, it omits any reference to Raymond Williams, Gwyn Thomas, Glyn Jones and most other English-language novelists in Wales, save to express envy of the Anglo-Welsh novel's 'colour' and 'extroversion'. Only one study, M. Wynn Thomas's stimulating *Internal Difference*,[12] endeavours to read across the linguistic divide, although his discussion of recent fiction is framed in a discourse of national crisis which privileges certain readings of the Welsh condition. In general, discussion of Welsh fiction has been driven by ideologies of Welshness which have engaged more comfortably with poetry and have tended not to move far beyond discourses of national identity and representational authenticity, severely limiting what is admitted into the forum of debate. Ironically, a crisis of recognition is manifested most clearly and self-defeatingly in the failure to admit into a Welsh field of vision texts of radical ambiguity which cannot be adduced to reinforce one or another totalizing narrative. In choosing novels for discussion, therefore, I have presumed no sanctioned mode of 'knowing' Wales and no privileged centre of authorship. I have admitted, in other words, the possibility of Aztecs in Troedrhiwgwair; the reality of authors who write simultaneously from Tredegar and London, Pandy and Cambridge; and the reality of those, like myself, who read as migrants, with ambiguous affiliations, rather than as members of an ideal, homogeneous readership.

Some forms of fiction are themselves, of course, committed to closing off ambiguity and reducing problems of recognition to simple mechanistic aspects of plot resolution. This is particularly true of the tradition of historical romance in which a succession of writers, from Allen Raine to Iris Gower, have succeeded, uniquely, in conveying an image of Wales to a mass audience. The limiting features of this genre do not, by any means, preclude serious attempts at representing the complex forces of historical change and the texture of everyday life. Iris Gower's *Copper Kingdom* (1983),[13] the first of numerous best sellers, conscientiously details aspects of nineteenth-century industrial Swansea, including the process of smelting, conditions of work, the growth of competition from Chile and Australia, and the mixed population of the city. The casualty is not representation *per se*, but the full articulation of the subject with the world that is represented. Whilst there is a recognition of human agency, its significance is ultimately subordinated to the requirements of the romance plot, with its 'dark and vital men', passionate amours, explosions, illegitimate babies and statutory revelations about parentage. The conflict between capital and labour is, as so often, closed off in the personal romance of boss and worker's daughter. The subject, displaced in and by history, is reconstituted in a habitation which transcends that history. 'Nothing will ever separate us again,' the novel concludes: 'I'm taking you home.'

In Alexander Cordell's more rigorous engagement with historical process, the use of the family-saga form has the opposite effect. The subject is afforded a fixity, not outside time, but within the prescribed historic roles in which all subjectivity is cast. In *Rape of the Fair Country* (1959),[14] the Mortymers are implausibly visited by both Crawshay Bailey and Zephaniah Williams as this is the only means by which they can be seen as significant in a narrative of representative individuals. Characters, in the end, are condemned to fulfil their historical destinies as hindsight perceives them. The whole is drawn together in a vivid first-person effusion, celebrating 'pride of place' and 'love of country' and conjuring dramatic tableaux of significant moments in a remembered past. Although conflict is foregrounded, it is finished, its outcome known. The single articulating voice could never address itself to the openness of the present, or of a past re-created – as it is in a different kind of historical fiction – as though it were present and still ambiguous.

Genre fantasy employs more extreme strategies to maroon Wales within fixed orbits of meaning. Most frequently, this meaning consists of an essential inscrutability: an orientalization of Wales in terms of a normality established elsewhere. As a device of defamiliarization, Welsh locations have served the purposes of numerous horror writers. In John Blackburn's *For Fear of Little Men* (1972),[15] for example, the English protagonists find the locals a 'difficult people to understand . . . so pagan, so morbidly superstitious': a trait manifested, ludicrously, in their worship of the pre-Celtic deity, 'Daran'. Phil Rickman's popular *Candlenight* (1991)[16] offers a similar scenario, but is invested with considerably more circumstantial verity and a contemporary political message. Here, the outsiders discover an 'insidiously primeval form of nationalism' and, notwithstanding their efforts to 'go native', suffer the grizzly fate visited upon all not 'protected by [the] aura of Welshness'.

It is in the field of children's fiction, however, that oriental Wales comes into its own, most often supplying the magical or sinister backdrop for visiting adventurers or holiday-makers.[17] Of the ten English-language novels considered for the 1990 Tir na nOg Award, four were within this category. In another, Jenny Nimmo's *The Chestnut Soldier* (1989),[18] primordial Welshness is attained through a miraculous rite of passage: as Gwydion Glyn enters the world of magic, 'he forgot his English and wrote Welsh poetry that no one understood'. A children's imprint has recently emerged, dedicated specifically to the correction of this representational bias. In one of its most interesting titles, Pamela Purnell's *Denny and the Magic Pool* (1993), the native boy hero is himself the author of the magic story through which disrupted order is restored.[19] The novel also establishes marginal, multi-ethnic, urban Cardiff as a valid site for that magic and does so in a way which fulfils rather than negates the contemporary realist plot.

Wales is also used as a site or metaphor for more complex narrative concerns where the question of expediency is not always so easily resolved. Anthony Burgess's *Any Old Iron* (1989)[20] revisits the myth of the Welsh as the 'lost tribe of Israel' and as peers of all those marginalized and dispossessed throughout history. It concludes with the Welsh/Russian migrant hero Reg Jones, despairing at the ceaseless ravages of war, aspiring in vain to a 'reality transcending time'. The survival of Wales *in* time, however, is largely restricted to the Karno-like ultra-nationalist 'Sons of Arthur', a prototype of groups beloved of so many writers dabbling with the 'matter' of Wales, and a descendant of the idealized hyperborean of traditional Welsh romance.

Kingsley Amis's *The Old Devils* (1986),[21] too, can be read as a novel only circumstantially relevant to Wales. The return home of professional Welshman Alun Weaver provides the author with ample material for his campaign against bullshit, manifested here as a 'whole way of writing' which need not be about Wales 'but always is'. The sub-text, it has been argued,[22] is much more the lament of English Old Fogeyism at the perceived decline of cultural difference – 'Everywhere new here is the same as new things in England' – than a serious attempt to satirize bogus Welshness. Although shallow and dated in its reading of Wales, however, the novel invites comparison with other works which engage with themes of exile and return. Weaver's vain attempt, in writing his novel *Coming Home*, to reinstate a chimeric continuity echoes the nostalgic lie knowingly and avariciously peddled by Alun Richard's Melville in 'The Former Miss Merthyr Tydfil'.[23] It is the same endeavour which Emyr Humphreys's Jones, 'murmuring bullshit loudly to himself', perceives as the 'absurd vestiges of outworn obligations'.[24] And it is the same ambivalence concerning 'obligations of attachment' and cultural authenticity that we see in Richard Jones's novel of return, *A Way Out* (1969):[25] a novel similarly located in a provincial no man's land ('a place to get away from') by an author exercised, like Amis, by a sense of national (British) decline. Reading Amis simply in terms of false representation and displaced Englishness sets up too easy dichotomies between 'inside' virtue and 'outside' contempt.

Wales is also used by Alice Thomas Ellis to frame two of her fables of interpersonal malice. Again, however, they cannot be read simply within a discourse of realistic representation. In *The Sin Eater*

(1977)[26] the protagonists, most of whom are themselves Welsh, 'would sooner have admitted to a strain of hobgoblin, or even jew' than the common Welshry of the town. The latter 'were all the same, undifferentiated . . . sliding out sly Welsh words'. The real subject, however, is a form of internal alienation for which such stereotyping is both manifestation and Gothic metaphor. The family's failure to communicate, with themselves or others, is projected in the semiotic confusion of Llanelys: a place blighted by modernity, tourists 'all somehow misshapen', nuns in lipstick and souvenirs made in Stoke. The sense of enclosure by 'loony aboriginals', of a 'superstitious people seeing signs and potents in everything', prepares the way for the more sinister dislocations with which the novel concludes. Wales, in this formulation, is the site of lost meanings, of homes which are not homes, of returns which only confirm exile. Ermyn, through whom these experiences are articulated, seeks consolation by inscribing herself within alternative narratives – including the Bible and the Mabinogion, and in particular that of the shape-changing, banished Blodeuwedd – but these only confirm her isolation, her ultimate regression to a state where 'I was never born'. The novel presents a crisis of the subject for whom Wales is inevitably, as implied by the self-referential place-name, Llanelys, an internalized landscape.

Unexplained Laughter (1985)[27] employs the more conventional holiday cottage stratagem to a similar end. The visitors, Lydia and Betty, fear 'mad axemen' and 'nationalists'. Instead, they hear the 'ethereal voice of the dead Angharad', who is 'not normal', and, like Ermyn, invokes Blodeuwedd and belongs to a family 'cut off from the rest of society'. The story serves to demonstrate, in the words of Angharad's brother, Beuno, that in a small community, 'passion . . . became distilled and reduced to poison . . .': the only peace achievable, the only form of authenticity, is 'a kind of pagan solitude'. The real subject of the novel – Lydia's 'sorrow of not belonging' – is transmuted, on the one hand, into an aspect of the human condition and, on the other, into a trait of the unwelcoming natives. She has, however, an ironic awareness of this process: 'I always used to wonder what they did when I wasn't watching them. Sometimes they were eating their babies.' Again, the stereotype is a consciously deployed Gothic projection of isolation, not only *from* place but as a defining characteristic of people *in* that place for which the disembodied Angharad is *genius loci*. It is a figuration by which the narrator and implied reader – reading across the displaced voices – can both feel and assuage the perception of self as 'a migrant bird'. The strategy is a compensatory, even an evasive one. It can be excluded, however, only by a strictly bordered concept of Welsh writing which does not admit migrancy except as part of the pathology of national dissolution.

Migrancy is even more centrally the subject of Adam Lively's *The Snail* (1991),[28] in which Welsh narrator-in-exile Harry Morgan, 'a minor planet on the outer edges of the Belgravian galaxy', embarks on a quest for two Polish refugees in wartime London. Through the eyes of these liminal figures, place is perceived as 'disturbed', alien, and full of puzzling and contradictory signs. Finding Antonin Trenter, Morgan believes, offers 'an end to the internal migration that was taking me further and further from the war, from the world . . .' and a means of knowing 'what was at the centre'. The labyrinth, however, duplicitously signed like the 'sugared cottage' of Hanzel and Gretel, recedes endlessly and 'the film never finishes. The national anthem is never played.' Like *White Chappell: Scarlet Tracings* (1987)[29] and *Downriver* (1991)[30] by Ian Sinclair (of Bridgend and London), *The Snail* is a novel of the post-modern city, in which the condition of migrancy is definitive and cannot be consoled by reference to a past or another life. Everything is 'inside the tunnel'. 'Things that spoke of outside' are mere 'dissociated fragments'. Morgan as autonomous subject – which includes Morgan as Welshman – no longer exists in a world which negates personal histories and attachments: he is, as he himself perceives, merely a character in others' 'stories'. By the same token, of course, the first-person narrative is unable to 'measure', in Raymond Williams's sense of the word, the distance traversed by Morgan as exile. The effect is, again, to render his Welshness an expedient, although the author's refusal to pursue a fiction of origins and connections makes the novel interesting when read alongside a literature for which this has been a dominant, even obsessive, means of constructing the Welsh subject; it also offers parallels with recent developments in Welsh-language fiction.

That fiction of connections has, since the late 1960s, been articulated predominantly around issues of nationality and more specifically around a discourse of cultural nationalism. Again, it is the unsettled exile who is centred as subject, seeking new forms of authenticity across the fault lines of that discourse. This fiction, too, has its reductive formulations, particularly in the crude roots romance of which Marion Harris's *Amelda* (1989)[31] is a representative example. Here, the granddaughter of 'Dragon', a nationalist grandee, languishes in Liverpool, is briefly seduced by the bright lights of London, resists emigration with her American lover, and finally, choosing patriotism before materialism, returns to her ancestral hearth. The conclusion is without doubt affirmative, but of a Wales that can only exist as an object of heroic, individual dedication. Ironic, non-heroic narratives are more typical. In Paul Ferris's *A Distant Country* (1983),[32] for example, return to Wales is the occasion for a quite contrary reorientation. Harry Jenkins, PR officer for the National Energy

Board, is dispatched to his home town in connection with a scheme to sink a new coal-mine. The project is opposed by the Sons of Llewelyn, a shadowy nationalist group 'from that other Wales that (Harry) hardly knew'. He seeks its leader, ap Einion, 'in the hills somewhere', and gets lost because 'the place was not on the map'. Instead, he finds the 'scattered remnants of a nearly extinct people': 'All around him was the quintessence of Wales, a bitter inhospitable nothingness that he shrank from . . . the place, like the past, had nothing to offer.' In so far as those remnants are granted a voice, it is one which Harry can easily dismiss: 'The whole Welsh movement is a bad case of melodrama.' The 'reality' of the modern (pit, power station, machinery) is set against the 'mystical claptrap' which is all that the 'other' Wales can muster in its defence. Ultimately, however, alienation from that Wales becomes a trope for those 'layers of ghost' which Harry must exorcize from his personal history (particularly the death of his wife). His affair with nationalist saboteur Pen ('Welsh on her tongue was disturbing') and its termination are part of a process of growing away from a dead past. Pen, together with the memories of wife and Wales which she awakens, can then safely be assigned to 'some remote ap Einion land that might as well have been the planet Neptune'. Equilibrium is restored through return to Surrey's 'management course' country: also a 'wilderness', but one at least in which no illusions are harboured. The novel's stark polarization of personal integrity and political wish-fulfilment is, once more, representationally crude. It does, however, provide metaphors for those real feelings of exclusion and disillusion which surrounded the devolution debate and the high-tide of seventies nationalism.

Robert Watson's *Rumours of Fulfilment* (1982)[33] attempts a more even-handed engagement with the same subject. However, the privileging of displacement over the too-prescriptive belonging of political nationalism is already evident in the opening quotation from Emerson: 'People wish to be settled; only so far as they are unsettled is there any hope for them.' The narrative proceeds to describe the political unsettling of Rhiannon and the apolitical domestic settling of her sister, Ruth, during the period surrounding the devolution referendum. Rhiannon rejects the 'political concoction of misery and nostalgia' which she associates with the devolution debate and resents 'the peculiar compulsion to have an attitude in the first place' regarding Wales. Attending a campaign meeting, she is confused by an 'onslaught of metaphors and emblems . . . St George, the Welsh dragon, fire, the treason of the blue books, the Tudors, roses, leeks, motorways . . .' Like the English 'eavesdroppers' in the audience, the welter of signs leaves her 'bewildered, uninspired and somewhat snubbed by her own ignorance'. Subsequently she moves beyond that cynicism and discovers that the referendum 'had had nothing to do with their lives after all'. The shattered fragments of her life, the deaths of her brother and father, the crisis of nationality – all are successfully internalized. 'A stranger in a maze devoid of clues', she departs with her English lover, but not before burning down the 'sad burden' of the family house. Ruth, meanwhile, gets on with life, marries a Welsh speaker, learns Welsh herself and shows fidelity to the past through caring for her grandfather. The wider business of Wales is left (once more) to a nascent guerilla group, 'Wales Now', led by a man with a 'misty, visionary gleam' in his eyes, whose first political act is to burn down Rhiannon's lover's cottage. Packaged as a novel which attempts to answer the question 'Why did the referendum go the way it did?' it is at pains, like Rhiannon herself, not to offer simplistic answers, and delineates at least two modes of authenticity, neither of which fits any glib political agenda of stock notions of identity. There remain, however, two problems which characterize this kind of writing. One is the symbolic over-determination of narrative and character, which constantly strains the realist terms in which the novel is framed and threatens to deteriorate into apocalyptic or sentimental melodrama. The other is seen in a conclusion which is deterministically pessimistic because a particular discourse of identity is both valorized and demythologized. 'There's a lot of Welshness everywhere, but no sense of a nation' sums up the self-defeating regret which permeates not only the character of Rhiannon but the novel itself and the period of its composition.

A similar process is at work in Aled Islwyn's *Cadw'r Chwedlau'n Fyw* (1984) ('Keeping the Legends Alive'),[34] which focuses on the period between the Investiture and the Referendum. Disillusion with traditional notions of Welsh identity is the prevalent mood: as for Watson's Rhiannon, the nation is just a rumour, a prop of false consciousness. In reality, 'there is no longer any nation there. Only individuals keeping the traditions alive . . .' Redemption, it is tentatively suggested, may be possible through those individuals' personal fidelity to each other. With the pregnant heroine looking to the future, the narrative once again leaps from a putatively gimlet-eyed scrutiny of the real Wales to a symbolic gesture. Disillusion with nationalist aspirations gives way to a more honest but severely pared-down personal resolution. Social purpose is undermined, but in large measure because the social agenda established at the outset is so selective.

A number of formal strategies have been used to evade the problem of symbolic over-determination. Moira Dearnley's *That Watery Glass* (1973)[35] employs a first-person narrator who constructs her identity in imitation of literary characters, notably Milton's Comus. In this way, another liminal figure explores her estrangement

53

from her working-class background, from the English middle-class background of her lover and from Welsh-speaking militant nationalists, whilst at the same time appearing as though it is she, not the author, who is 'too much given to performing symbolic actions'. Mary Jones's first-person Gothic novel, *Resistance* (1985),[36] also explores the relationship between English speakers and Welsh speakers, but departs much more radically from realist expectations. Here, the topos of the oppressive house becomes a metaphor for national decay, its 'interminable passages' and 'spying walls' discomfiting the outsider, Ann Thomas, who has 'no sense of being anyone or being anywhere'. The surrounding landscape, with its ruins, burned-down cottages and nationalist slogans is inhabited by ghosts which reproach her unbelonging: 'just when you thought you were safe, choosing the middle of nowhere to lose your identity in, the struggles inherited from defeated ancestry leapt out at you from country waysides.' Ann, however, overcomes distrust and develops a relationship with Aled, a local 'Mohican' and Saunders Lewisian nationalist. In the end, he is killed by his own bomb, setting the hotel on fire in the process. This purgation and her battle against cancer lead to Ann's realization that survival is all and that the only significant belonging is to the great 'constellations' of humanity. Again, a particular construct of Wales is conjured and exorcized to facilitate an essentially personal revelation. Although the novel's Gothic frame does permit that experience to be generalized without a sense of excessive tendentiousness, it nevertheless remains cast in fixed and limiting oppositions between inside and outside, closed and open, parochial Welsh speaking and rootless English speaking, and the dominant pathological metaphors of health and decay.

The real-life Mohicans of Mary Jones's hotel have, in Welsh, produced their own very different narratives of passage, displacement and epistemological confusion, favouring a loose, picaresque form which does not constantly tend towards resolution. Goronwy Jones's *Dyddiadur Dyn Dwad* ('A Stranger's Diary') (1978),[37] Siôn Eirian's *Bob yn y Ddinas* ('Bob in the City') (1979),[38] Gareth Miles's *Treffin* ('Bordertown') (1979),[39] Twm Miall's *Cyw Dôl* ('Dole Queue') (1990),[40] and Angharad Tomos's *Yma o Hyd* ('Still Here') (1985)[41] all employ geographical shifts to explore cultural and class borders and notions of authenticity. In addition, they represent a deliberate violation of sanctioned modes of writing and representation in Welsh. The satirical, *faux-naïve* narrative of *Dyddiadur Dyn Dwad*, for example, relates the story of its own condemnation in a local newspaper as an 'insult to the Christian Welsh tradition'. Siôn Eirian's *Bob yn y Ddinas*, again in diary form, and vilified by an Eisteddfod adjudicator as 'a waste of genius', traces a passage *away* from such respectability, to working-class, multi-ethnic Cardiff: an experience which resists narration within the terms of his previous cultural certainties and modes of expression. The narrator attempts repeatedly to achieve an adequate style and subject but is always thrown back on the self-conscious rehearsal of isolation. The work concludes, unable to shape its story in English or in Welsh, with the sole conviction that 'there is no truth or falsity, only facts and the absence of facts'. In Angharad Tomos's *Yma o Hyd* the narrator – another Blodeuwedd – is doing time in an English gaol for her Welsh Language Society activities. The novel translates the frustrations and contradictions of this situation into tropes for the national condition. It is also, like *Dyddiadur Dyn Dwad* and *Bob yn y Ddinas*, concerned with the problem of writing about a Wales in which the imagined communities of Saunders Lewis and Waldo Williams and their closed rhetorics of 'beasts', 'towers' and 'vineyards' have been rendered obsolete or appropriated by a materially comfortable and politically quiescent middle class. An alternative text – the Dafydd Iwan song which gives the novel its title – provides a more honest and ambiguous motto, but the narrator, ironically and knowingly, remains locked and increasingly isolated within the imperatives of the older formulations – an 'anxiety of influence' explored further in Aled Islwyn's *Os Marw Hon* (1990)[42] and Gareth Miles's *Trefaelog* (1989).[43]

All of these novels are, in one sense, essays in a new kind of realism: a radical stripping down of illusions for which the seeming ingenuousness of the diary form, or equivalent, provides a suitable vehicle. In their metafictional preoccupations, however, they point to other novels which adopt a more radical scepticism towards all narratives and the agencies which construct them. Wiliam Owen Roberts's *Bingo* (1985)[44] is something of a formal exercise in such scepticism. Unlocated in time and space, and doubly fictive through borrowings from Kafka, it employs the form and rhetoric of the psychological thriller to tease the reader's sense of recognition and frustrate confidence in the narrator. The story opens in clichéd genre mode; its stylistic predictability, however, is subverted by the ambiguous signs and uncertain identities which it narrates. Before its conclusion, it is revealed to be not the novel's 'real' story at all but a film observed by the narrator, who then embarks on his own, 'true' story: a story which, in turn, degenerates into a parody of the earlier film. The text itself takes on the form of a film script, the conventions of which alone hold together its random, unresolved convolutions. The narrative permits no settling of reality beyond its manipulation of signs and structures.

Mihangel Morgan's *Dirgel Ddyn* ('Secret Man') (1993)[45] also constructs an unidentified location 'full of mysteries, secrets and unanswered questions': a city-as-labyrinth, like that of Adam Lively, in which the displaced hero's efforts to secure fixed meanings are constantly undermined. Characters are never as they appear or claim to be, although the most insubstantial of them – invented by the narrator, Cadwaladr, to achieve the required number of students for his night class – emerges as the novel's dominant figure. Formally, Cadwaladr's home narrative is the Welsh literature he teaches, but he glosses his experiences instead through reference to American and European films. The story gradually acquires the inscrutability of one of his favourites, *Duel*, which dramatizes a 'mystery without solution'. In a parody of narrative manipulation and improbability, Cadwaladr's creation climbs to high rank as a Tory politician. At this point, however, Cadwaladr wins a small measure of control over his narrative and, through purposeful use of the image (blackmail with photographs), achieves partial escape from the trap of epistemological and moral relativism.

In Robin Llywelyn's *Seren Wen ar Gefndir Gwyn* ('A White Star on a White Background') (1992),[46] the discourse of disrupted recognition is transferred to the global plane in a fantastic parody of international warfare. The belligerent parties echo, variously, Nazi Germany, the Gulf War and Celtic mythology, but their anachronistic juxtaposition renders them essentially indistinguishable. The empty, borderless land of Haf Heb Haul is a conceptual joke directed ironically at these excessively bordered spaces, as is the heraldic emblem of the title, in which the boundaries of the star (and by implication of the nation) *can* have only a conceptual status. These are 'imagined communities' in a radically literal sense. The subversion of the signifier's anchorage in a stable reality is completed by the reader's alienation from the narrative, which is observed in snatches on the video screen of a sleeping functionary.

It is perhaps only in Wiliam Owen Roberts's *Y Pla*[47] and Robat Gruffudd's *Y Llosgi*,[48] however, that this scepticism supports a fully developed engagement with the social agencies which circumscribe what is available as reality. Both novels are, to different degrees, essays in decentring Welsh identity whilst at the same time seeking new ways, not only of breaking the code, but of regrounding moral purpose. *Y Llosgi* is constructed as an increasingly puzzling detective story – the quintessential form of epistemological enquiry – in which the quest to discover who burnt the hero's car becomes sidelined by a welter of other conundrums. That hero, John Clayman, is both perpetrator and victim of semiotic confusion about the Wales in which he lives. As External Relations Officer for the Wales Development Council, he is a 'conjuror of images', attempting to sell Wales as a 'dynamic, modern' location for foreign investment, while at the same time needing to project quite contradictory images of old-fashioned quaintness in order to seduce the investor-as-tourist. The reader is not absolved of this confusion, however, as the text itself is equally unreliable. Clayman has fictionalized his own story in order to provide him with an income; but that story has in turn been edited, perhaps rewritten, to meet the requirements of the Welsh Publishing Corporation. Within that fiction, Clayman occupies a world of ambiguities. Like Raymond Williams's Manod, Newtown is both a 'real' place and a site for contesting interest groups. The Welsh Development Council is run by a man who 'couldn't care a fart for the Welsh language', only the survival of his own bureaucracy, and another who is a secret member of the British National Party. Trenkler, the Eurocrat responsible for negotiating the Minority Culture Material Basis grant, also has a hidden agenda. Is former language militant Robyn now just a businessman, or is the business organization to which he belongs a front for the Soldiers of the Welsh Republic? As Clayman observes of the negotiation between Trenkler and his boss, Bishop: 'What parts are they playing now? Are they following their official scripts?' In a world where individuals possess or act out a range of contradictory identities, the answer seems beyond reach.

The sites where formal negotiations take place are rich metaphors for these ambiguities. At the Berlin transvestite club where Llangollen and Brussels vie to be the future cultural mecca of Europe, 'you can choose whatever sex you wish'. 'Real transvestites', however, are distinguished from the 'pretenders': 'to be completely convincing and natural you must transcend your sexual stereotype, not only to act well, but to *live* well too.' Clayman begins dancing, but his partner spins away in a 'feigned ecstatic gesture': 'This was not dancing, it was satire.' In this world, however, parody and reality are indistinguishable. At Plas Bodhywel – a 'genuine Tudor' half-timbered country house 'with Celtic-style all-inclusive weekend packages' – the negotiations it hosts are a 'deception . . . it is an arena for political battles where the innocent lose and are cast out to the ravens'. Indeed, the hotel itself, we learn, is a sham, largely used by the Tourist Board to justify its subsidy.

Clayman as semiotic anti-hero attempts to mask such contradictions. In the promotional film he produces for the Development Council, Wales is 'the ancient land . . . where opposites meet, embrace and kiss'. His life, however, is riven by contradiction. His English wife claims, plausibly, that 'I live here, in the real Wales, not you'; and his sixties language activism has been reduced to a mere memory and a failed attempt to pass on the language to his daughter. From this vantage point Wales is, as in Angharad Tomos's dystopic vision,

> a meaningless pre- or post-historical wasteland . . . a few large-
> headed monsters will harbour a faint recollection, a private
> phantasmagoria . . . the Soldiers and their Welsh Jerusalem, the BNP
> and their Pure England, the AEL and their Red Europe; the
> Development Council and its Wales of motorways and hi-tec parks
> and artificial ski-slopes and Celtic feasts.

This insight into the crisis of ideologies, however, then contracts into a
more conventional, albeit affirmative, story of personal reorientation.
Clayman embraces his friend Dic's manageable and tangible
aspirations ('he exists, he is here, in and on the bog') as a first step in
piecing together a new order and authenticity. His *bildung* is complete
when he refuses to accept another compromising PR job, promoting
nuclear power, and the narrative is recast as a parable of false
consciousness, existential choice and the recentring of John Clayman
as a reliable narrator and an agent in his own future.

In *Y Pla*, however, the ironic mode is maintained throughout, so
that only the reader has complete access to a sense of overriding
agency. Set in the fourteenth century, it relates parallel and ultimately
converging stories: that of Salah Ibn al Khatib of the Madras Academy,
Cairo, a wide-eyed innocent dispatched across Europe to avenge his
grandfather's death – according to a text of uncertain authority – at the
hands of the French king's grandfather; and the sordid travails and
intrigues of the community of Dolbenmaen in north Wales. As the
stories unfold, the shadow of the Great Plague is cast over both,
precipitating social crisis, hastening the development of capitalism and
exposing to view the means by which power is won and maintained
and 'truth' constituted to that end. It is a novel, therefore, both about
historical change and the representation of that change. Within the
narrative, as in *Y Llosgi*, nothing is as it seems. A merchant mimics a
dog, a jester the Pope (and, by inter-textual allusion, the modern-day
critic, Bobi Jones), Salah dresses up as Archbishop, his Abbot
companion turns out to be a woman and he himself finally dons
woman's clothes to protect himself, in accordance with the prevailing
wisdom, against infection. Meanwhile, in Dolbenmaen, the local
steward attempts to enforce the king's law amidst burnings,
disappearances, signs of the coming Antichrist, and 'Einion Fychan the
leper . . . fucking his goat'. At every turn the discourses of church and
state are parodied and subverted in the 'terrified gabbling' of epic
verses, in the bardic practice of hired sycophancy, in the physicians'
absurd prescriptions against the plague, and in the apocalyptic
expectations of the nuns of Genoa, answered by the arrival of a giraffe.
The progress of the narrative is interrupted throughout by reversals,
stories-within-stories, anachronisms and sudden shifts in register, to

draw our attention to its fictive nature. At the end, a new story begins, already full of ironies. Chwilen Bwm, released from prison, contemplates the demise of serfdom and the prospect of selling his labour, perceives 'a crack in the wall' through which he might bring 'the whole house down', but is rapidly seduced by a new story of which he is not the main narrator: a story for 'the age of the market, the age of production'. Abjuring mimetic realism, purity of genre and any explicit reference to a bordered Wales, *Y Pla* has been as significant in Welsh as Gwyn Thomas's *All Things Betray Thee* (1949)[49] was in English in offering a way beyond the enclosed historical novel, and in subverting the simplistic use of that form to construct allegories for contemporary nationalist concerns. In doing so, it also invests the act of decoding with a sense of social purpose and inscribes the reader – privileged with an overview of Chwilen's ideological entrapment – as a potential agent of that purpose, as a potential narrator of his or her own history.

In English, Christopher Meredith's *Griffri* (1991)[50] offers many parallels with *Y Pla* although, lacking the latter's Marxist sense of *telos*, its scepticism is darker and more pessimistic. Set in twelfth-century Wales, it records the self-doubting testimony of Griffri ap Berddog, court poet, as it is related to a Cistercian monk. Griffri, as a kind of medieval Clayman, is both 'paid arselicker' and 'keeper of memory': he believes that 'truth is the best song' but 'in the meantime . . . praise for the mighty pays nicely'. His autobiography unfolds as an epistemological quest, moving out from the self into wider spheres of unknowing. Although he is the 'lister of the dead' for many generations, even his own father's life is 'obscure' to him. His childhood offers a world better 'known' than any other will be, and yet 'in another sense I didn't know it. I didn't know where or how it was.' That different kind of knowing comes through the discovery of time, the seasons, myth and then, disturbingly, through the history of his people: on first hearing of the French '. . . I remember thinking . . . that it was odd to suffer every year for things that had happened before we were born'. Historical narratives, however, are especially opaque. Griffri chants genealogies, law triads and grave verses 'without understanding'. Rhys the storyteller invents 'histories' to relate as fact. And Meilyr the oracle gives advice to soothe 'the memory marred' and then spends 'whole evenings trying to work out the meaning of what he'd said'. It is a world which 'teemed with puzzles'. At the same time, the narrative struggles with actual memory – its selectivity, its dependence on coincidence and the problem of collective memory. Caught within events, 'you stand at the heart of things but you don't see the boundaries'. Stories (as in the story-within-a-story here) are used to provide such boundaries, but 'telling' is in turn qualified by the hearer. 'What counts' for the Benedictine monk's narrative is 'lists of dead bishops'; for Griffri's war-band, the promise of survival through military conquest. Griffri's personal history, meanwhile, unfolds as a farrago of murder, rape, kidnap, torture and delirium, which concludes with the realization that 'we know nothing, we don't know one another or ourselves'. The last-page discovery of his long-lost mother is, in the failure to acknowledge recognition, consistent with this realization but it also teases and frustrates the reader's expectations of resolution and denouement.

Meredith's earlier *Shifts* (1988)[51] is also centred on the figure of a 'remembrancer'. Keith, a local historian, tries to locate his time and place, particularly the imminent closure of the town's steel works, within some context of historical purpose. The unravelling of his personal life becomes a metaphor for his failure in this task. The novel approaches its theme with those careful, exploratory essays at measurement which are such prominent features of the work of Raymond Williams and Emyr Humphreys. The journey home of the significantly named 'O' at the outset establishes the felt dimensions of space and time as they are traced in daily life, pointing to a stubborn will to live within its routine, quotidian time. Projected behind that sense of solidity is the figure of Keith himself, also·moving through town, but with less obvious purpose, speculating within a wholly different time-frame about the age of houses, testing alternative openings for a public lecture on the origins of the town's industrial growth, and puzzling over changes and omissions in contemporary documentation of that history. And projected again behind Keith's understanding of space and time, trapped as it is within its excessive and formless detail, are the 'huge ideas' of the professional historian, delineating those broader frontiers of 'rural and industrial', 'farmland and desert', which place the town in a wider world and a wider history. And yet again beyond that placing are the barely decipherable images of the grand narratives by which the past explained itself: represented here by the sermon crib, with its apocalyptic vision of the Destruction of the Temple: 'like a parallel universe in science fiction . . . though for real, and too complex to find words for, and in another language.'

Cutting across Keith's search for historical meaning is the affair between Judith, his wife, and Jack. Jack, a liminal, ambiguous figure newly returned from England, recoils from the sense of 'time wasted' by projecting his own fiction, centred on a timeless Judith. Together, they reject the comforting certainties of all grand narratives – represented on their visit to Hereford by the Jerusalem-centred Mappa Mundi – and the historical meanings sought by Keith, 'stuck in a time warp'. They are satisfied, instead, with the 'historical significance of fucking ballocks'. The strip mill closes as an ironic replay of the Destruction of the Temple – a 'non-event' with 'no mysteries' – and the novel is rounded off within the habitual world of 'O', the mill now replaced by 'a nice, solving blank space' and life shaped only by the endeavour to reduce it 'to anecdote'. At the same time, however, Keith is recentred as a credible narrator who rises above these contingencies, seeing, if imperfectly, how 'invisible history . . . transformed things without their understanding it'. His vision concludes, disconcertingly, with another partially deciphered message from the past, in which the Welsh word for 'leaders' remains opaque. He will unveil this meaning, but the novel projects no context for turning that knowledge into practice: knowledge, it seems, is private and can replace confusion only with a sense of impotence.

Where Christopher Meredith inscribes the subject within a discourse of historical meanings, however exhausted, the novels of Duncan Bush, Ron Berry and Alun Richards occupy a world where relationships have become almost entirely spatial. Duncan Bush's *Glass Shot* (1991),[52] like Wiliam Owen Roberts's *Bingo*, uses the crime thriller form and the metaphoric possibilities of film to investigate the complexities of an identity which defines itself only in that dimension. The title refers to a technique of filming action through a plate on which a scene has already been painted: a metaphor for the way in which fantasy and reality are confused by the novel's central character, Steve Boyle, but also for the way identities are seen here to be partly constituted from fictions. Boyle, a Quick Fit fitter, is another liminal figure: a Maltese-Irish Cardiffian, separated from his wife and children, who dreams of emulating Hollywood loners like Martin Sheen in *Badlands*. The places represented in those films – by the 'State Capitals I learnt by heart once' and by the destination of a casually observed airliner – are the chimeric 'somewhere' by which he orientates his movements and actions in an increasingly desperate effort to construct a purposeful self: the 'somebody' he might have been had he been born 'in Worcester, Massachusetts or Newport, Rhode Island instead of Cardiff, Glamorgan'.

The novel unfolds as a map of the territory traversed in this process, and indeed maps, journeys and problematic spaces have in this narrative a dense significance comparable with the novels of Raymond Williams – and also, within a different frame of influence, with the work of Raymond Carver. For Boyle, empty space and its open possibilities are always present at the borders of the known: opposite the house of Rusty, the woman he desires, is a 'big uninhabited darkness . . . an island in the lit map of the city's streets and arterial roads and roundabouts and junctions . . .' Boyle, we discover, was himself a child cartographer, reifying the places of his desire like those early explorers who 'didn't know what lay out in the ocean to the west so they'd just draw an island where they felt like having one, and trying to find that island was the only thing that made them put out from the shore'. His journey to Powys is at the same time a quest for his estranged wife and past, and also the creation of this kind of imaginative hyper-reality. Passing the miners' pickets (for this is 1984), the real world suddenly turns into image:

> it's like Wyoming must be or Montana, like a background you'd see in a film. Or some Shangri-la, another mountain land painted on glass . . . it's suddenly like you're not in Wales any more. You're in America.

Here he dreams living out a *Deer Hunter* role, reunited with his family. Ultimately, pursued by the police and without adequate maps, he achieves only a sinister parody of that role. Looking for a 'last-ditch hiding place', he discovers a patch of land 'blank on the maps in everybody's mind and memory' which – this time emulating Harry Stanton in *Paris, Texas* – he claims for his own and names 'Boyle's Peak'.

Parallel with this exploration of landscape is a continuing critique of interior spaces, particularly the remembered front room of home, 'joyless as a tomb', the violated space of Rusty's flat and the interior of his wife's cottage, '. . . another colour plate for the Coffee-Table Book of French Farmhouse Cooking': a film set from the very 'different movie' which she had been trying to live out. Paradoxically, he can only define the desired, authentic 'other place' in terms of further fabrication: 'Like in *Last Tango in Paris* . . . Brando doesn't want them to have any identity, any existence for each other, outside those rented rooms'.

Glass Shot is, at one level, a study in psychopathic derangement. In common with the work of Roberts, Meredith and the later Raymond Williams, however, it is also concerned with problems of cognition. The world it describes is one in which, like that of Baudrillard, 'the territory no longer precedes the map, nor survives it . . . it is the map that precedes the territory – precession of simulacra – it is the map that engenders the territory'.[53] As anticipated in the prefatory quotation from Rimbaud ('*C'est faux de dire. Je pense. On devrait dire: On me pense.*'), Boyle sees each of the protagonists as 'thinking' each other – the police 'putting together a picture' of Boyle, Boyle 'building a dossier on Rusty' – so that there is never a stable, unitary knowledge of reality: never the 'whole picture' of which the newspaper's identikit image of Boyle is such a poor imitation.

Bush's Cardiff, in its streetwise American accenting, its constant, restless looking beyond itself, and its sense of detachment from its hinterland, emerges in *Glass Shot* as a new fictional subject in Wales. The novel is related, however, to a wider mode of writing which has been marginalized by preoccupations with more explicit narratives of nationhood. *Glass Shot* echoes, in particular, Ron Berry's *So Long,*

Hector Bebb (1970),[54] although in the latter isolation and the uncertainties of knowing and being are conveyed not by an increasingly solipsistic first-person narrator but through the atomization of the narrative into fourteen self-contained internal monologues. Hector, a boxer and lorry-driver, is projected by the others as 'authentic' in a way which they can achieve only 'in spasms'. In comparison with Hector, 'We're adverts'. He is lonely but heroic: like 'the only soul left to perish', a 'strange alien' who transgresses conventional social boundaries, running over the hills like 'the only man alive in the whole world'. After killing the man he suspects of having an affair with his wife, he escapes to 'bow and arrow country' where, playing 'Ghost Riders in the Sky' on the mouth organ, he holes up in a parody of the outback shack – a derelict colliery building. He is finally run to ground, dying in a fall before being captured. Running alongside the narrative of crime and pursuit are the many stories of isolation, loss of 'inner strength' and the inability to love adequately: conditions which are part of a Wales that is 'going to rack and ruin'. Hector's flight at once represents the need to 'wipe the slate clean, start all over again' and indicts a community in which it is becoming increasingly difficult to 'help one another'. Both Berry and Bush, in projecting the anti-hero into a space that is open-ended but ambiguous – the site of escape and self-discovery, survival and destruction – develop the 'ap Einionland' of Ferris into a powerful metaphor for the process of self-definition.

Whereas *So Long, Hector Bebb* is spatially organized, Berry's earlier *Flame and Slag* (1968)[55] resembles *Shifts* in its articulation of place, movement and time. Beginnings (here in Caib colliery) are traced in a discovered contemporary diary and contrasted with the first-person story of aspiring 'penman' Rees, observing the final dissolution of a Wales now held together only by the memory of memories, and no worse than 'Detroit, hinterland Africa or Llasa'. The diary narrates the departure to England and return to Daren of John Vaughan, together with daughter Ellen. That return is prompted by a 'renewed sense of purpose' founded on the 'fundamentals' of 'food and fuel' and the 'want of home': coal being the agency which 'delivered Daren into being out of a long bank of time'. Ian Rees, who marries Ellen, is unable to embrace 'John Vaughan's time' and its sense of linear, historical purpose and recommends, instead, 'long-term trial and error disintegration, perhaps as opposed to compulsory One-ness. Perhaps there's more information in disintegration . . .' For their world, the past is as foreign and displaced as 'Gran', deranged, cursing in Welsh, alien like 'a Khirgiz peasant woman'. Ian concludes his narrative, clinging to the only survivals of that past, purposeful time: a refusal 'to be overcome', and mutual love.

Alun Richards, too, has been compared with Ron Berry for his open engagement with contemporary, urban Wales, free of the compulsion to adopt a position within narratives of nationhood and historical destiny. The world of Richards's *Home to an Empty House* (1973)[56] is also a fragmented one. It employs five narrators who, liminal and isolated at the outset, progress only to a better understanding of their isolation. Walter is debilitated by TB and he and his wife Connie, both orphans, separate at the end of the novel. Connie's lover, Ifor, is Welsh speaking but rootless and uses Connie to recover some kind of authenticity; but their love becomes like 'something on the commercials'. Rachel, her aunt, represents for Connie a Wales that prefers 'remembering to living', 'a club for the elderly that was soon to vanish'. And Hilda, Ifor's wife, is driven to attempt suicide by loneliness, self-hatred and betrayal. The bleakness of their world is somewhat relieved by the final centring of Rachel, who alone displays personal loyalty – is 'there, formidable, concerned, involved'. But her virtue serves largely to intensify Connie's sense that 'beneath the surface everything is cracking really'. As in *Flame and Slag*, the disintegration of community catastrophically damages people's ability to transfer moral choice and purpose from one generation to the next. And, in each case, the novelist faces the need to depict or project survival and some form of reconstitution of self without the props of received teleologies.

No writer has been more concerned with the social transmission of meanings, across both space and time, than Emyr Humphreys. He is also the novelist who has most explicitly placed this issue within the discourse of national identity and representation: a fact reflected in his critical reception. He is read as 'the most Welsh' of English-language novelists and the saviour of Welsh representation from generations of caricature and vilification.[57] His work is incorporated – 'like Charles Edwards's *Hanes y Ffydd yng Nghymru*' – into a literature of national redemption, which sees Wales as an 'Israel awaiting the coming of the Son to save her'.[58] He has been elevated as the Welsh writer who, above all others, has accomplished what Seamus Heaney calls a 'Ptolemaic revolution', reconstituting the region as a new centre: a process enhanced, it is argued, by the deliberate eschewing of egregious Welshisms, achieving a transparency of style which is the 'Welsh equivalent of Barthes's "white writing" or "writing degree zero"'. The reader is inscribed within this interpretation as fellow agent in the reclaiming of 'our relationship with the nation's past'.[59] This is, the critics recognize, to reinforce an inscription already embedded in the texts themselves: an inscription achieved, behind the guise of narrative detachment, chiefly through allusion, metonym, the privileging of certain voices and the weighted juxtaposition of events. Most of all,

Emyr Humphreys's elevation of the moral dissident – not as exile but, paradoxically, as liminal native, like Angharad Tomos's Blodeuwedd – has provided a usable mirror for an embattled intelligentsia.

Throughout, Emyr Humphreys constitutes the subject as a moral agent in a world of conflicting choices which are, at any given juncture, only partly known and understood by the subject. In what is becoming one of the most canonical of modern Welsh novels, *Outside the House of Baal* (1965),[60] he uses a double time-frame to counterpoint, on the one hand, the lived consequences of choices made with, on the other, the accumulation of cultural and material circumstances which always limit choice. Those limitations derive, within the author's narrative of national dissolution, from the atrophy of Nonconformist Wales and the usurpation of its values by the individualism and materialism which have accompanied progressive incorporation into the British state. Within this narrative the characters have somewhat typological roles, although these are effectively realized within the lived experience of each. The Wales of JT, the idealist minister, is for his sociologist son 'a world of fantasy related to something that might have existed before 1914' and which obstructs freedom and progress. Brother-in-law Dan Llew's own pursuit of progress, however, through developing the site of the family home, Argoed, leaves him utterly disorientated. Ultimately, failures of will, understanding or foresight, or the force of historical circumstances, conspire to isolate each. The novel closes with JT's sister, Kate, as yet another isolated survivor, a radically reduced, unfulfilled and unpropitious keeper of virtue, living 'in a water-tight compartment . . . if I shouted nobody could hear me'.

This basic typology is expanded and elaborated in Emyr Humphreys's most ambitious undertaking, the seven-volume sequence, 'The Land of the Living' (1971–1991). Cast more resolutely and expansively in the mould of national allegory, the sequence interrogates those positions which contend for hegemony following the collapse of Liberal Nonconformist Wales: the politics of class, represented by miners' leader Pen Lewis, the politics of reform and accommodation pursued by Amy Parry; and the idealistic nationalism of Val Gwyn and the poet John Cilydd More – a kind of artist-in-philistia who strives for ways to articulate this world, but whose work is spurned as a 'heap of filth'. Authorial comment and control are achieved, not directly, but by careful juxtaposition of scenes: in *The Best of Friends*,[61] for example, Cilydd's measured, academic plea for the establishment of a 'new cultural pattern' is contextualized by the succeeding description, in more erratic rhythms, of Pen's injury at a political demonstration. The theme of disjuncture between principle and practice is interrogated in this way throughout the sequence, allowing the reader to supply the connections and moral judgements.

Behind the sustained semblance of detachment, however, there are at work a number of techniques for privileging certain characters and points of view. The symbolic landscape of interiors, in particular, is used to inscribe characters within continuities of space and time. In *Salt of the Earth*,[62] the interior of Glanrafon Stores is 'something of a shrine' to John Cilydd's grandfather William Lloyd. It is 'densely crowded with the artefacts of that time' including, in Lloyd's 'History of Calvinistic Methodism in Rhosyr and Dinody' and the aquatint of 'The Board and Narrow Way', metonyms of its cultural and moral certainties. In *Open Secrets*,[63] the furniture at Glanrafon Stores has become, literally and symbolically, too big for its 'shrivelled' inhabitants. And in *Bonds of Attachment*[64] the edifice – now a 'lost interior' – has become a pub, although still offering fragments of meaning to be pieced together by John Cilydd's son, Peredur.

For Amy Parry's family, 'the furniture that crowded the small room' defines their material impoverishment and the narrow horizons of achievement it can offer Amy. For Val, Amy's promise of a better future, 'there was just enough room . . . to stand between the dresser and the table'. It does, however, afford him a 'precarious sitting space' from which to converse with Amy's Christian socialist uncle: space has narrowed, but accommodating the old in an impoverished new still seems possible.

In the terraces of south Wales, however, furniture and home are radically reduced in status. Poverty, in the form of the bailiff's removal van, 'looked big enough to swallow all the cottages and their contents'. Furniture is afforded significance only when displaced – 'a kitchen chair stood on the pavement'. Home becomes a transitory property relationship: 'she seemed to view the proceedings with the stolid and indifferent impartiality of a lodger who has paid her rent for her room.' And the sense of personal identities embedded within specific interiors is replaced by a nameless and manipulable crowd. The desultory representation of interiors in South Wales, in the eviction scene and elsewhere, provides a context not for a sympathetic engagement with historical process but for the ideological duelling of Val and Pen Lewis. Although Val's authority is qualified by being perceived as an outsider, 'even more foreign than those do-gooding English Quakers', the meagre detailing of what constitutes being 'inside' means that Pen's typological role is inadequately anchored in the fictive world of the narrative. Whilst John Cilydd may acknowledge that 'they valley marxists are right to laugh at us', it is that 'us' which retains centrality.

This privileging is also evident in the representation of character. A farmer in *Bonds of Attachment* and the dialect of Welsh-speaking bus passengers in *Open Secrets*, although incidental to the plot, are invested with historical significance: a 'glorifying the commonplace' justified because of the 'threat of extinction'. The failings of Val Gwyn and John Cilydd are placed within a hard-won integrity and self-knowledge which become figurations of the sequence's whole problematic. The representation of Pen Lewis, in contrast, is reductive and gratuitously projects his political position through the filter of sexual opportunism: a treatment meted out later to the other South Walian socialist, Gareth Hopkin. This process is consolidated in the use of 'standard' English primarily as the authoritative argot of the Welsh speakers in each novel, and the reservation of truculent dialect to represent proletarian South Walians ('How you do dant me, you ignorant bugger') and English refugees ('Can we 'ave summat to eat? We're bloody starvin'). Embedded within the language of the text, too, are what have been described as 'codes of allegiance',[65] which privilege readers from the same cultural grouping as that foregrounded in the narrative. John Cilydd's allusions to D. J. Williams and Waldo Williams are followed closely by his son Peredur's encoded reference to J. R. Jones, the nationalist philosopher, establishing a rhetoric of continuity for which the only equivalent in the speech of South Wales is the shallow rhetoric of exhortation and slogans.

The proper, and narrower, subject of the sequence therefore emerges as the struggle of a Welsh-speaking intelligentsia to retain influence as an agent of national formation in a world which has largely rendered it redundant. This more restricted focus becomes clear in the final volume of the sequence, *Bonds of Attachment,* in which desired historical continuities are articulated within the inevitably more partial first-person narrative of Peredur who, like his mythic namesake,[66] is cast in the role of authoritative decoder of signs: a role exercised, in particular, in reconstituting John Cilydd's diary as the point of origin of his own narrative. The counter-histories remain the same. Amy and Bedwyr, preparing for the Investiture, plan the conversion of Brangor Hall into a royal residence in a time-honoured Lloyd Georgian effort to pursue power through British institutions and at the same time impose on the establishment 'as much Welshness' as possible. Gwydion tries to engage Peredur in making a 'film on the Eisteddfod for worldwide consumption', just as journalist Eddie Meredith had pressed John Cilydd to use his writing abilities to 'put the original Britishness back in the British Army and the British Council'. Gareth Hopkin no longer represents an available alternative, merely seeking witnesses 'to the purity of his Marxist faith' and ultimately proposing the indulgence of 'strategic withdrawal'.

The death of Peredur's lover, Wenna, killed by her own bomb, serves to clarify his allegiances. He rejects the efforts of Gwydion, as post-modernist semiotician, to reduce the world to a 'display' of undifferentiated simulachra, in which the Investiture is 'just a colourful flicker on the TV screen – signifying nothing' and 'hardly worth dying for'. The alternative, however, is difficult: 'My father's papers were locked in with the detonators and it wasn't a door I wanted to open.' Amy's apparent death-bed anagnorisis renews the challenge to Peredur to be his 'father's son', but we are left characteristically uncertain of the status both of the challenge and its acceptance, an uncertainty increased by the ironic parallels with the proving-the-hero fable. In any event, the narrative fails to bridge the symbolic gulf which divides Peredur, locked in the manse, from the village, which 'had become as inaccessible as a settlement in Outer Mongolia'. His aspiration – to save 'your class and your country and yourself' from 'a condition of permanent grovelling servility and sycophancy' – remains as a guide to action. The narrative, however, is not equipped to question that agenda in the way that had, to a degree, been established in the earlier volumes. Conflicts are internalized and the fidelity to dissonant voices inevitably compromised.

This closing limitation is, in part, a chosen, even an autobiographically determined one. Emyr Humphreys's concern is to recentre Wales within a continuity which can and must be realized within the consciousness of single, real individuals. Indeed, as his history of Wales is one of 'unending resistance' to 'historical necessity',[67] authentic Welshness becomes almost synonymous with isolated dissidence. The pivot around which the narrative moves, therefore, is the hero-in-waiting for which Michael in *A Toy Epic*[68] is an early prototype, accepting 'the burden of being utterly alone'. Michael and Peredur alike appropriate the lives of others to represent 'the soul of Wales' they wish to safeguard, but it is their experience of cultural conversion which is centralized, and which becomes the figure for the beleaguered intellectual which in real history finds its paradigm in Saunders Lewis.

Raymond Williams's experience of dislocation presented challenges for which the realistic representation of difference, under strain in Emyr Humphreys's work, ultimately proved inadequate. The early intentions of both authors, however, have much in common. Like Humphreys, Williams endeavours to avoid the 'Welsh style' and the temptation to counter cliché with alternative totalizations or by retreating into a 'fiction of private lives'.[69] Like Humphreys, he is concerned with how, through dislocation or exile, realities are frozen into detached images and real meanings lost. In *Border Country* (1960),[70] Morgan Rosser's transformation of the Holy Mountain into an advertising logo echoes the commodified space of Gwydion in *Bonds of Attachment*. Matthew, the exile returned, is constantly checking himself against the temptation to turn the familiar into a transcendent identity in order to negate change and repress history: 'This was not anybody's valley to make into a landscape. Work had changed and was still changing it, though the main shape held.' Above all, the starting-point for each is a centre which is already fully understood as an ambiguous space, at once itself and other and only remaining itself by becoming other. Neither Argoed nor Manod is presented as a hallowed, pristine ground of authenticity – the space of 'tower' and 'vineyard' in which Angharad Tomos's discourse was confined.

The differences, however, are equally important. Both authors would concur with Matthew's view that, for the dislocated subject, it is 'measuring' that matters: 'By measuring the distance, we come home.' For Humphreys, however, as we have seen, that measuring tends to have a single, defining point of orientation: the method is polyphonous, but internal weighting always centres those 'dedicated minorities prepared to bond their entire life energies towards the salvation of the whole nation'.[71] For Raymond Williams, that national centring is neither sought nor available. His Wales, although always acknowledged as a repository of real and distinct values, is defined in terms of the radical ambiguities of his own experience, perceived as representative of the modern condition: the experience of living on an actual border, of personal displacement, and particularly of engagement in the wide spatial relations of industrial working-class life and political struggle. The history of enforced mobility in *Border Country* and *Second Generation*[72] is, from this vantage point, a 'Welsh' history as much as the history of rooted continuities. Within the intellectual careers of both Matthew and Williams, the acquired knowledge of metropolitan power becomes, it is insisted, an essential knowledge of Wales itself, in its inescapable integration with a larger world. The consequences of this analysis for a Wales-centred fiction are profound. As ambiguity and exile emerge as new authenticities, the subject can no longer be constituted in a single centre: 'you cannot write a fully realist novel about Wales', argues Williams, 'without writing about England.'[73]

Border Country (1960) and *Second Generation* (1964), like ' Land of the Living', use the knowable community as the touchstone with which to measure movement and dislocation. In *The Flight of Manod* (1979),[74] however, the ambiguity of space is too fundamental to be accommodated within these limits. This is partly because of the tentative, futuristic nature of the subject (the planning of a new city), but more importantly derives from the dense web of interconnections it investigates which cannot be 'lived' together:

> What could now be heard . . . as this actual movement, had conditions of time, of growth quite different from the condition of any single life, or of any father and son.

The earlier investigation of specific identities through measuring distance and time has been superseded by a more radical questioning of what constitutes identity. Manod is not a place-in-itself, it is the 'name, a codesign' for a particular convergence of interests, local and international: an inhabited place with a distinct history, but also the incarnation of interests for which space is never local but always relative, transferable. Significantly, it is through the agency of local capital – always present but only now mature enough to make its own wide connections – that the two worlds are yoked. The detective-like decoding of evidence concerning the complex network of land deals, revisions of plans and power-broking ultimately reveals the oil and banking interests which underwrite the scheme. Nevertheless, a new Manod of some kind will be necessary because, as in Glanrafon Stores, the alternative is atrophy. That development can be seen, within the discourse of nationalism, as 'just the old penetration' of English colonization. It can be seen, within an alternative discourse of left-wing internationalism which denies Welsh specificity, as merely a local example of an 'actual history . . . back there in the bloody centre: the Birmingham–Dusseldorf Axis, with offices in London, Brussels, Paris, Rome . . .' Or, as Matthew Price urges, it can be seized as an opportunity to fight for ownership and control of change. But that change – like the mixed immigration which, in South Wales, formed the basis for 'one of the strongest autonomous cultures in Europe' – will necessitate a 'culture people made, not inherited'.

Raymond Williams's other futuristic detective novel, *The Volunteers* (1978),[75] explores similar themes and arrives at conclusions which even more radically undermine the holistic narratives of selective traditions.[76] As in *The Fight for Manod*, apparently disconnected 'local' events – the killing of a miner on strike at Pontyrhiw and the shooting of a minister of state at St Fagans – are connected and understood only through engaging with transnational space. Within that process of discovery a range of partial and contradictory views of reality is investigated: through the alternative narrations of events, including that of the Gwent Writers' Group, which is itself not what it seems; through the incongruous 'clash of scene and action' within a 'national' museum which cannot accommodate such realities; through the blinkered investigation of the police, 'misdirected by their own stereotypes'. The 'solution' to the plot lies in piecing together the bewildering jigsaw of covert sponsorship, deception and unwitting collaboration which surround the activities of the ironically named Volunteers. For them, as for the narrator, Redfern, choice and instrumentality are never available outside a wider process which necessitates that 'radically divergent potentials continue to inhabit them. Their ordinary active condition is profoundly divided

. . . Most people go about with a score of faces.' Redfern, a detached 'cartographer' of political space most at home on 'a road of long-range mobility', longs for a less compromised authenticity: for 'the cement . . . of belonging to something, of confirming an identity in the identification with others'. No resolution is achievable, however, beyond the interminable task of making connections: 'there was no available identity outside it: only the process itself which could never be properly told in any single dimension or any single place . . .' It is a process, nevertheless, which provides the basis for Redfern's renewed political commitment: a basis which neither the fixed and partial realities identified in the novel nor the simulated realities of the television network for which Redfern works can provide. It is also a way back to the lived realities of Pontyrhiw, to which Redfern symbolically returns at the conclusion.

That passage of departure and return is traced, in some form, by all of Raymond Williams's fictional heroes: Matthew Price, Gwyn in *Loyalties*,[77] Redfern, and Glyn in *People of the Black Mountains*.[78] Whilst the novels cannot be read simply as a personal, autobiographical quest for self-knowledge – for reconciliation with 'the world you grew up in and left' – they are, like Emyr Humphreys's work, centrally concerned with the ambiguous position of oppositional intellectuals in bourgeois society. This concern is manifested in the need to answer Gwyn's reproach of the bourgeois radical whose socialism is merely 'a frame for your ego', and Evan's castigation of the technocratic intellectual: 'You have nothing to say for us. You have plenty to say to us. You beam in from another world.' The seeker of an authenticity beyond these limitations must accept a necessary alienation: 'In a culture like that', observes Redfern of Pontyrhiw, 'belief is not a problem, in the way it is for the rest of us.' And it is that 'us' which is the implied readership here, as elsewhere. 'Connecting', then, is a way of recentring oneself within 'a society . . . with its own bonds, its own loyalties'. The task Williams sets himself is to understand and then to break through that 'bleak sense of human entrapment in Discourses of Power'[79] which close down the possibility of human agency. It is to work within the 'excess of belongings'[80] which define the modern migrant intellectual, and then to construct new narratives of authenticity which do not deny that necessary pluralism. While it is true that a historical Welsh working class is the site of this process, the primary task is that recentring itself, as it is in the work of Emyr Humphreys.

It is difficult not to frame a discussion of contemporary Welsh fiction in the self-defining discourses of Emyr Humphreys and Raymond Williams. Their respective projects have a breadth and chronological span which tend to overshadow other endeavours. It is all the more important, therefore, to recognize their foregrounded subjects as themselves historically specific and to resist the temptation to close off the critical narrative simply by invoking their case histories. Instead, we must recognize that the texture of Welsh fiction remains, like Williams's *The Volunteers*, remarkably 'bumpy'[81]: a texture which reflects the complex, uneven problematic of difference rather than any of its individual renditions. The investigations of that problematic have, nevertheless, important features in common. Their subjects are most often constituted as exiled narrators in a world of redundant or ambiguous meanings, each facing a dilemma similar to that of Gwyn Thomas's harpist in *All Things Betray Thee*, whose traditional songs are rendered useless in the new, uncharted territory of Moonlea. Engagement with that dilemma may unfold as a search for alternative authenticities, either social or personal, or as an ironic commentary on the very concept of centred authenticity. In each case, however, Wales or Welsh subjectivity is rendered as a site for renegotiation of the relationship between available identities and perceived realities.

For the pessimistic reader, the manner of this renegotiation is increasingly associated with an attenuation of the possibilities of a Welsh fiction. A shift of attention from representation to problems of subjectivity has, it is argued, through appropriating space as metaphor, further frustrated the growth of a broad, capacious realism. This is particularly true of Welsh-language fiction, where non-realist strategies, like earlier preoccupations with the enclosed domains of childhood, domesticity and the past, are deemed to have deferred the formally complex task of engaging with actual linguistic behaviour and the social relations it signifies. In both languages, there is echoed the general fear that interrogation of the code is fast usurping engagement with social relations: that a process of cultural privatization is under way which devalues action, reduces moral dilemmas to matters of style, and confirms the final redundancy of those oppositional intelligentsias for which Emyr Humphreys and Raymond Williams have attempted to forge a new purpose and legitimacy. More optimistic readers will see the jolting of epistemological complacency and the rejection of stable anchorages of subjectivity as a way of moving beyond a deadening regret for lost authenticities. Welsh fiction, according to such a reading, is progressive precisely to the degree that it does not mimic the centre by seeking counter-authenticities and counter-canons, but instead embraces a hybridity that abrogates all centres. The model for that writing lies not in those post-colonial narratives of emergent or recovered nationhood which have been invoked in the past, but in more fluid cultural formations which at once focus on but are uncertain of the boundaries of their identity and the margins of their literature.[82] The recasting of Wales as a site of ambivalent identification clearly places Robin Llywelyn's Gwern and

Wiliam Owen Roberts's Salah Ibn al Khatib within the typology of the post-modern migrant subject. As a practice of reading, however, it also offers new ways of understanding the liminal heroes of Alun Richards's sea stories in their homes-which-are-not-homes, the 'outcast' Josi Evans of Siân James's *A Small Country*,[83] brutalized and alienated Evan Price in Russell Celyn Jones's *Soldiers and Innocents*,[84] the fugitive inhabitants of Aztec Wales, and other subjects conventionally understood as local, atypical or mere genre stereotypes. Ultimately, of course, such a reading realizes its optimism only to the extent that both subject and reader perceive the possibility of exercising control over the choices available.

References

1 Christopher Evans, *Aztec Century* (London, Gollancz, 1993), p.11.
2 This was true at the time of writing. My accidental discovery of the novel, however, led ultimately to its inclusion on the short list for the Welsh Arts Council's Book of the Year Award.
3 On issues raised in this paragraph see in particular Graham Day, 'A million on the move?: population change and rural Wales', in Graham Day and Gareth Rees (eds.), *Contemporary Wales*, Vol. 3 (Cardiff, University of Wales Press, 1989), pp.137–59; and John Giggs and Charles Pattie, 'Wales as a plural society', in ibid., Vol. 5, pp.25–63.
4 Dai Smith, *Wales! Wales?* (London, Allen and Unwin, 1984), p.165.
5 Penmachno Woollen Mill: promotional leaflet.
6 Knights Caverns, Rhyl, promotional leaflet (HB Leisure Group).
7 Development Board for Rural Wales: newspaper advertisement.
8 Development Board for Rural Wales: promotional pack, *The New Wales Solution*.
9 D. Tecwyn Lloyd, 'The romantic parody', in *Planet*, No. 29 (March 1976), pp.1–6.
10 See in particular Raymond Williams, 'The Welsh industrial novel', in *Problems in Materialism and Culture* (London, Verso, 1980), pp.213–29; 'Working-class, proletarian, socialist: problems in some Welsh novels' in H. Gustav Klaus (ed.), *The Socialist Novel in Britain* (Brighton, Harvester Press, 1982), pp.110–21; 'Region and class in the novel', in *Writing in Society* (London, Verso, 1984), pp.229–58; and Dai Smith, 'Myth and meaning in the literature of the south Wales coalfield', in *The Anglo-Welsh Review*, Vol. 25, No. 56 (Spring 1976), pp.21–42; 'A novel history', in Tony Curtis (ed.), *Wales: The Imagined Nation* (Bridgend, Poetry Wales Press, 1986), pp.129–58; 'Relating to Wales' in Terry Eagleton (ed.), *Raymond Williams: Critical Perspectives* (Cambridge, Polity Press, 1989), pp.34–53.
11 John Rowlands, *Ysgrifau ar y Nofel* (Cardiff, University of Wales Press, 1992).

[12] M. Wynn Thomas, *Internal Difference: Literature in Twentieth-Century Wales* (Cardiff, University of Wales Press, 1992).
[13] Iris Gower, *Copper Kingdom* (London, Century, 1983).
[14] Alexander Cordell, *Rape of the Fair Country* (London, Gollancz, 1959).
[15] John Blackburn, *For Fear of Little Men* (London, Jonathan Cape, 1972).
[16] Phil Rickman, *Candlenight* (London, Duckworth, 1991).
[17] On this subject generally, see Sally Roberts Jones, 'Star Wars and settlers', in *Dragon's Tale*, Vol. 1 (January 1984), pp.4–7; and C. W. Sullivan, 'A wizard behind every bush' in *Planet*, No. 64 (Aug/Sept 1987), pp.48–51. The latter argues the case for an 'Anglo–Welsh children's fiction . . .' of 'bards and wizards, magic and mysteries' primarily, it seems, to meet the needs of Americans and Canadians dissatisfied with 'the scientific and technological revolution' and their lack of an extended history.
[18] Jenny Nimmo, *The Chestnut Soldier* (London, Methuen, 1989).
[19] Pamela Purnell, *Denny and the Magic Pool* (Llandysul, Pont Books, 1993).
[20] Anthony Burgess, *Any Old Iron* (London, Hutchinson, 1989).
[21] Kingsley Amis, *The Old Devils* (London, Hutchinson, 1986).
[22] See M. Wynn Thomas, op. cit., pp.170–9 and John Barnie, *The King of Ashes* (Llandysul, Gomer Press, 1989), pp.52–7.
[23] Alun Richards, *The Former Miss Merthyr Tydfil* (London, Michael Joseph, 1976).
[24] Emyr Humphreys, *Jones* (London, Dent, 1984), p.40.
[25] Richard Jones, *A Way Out* (London, Macmillan, 1969).
[26] Alice Thomas Ellis, *The Sin Eater* (London, Duckworth, 1977).
[27] Idem, *Unexplained Laughter* (London, Duckworth, 1985).
[28] Adam Lively, *The Snail* (London, Hutchinson, 1991).
[29] Ian Sinclair, *White Chappell: Scarlet Tracings* (London, Goldmark, 1987).
[30] Idem, *Downriver* (London, Paladin, 1991).
[31] Marion Harris, *Amelda* (London, Sphere, 1989).
[32] Paul Ferris, *A Distant Country* (London, Weidenfeld & Nicholson, 1983).
[33] Robert Watson, *Rumours of Fulfilment* (London, Heinemann, 1982).
[34] Aled Islwyn, *Cadw'r Chwedlau'n Fyw* (Cardiff, Gwasg y Dref Wen, 1984).
[35] Moira Dearnley, *That Watery Glass* (Llandybïe, Christopher Davies, 1973).
[36] Mary Jones, *Resistance* (Belfast, Blackstaff Press, 1985).
[37] Goronwy Jones, *Dyddiadur Dyn Dwad* (Penygroes, Cyhoeddiadau Mei, 1978).
[38] Siôn Eirian, *Bob yn y Ddinas* (Llandysul, Gomer Press, 1979).
[39] Gareth Miles, *Treffin* (Talybont, Y Lolfa, 1979).
[40] Twm Miall, *Cyw Dôl* (Talybont, Y Lolfa, 1990).
[41] Angharad Tomos, *Yma o Hyd* (Talybont, Y Lolfa, 1985).
[42] Aled Islwyn, *Os Marw Hon* (Llandysul, Gomer Press, 1990).
[43] Gareth Miles, *Trefaelog* (Caernarfon, Annwn, 1989).
[44] Wiliam Owen Roberts, *Bingo* (Penygroes, Gwasg Dwyfor, 1985).

[45] Mihangel Morgan, *Dirgel Ddyn* (Llandysul, Gomer Press, 1993).
[46] Robin Llewelyn, *Seren Wen ar Gefndir Gwyn* (Court of the National Eisteddfod of Wales, 1992).
[47] Wiliam Owen Roberts, *Y Pla* (Caernarfon, Annwn, 1987).
[48] Robat Gruffudd, *Y Llosgi* (Talybont, Y Lolfa, 1986).
[49] Gwyn Thomas, *All Things Betray Thee* (London, Michael Joseph, 1949).
[50] Christopher Meredith, *Griffri* (Bridgend, Seren Books, 1991).
[51] Idem, *Shifts* (Bridgend, Seren Books, 1988).
[52] Duncan Bush, *Glass Shot* (London, Secker & Warburg, 1991).
[53] Jean Baudrillard, *Selected Writings* (Oxford, Polity Press, 1988), p.166.
[54] Ron Berry, *So Long, Hector Bebb* (London, Macmillan, 1970).
[55] Idem, *Flame and Slag* (London, W. H. Allen, 1968).
[56] Alun Richards, *Home to an Empty House* (Llandysul, Gomer Press, 1973).
[57] Glyn Jones and John Rowlands (eds.), *Profiles* (Llandysul, Gomer Press, 1980), p.313.
[58] Derec Llwyd Morgan, 'Llenor y Llwyth', in J. E. Caerwyn Williams (ed.), *Ysgrifau Beirniadol*, Vol. 8 (Denbigh, Gwasg Gee, 1971), p.296.
[59] M. Wynn Thomas, op. cit., pp.76–7.
[60] Emyr Humphreys, *Outside the House of Baal* (London, Eyre & Spottiswoode, 1958).
[61] Idem, *The Best of Friends* (London, Hodder & Stoughton, 1978).
[62] Idem, *Salt of the Earth* (London, Dent, 1985).
[63] Idem, *Open Secrets* (London, Dent, 1988).
[64] Idem, *Bonds of Attachment* (London, Macdonald, 1991).
[65] Gerwyn Williams, 'Options and allegiances: Emyr Humphreys and Welsh literature', in *Planet*, No. 71 (October/November 1988), pp. 30–6.
[66] See the commentary on *Peredur* as 'sovereignty myth' in Proinsas Mac Cana, *The Mabinogi* (Cardiff, University of Wales Press, 1977), pp. 109–16.
[67] See Emyr Humphreys, 'The dissident tradition', in *Planet*, No. 71, op. cit., pp.23–9; and *The Taliesin Tradition* (Bridgend, Seren Books, 1989), pp.1, 228.
[68] Emyr Humphreys, *A Toy Epic* (London, Eyre & Spottiswoode, 1958).
[69] On these issues see Raymond Williams, *Politics and Letters* (London, New Left Books, 1979), pp.271–302.
[70] Raymond Williams, *Border Country* (London, Chatto & Windus, 1960).
[71] Emyr Humphreys quoted in Dai Smith, *Wales! Wales?*, op. cit., p.167.
[72] Raymond Williams, *Second Generation* (London, Chatto & Windus, 1964).
[73] Idem, *Politics and Letters*, op. cit., p.267.
[74] Idem, *The Fight for Manod* (London, Chatto & Windus, 1979).
[75] Idem, *The Volunteers* (London, Eyre Methuen, 1978).
[76] On the subject of selective traditions see Raymond Williams, 'Wales and England', in John Osmond (ed.), *The National Question Again* (Llandysul, Gomer Press, 1985), pp.18–31.
[77] Raymond Williams, *Loyalties* (London, Chatto & Windus, 1985).

[78] Idem, *People of the Black Mountains* (London, Chatto & Windus, Vol. 1 1989, Vol. 2 1990).

[79] The phrase is from Ajaz Ahmad, *In Theory: Classes, Nations, Literatures* (London, Verso, 1992), p.130: a work which challenges established (nationalist) readings of post-colonial literature.

[80] Ibid., p.127.

[81] Raymond Williams, *Politics and Letters*, op. cit., p.228.

[82] For positive readings of cultural hybridity and migrancy see Ajaz Ahmad, op. cit.; Bill Ashcroft, Gareth Griffiths and Helen Tiffin (eds.), *The Empire Writes Back* (London, Routledge, 1989); Homi K. Bhabha (ed.), *Nation and Narration* (London, Routledge, 1992); and Paul Gilroy, *The Black Atlantic: Modernity and Double Consciousness* (London, Verso, 1993).

[83] Siân James, *A Small Country* (London, Collins, 1979).

[84] Russell Celyn Jones, *Soldiers and Innocents* (London, Jonathan Cape, 1990).

Writing on the edge of catastrophe

WILIAM OWEN ROBERTS

I'm a playwright, short-story writer and a novelist. I write full time and earn my living from what I manage to produce. I've published two novels, one volume of short stories, staged about a dozen plays, radio plays, situation comedy, TV drama series, two films and even managed a musical. So what? What's so special about that? I wrote everything in Welsh.

On a recent British Council tour in southern Germany I was asked certain questions time and again: where is Wales? what is Wales? what is Welsh? where did the Welsh come from? is Welsh a dialect of English? how many people speak Welsh? you actually mean to say that there are other languages in England etc. . . . Time and again I had to give a brief history lesson. The same lesson I've given to English people who live much closer to us than the Germans. At least the Germans could be excused for their ignorance.

The population of the UK is about 56,000,000. The population of Wales in about 2,500,000. Out of this, about 400,000 to 500,000 speak Welsh. This includes everyone and as a writer that's my entire possible audience. The percentage of people who actually read literature in Welsh must be anyone's guess. Operating as a writer with such a small audience has obvious disadvantages. First, there are few reviews. By and large, the reading public and, indeed, most reviewers tend to be pretty conservative, and it is fair to say that there is very little truly exciting experimentation or innovation in the arts. Breaking away from the accepted norms is generally painful and difficult. Also, there are other problems which arise from the historical context.

Wales was politically, economically and linguistically joined to England by the Acts of Union passed between 1536 and 1543. English was made the official language and Wales became the first of a long list of colonies which England acquired over the centuries. Wales is still annexed to her neighbour and therefore I can quite legitimately claim to be a colonial writer. This gives me a shared experience with a host of other writers around the world.

'A language chooses the writer,' as my fellow novelist Christopher Meredith says. Welsh, however is an unofficial language even in Wales. You might find this curious. But it happens to be true. Even in 1995 the Welsh language has not been recognized as having equal status with English on the statute books of the Parliament of Westminster. Conferring official status on it would be the undoing of the Acts of Union which first classified it as a non-language. The language therefore has no standing before the law and users of Welsh have no automatic rights to demand that public bodies respect their mother tongue. Welsh speakers are non-language users. As far as state institutions which recognize and legitimize reality are concerned we do not really exist. We are not truly human. We are ghosts. It's classic colonialism.

By withholding recognition, you eradicate the problem. Wales is no different from England. We are all the same really. Only, we're not. The British State doesn't want any of the people living within its borders to have an unofficial existence within its own reality. Conformism is always the aim. 'Sooner or later the language barrier between England and Wales will be erased. A policy which is politically and socially desirable,' to quote Matthew Arnold. Which is why equal status for Welsh was withheld in the new 1993 Language Act. The policy remains the same; kill the language, eradicate the differences. The language will still have to fight a rearguard action to survive the next century against all the economic, cultural and political forces over which we have little or no control. They have ensured the continuance of the ghosts, living their unofficial reality within the state, for another century. But, as history has also demonstrated, getting rid of ghosts isn't that easy.

It is no wonder that my first novel *Bingo!* published in 1985 was a re-working of the diaries of Franz Kafka. It is a work imbued with a frightening, almost violent, sense of fragmentation, persecution and alienation. Because the product of all colonial situations is power imbalance and racism. It's inherent in the relationship between ruler and ruled. We have no power thus we can never draw up the agenda. Other people draw it up for us as well as deciding priorities and the way we assess the importance of issues which affect our daily lives and the reality which we occupy. There is a never-ending discussion, for example, on the 'Welsh language problem'. Looked at in another way, it could be argued that there is no Welsh language problem, only an English language problem which is an immense barrier to the achievement of true bilingualism in our country. (The BBC news also constantly refers to the 'Irish problem', which in fact could be referred to as the problem of English imperialism in the occupied six counties).

It is no wonder that racism exists. I have had experience of this. The mere fact that someone has to explain to a very close neighbour who he is and what he's all about clearly demonstrates that the neighbour has little or no concern. It shows a certain contempt. And little wonder. Nothing is taught in English schools about Wales, its history or its literature. I find even amongst intelligent and enlightened English people a great ignorance. There isn't even an awareness of what's going on.

I wish to end with two questions:

Can any English author imagine getting up in the morning to sit at a desk for eight hours to write in a language which has no official status in its own country?

Can any English author imagine writing in a language which could quite easily die and disappear as a daily, living tongue in the first few decades of the next century?

This is why I have begun to feel recently that writing in Welsh is very much a classic twentieth-century experience. You are writing on the edge of catastrophe.

5

Constructed out of bewilderment: stories of Scotland

DOROTHY McMILLAN

It seems probable that if we were never bewildered there would never be a story to tell about us.[1]

On Wednesday 25 May 1993 *The Herald* published the results of an extensive System 3 Poll which showed 30 per cent of Scots in favour of a completely independent Scottish parliament and 49 per cent in favour of a Scottish parliament with substantial powers within the British framework. And this even if it proved more costly. The same issue of the newspaper reports the Bosnian Muslim president, Alija Izetbegovic, angrily accusing the world of appeasing Serb 'aggression and genocide' and urging his nation to 'fight to the bitter end'. Surely this tells a story in the popular use of the phrase? If stories of Scotland and Scottishness are constructed out of bewilderment, they share in a confusion that is at least European if not worldwide. 'Who would have thought', writes Benedict Anderson in the Preface to the second edition of his *Imagined Communities*, 'that the storm blows harder the farther it leaves Paradise behind?'[2] When he originally published his study of nationalism in 1983 he was 'haunted by the prospect of further full-scale wars between the socialist states. Now half these states have joined the debris at the Angel's feet, and the rest are fearful of soon following them. The wars that the survivors face are civil wars.'[3] At one of the crucial moments in Scotland's continuing quest for national definition, a quest complicated by the uncertainty about whether the aim is the revivification of an old sense of nationhood or the creation of a new, nationalism is once more getting a decidedly bad name. While life in the margins may be frustrating, there is perhaps something to be said for staying on the sidelines. Tom Nairn whose own book, *The Break-up of Britain,* broke new ground in studies of nationhood,[4] attacks the automatic, untheoretical excoriation of nationalism typified by a *Guardian* leader of 1990, 'Don't Put Out More Flags'. But his apologia for modern nationalism includes what he himself admits is the rather dodgy method of inviting us to recognize that the three thousand-plus who died in the ex-Soviet empire is 'fewer than most people think'. He is surely right that there are always sentimental universalists to claim that they told us so, that nationalism is inherently flawed, and new phenomena may well need new theoretical tools for analysis, but the optimism of his conclusion seems more *bien pensant* than empirically founded:

> Fifteen years ago I wrote something about 'The Modern Janus', likening nationalism to the two-headed Roman deity who couldn't help looking backwards as well as forwards. Since then the whole world has increasingly come to resemble him. But with an important difference. I believe that, on the whole, the forward-gazing side of the strange visage may be more prominent than it was in 1977. Perhaps because today the forward view is that much more open and encouraging than it was then.[5]

The metaphor begins to collapse under the weight of defence: a Janus with a more prominent forward-gazing side may simply be a more obvious monster and one much more likely to topple over.

Yet for contemporary Scottish novelists the nation, its myths and allegories, however monstrous, are probably inescapable. This is peculiarly true for novelists, since historically the very project of the novel involved the celebration and organization of that heterogeneity that also characterizes the raw material of nationhood. For Balzac the 'novel is the private history of nations' and its great flowering in the nineteenth century went hand in hand with European nationalism and the demarcation of national literary boundaries. And, of course, in Latin America and the Third World the novel is inextricably implicated in the formation or critique of national consciousness. Timothy Brennan neatly shows how the textual conditions of writing a novel figure the processes of creating the nation: 'It was the *novel* that historically accompanied the rise of nations by objectifying the "one, yet many" of national life, and by mimicking the structure of the nation, a clearly bordered jumble of languages and styles.'[6]

It may be a wish to frustrate the reading of their novels as national allegory that sends Alan Massie and William Boyd and Ronald Frame in flight to Rome or France or Africa or Bath, although Massie at least can leave his readers with uncomfortable questions about betrayal of country and collaboration with the enemy. The price they pay is the inevitable price of sophisticated dislocation: when they do return to Scottish places they seem to come as visitors. More commonly, novelists writing now have felt the pressure to engage with the affairs of the Scottish nation even to the extent of generating analogies to act like stickers on the book itself. Andrew Greig's *Electric Brae* announces its agenda on the fly leaf: 'You're not in love', Gerry said, 'you're in a state of dependence. Like this country of yours.' 'I bet he didn't say that,' I thought, and funnily enough when I got to the conversation in the text, I found that he hadn't quite – so anxious were the publishers to proclaim the work relevant to the Scottish dilemma that they did not check their reference.[7] Andrew Greig shares their anxiety; his project is wholly self-conscious and in reaction against what he feels as an urban centrist strain in the Scottish novel. Here he is in an interview with Rory Watson:

> RW: I notice that the characters from *Electric Brae* come from all over the country? You were saying . . .?
> AG: – Consciously and deliberately because I wanted to recognize the diversity of culture and place in my country, and I suppose it does have a strong anti-metropolitan bias; the point being that whatever Glaswegians may think, Glasgow and Scotland are not synonymous, nor is Edinburgh![8]

Yet this sounds perilously close to trying to convey the unity in diversity of the United Kingdom by telling stories about an Englishman, a Scotsman and an Irishman. The deliberateness of the project is in keeping with the general poetic tendency in the organization of *Electric Brae*, the three parts of which are firmly structured according to a predetermined plan which includes the relentless working through, as chapter headings and signifiers, of the objects used to play the child's memory game, 'Kim's Game' (Kim is the name of the speaker's lover). It may be that the process of imagining a nation calls for more redundancy and messy imbalance than Andrew Greig is prepared to tolerate in his writing.

Two years earlier Alan Spence in *The Magic Flute*[9] was more relaxed about redundancy but, of course, this may turn out to be because he hopes that all glorious diversity may be ultimately subsumed into the mystical 'One', and if it is, then that sense of communal difference which is at the heart of the idea of the nation must disappear. There is no one writing in Scotland at the moment who so effortlessly writes the idiom of the ordinary young or has so seeingly rendered urban Scotland during the period from the death of Kennedy to the death of John Lennon. The novel is unsystematically packed with references to Scotland and Scottishness, simply because that is the way things are. They are also frequently the result of deprivation, prejudice and violence. The novel traces the fortunes of four Protestant boys from Govan, Brian, Tam, Eddie and George, who join an Orange band in their last year of primary school. Eddie, from a miserable, hopeless broken home is at last killed in Northern Ireland; George, his small store of imagination early stifled, settles into a loveless marriage, a salesman's job and the vulgarity of the Masonic handshake. Brian becomes a schoolteacher and perhaps a writer, Tam travels in Europe, and goes to America with his American wife and his flute; the novel closes in the aeroplane which is bringing him back alone to Glasgow.

The flute is, of course, the organizing figure, its Enlightenment message of universal brotherhood and truth, embodied in Mozart's opera, is traced through its corruptions into a symbol of sectarianism and hatred, but the possibilities of its original optimism for humanity are never allowed to disintegrate. But in spite of the title, it is in the end the mysticism of Zen, that very sixties preoccupation, that is given precedence. Ruby constructs a backdrop in the hall where she and Tam are to marry: 'the central motif was a huge stylized figure of Krishna playing the flute, straddling images of Glasgow and New York.' (p.232) The priest who marries them remarks: 'This has to be the first . . . a Protestant and a Jewess being married by a Catholic in front of a Hindu image!' (p.233) This is persuasive up to a point but a recalcitrant Western pragmatism makes me refuse the novel's offerings of the actuality of vision and the wisdom of paradox. 'How do you play', the Zen koan asks, 'the flute of solid iron, with no mouthpiece and no holes?' (p.253). You might begin, I suppose, by saying that it is not a flute.

The novel's final attempt to reconcile all things is a noble one: Tam in his aeroplane is reading the *Bhagavad Gita* and listening to the radio on his headphones; happily through them comes James Galway's flute 'pouring out glorious Mozart':

> He pushed up the little plastic blind over his window and was startled at the sun's rays streaming in. *Die Strahlen der Sonne vertreiben die Nacht.* He pressed his head close to the glass, to see. They were flying into the sun. The great red ball was up over the Atlantic, hurrying to meet them halfway across. (p.412)

If the visionary real is so firmly privileged over the quotidian, however attentively that is rendered, then it does not matter if you have your epiphanies a mile high, but it is 5,274 feet too far up to have a view of Scotland that is more than a map. And although the novel seems to end in qualified optimism, its predominant tone is elegiac, the end, as it were of a new song, rather than the music of the future.

If it is working-class culture with which *The Magic Flute* initially engages, the novel's chief centres of consciousness are finally middle-class, for the mysteries of Zen are unlikely to engage the urban working class or the disempowered inhabitants of rural or coastal areas. Yet some engagement with the folk or the people has generally been found necessary in the construction of a notion of nation and it is, of course, in the urban discourses of James Kelman and his disciples that most critics north and south of the border have found the new centre of Scottishness; it is also this presumption about which Andrew Greig is complaining. It is less clear that Kelman is happy with the way he has been positioned, with the institutionalizing of his subversive disaffection, for in taking an alienated schoolteacher as the hero of *A Disaffection*[10] Kelman is committed to questioning the normalizing discourses of education, including those that attempt to validate the notion of the Scottish nation. One of the ways of legitimatizing the nation state is, as Jean Franco points out in her essay 'The Nation as Imagined Community',[11] through pedagogical discourse, and for Patrick Doyle pedagogical discourse is a means of oppression and control, notwithstanding Scotland's persisting boast that its educational system is a national mark of distinction.

Patrick Doyle needs to be a bad teacher since to be a good one would mean that he was complicit with a system that he holds responsible for stifling enquiry, just as he rather petulantly holds his family responsible for forcing him into the very education that has contaminated his relationship with them:

> They were all like that, these middle-class bastards, lying fuckers, so absolutely hypocritical it was a way of being, they never even bothered reflecting on it, all those lecturers and students, so smugly satisfied and content to let you say what you wanted to say and do what you wanted to do, just so long as it didnt threaten what they possessed, and what did they possess why fucking everything, the best of health and the best of fucking everything else . . . It was them wanted him to go to uni and no him, his parents and his fucking big brother. It was all so stupit. Really, so stupid. He had not wanted to go. (*A Disaffection*, p.53)

The revenge of the middle-class fuckers in my university has been to put *A Disaffection* on the second-year course and lecture on it to 200 students. But Kelman faces a more serious appropriation of his work. There is unsurprisingly a kind of parallel here with Third World writers: Timothy Brennan remarks 'a trend of cosmopolitan commentators on the Third World, who offer an *inside view* of formerly submerged peoples for target reading publics in Europe and North America in novels that comply with metropolitan literary tastes'.[12] To describe Kelman's poetry of 'fuck sake', 'keech' and 'tollie' as complying with metropolitan literary tastes might seem on the face of it unlikely – is he not after all the first writer really to privilege the people's speech by taking it out of inverted commas and placing it at the top of the novel's hierarchy of discourses?

When Kelman began to publish in the 1980s Scottishness was already becoming rather fashionable in metropolitan circles. It had something to do with Billy Connolly and with Bill Forsyth's *Gregory's Girl* in 1980, the success of which enticed Burt Lancaster into the Scottish Highlands in *Local Hero*; it probably had most to do with the need of those inside the London egg to validate their fragile authenticity by adopting as mascots artists that seemed closer to the 'real life' of the people. Into this climate came Kelman's pure, naturalistic fictions calling in question any totalizing myth of Scottishness and ending up, through no fault or desire of his own, seeming to embody such a myth. Kelman, like a number of other Scottish novelists was initially published by Polygon, originally a student-run branch of Edinburgh University Press, and again like others after him, he moved to Secker & Warburg – they are quite right to do so, writers must live. But the Polygon nursery does seem to have stocked the Secker stable at its cost, not least the cost of its distinctive cover, from the corner of a close sibling of which the Secker & Warburg logo now peeps. Would *A Disaffection* have got on to the Booker short list when it did, if it had been published by Polygon? It is a distressing irony that the man who took the quotation marks away from the vernacular may have instead placed them round his whole book.

For the Scottishness of *A Disaffection* is not as readily available as its linguistic experimentation might suggest, it is half-submerged, half-accidental. It is there in Patrick's support of the Junior League Football team, Yoker, or his imagining of the shock headline, 'Glasgow drinker buys tomato juice'; perhaps most of all it is there when he speaks to his nephew and niece about the pipes (ordinary builders' pipes found in the local arts centre) from which he hopes to produce a magical reconciling music:

> Naw I'm no kidding ye, what I did I actually lifted them both up off the ground and after I played them I smuggled them away home with me. And that's where they're lying right at this very minute in time, this very second in the universe, in my parlour, that selfsame old parlour where yous pair of weans always sit whenever yous come up to visit your stupit auld uncle Patrick MacDoyle. (*A Disaffection*, p.299)

It is at this very second in the universe, as he conveys to the young a belief in future magic, that this disaffected Glasgow schoolteacher with an Irish name, suddenly tacks on a half-comical 'Mac'.

If James Kelman's fiction resists some of the readings it has seemed to invite, Alasdair Gray's *Poor Things*[13] and Iain Banks's *The Crow Road*[14] explicitly invite readings as national allegory which they then subvert or complicate. It seems clear that both writers, already well-established by 1992, were feeling the pressure to speak for as well as from Scotland; indeed Alasdair Gray had already published his pamphlet, *Independence: Why Scots Should Rule Scotland*.[15] That is straight enough, but *Poor Things* is as relentless in its twistedness, its employment of pastiche, intertextuality, and the pseudo-pedagogy of the auto-didact as might be expected from the author of *Lanark*. The plot is declaredly modelled on *Frankenstein* (all, or almost all, of Alasdair Gray's borrowings and thefts are confessed within the text). Gray purports to be the editor of the found papers of a nineteenth-century public health officer, Archibald McCandless. McCandless tells how his monstrous friend, Godwin Baxter ('God' for short), himself perhaps unorthodoxly 'made' by his famous surgeon father, Sir Colin Baxter, makes the splendid and monstrous Bella, by uniting the body of a woman who has drowned herself in the Clyde with the brain of her unborn child. After a world tour with Baxter and a series of adventures in Europe with a foolish, randy lawyer, Duncan Wedderburn, who is at last driven mad by Bella's loving sexual voracity, Bella and Godwin defeat the attempt of her husband, General Aubrey de la Pole Blessington, to reappropriate her. Bella learns about her past and the secret of her 'birth'; she marries the rather null McCandless after her husband's suicide; God's artificial metabolism crumbles and he dies leaving his estate to the couple. Archibald remains a dull public health officer, Bella becomes one of the first Scottish women doctors, runs the Gordon Baxter Natal Clinic, writes Fabian pamphlets, supports female suffrage and becomes an international celebrity.

In two unmistakable ways readers are invited to think of Bella in terms of national allegory. McCandless's memoirs are purportedly illustrated by William Strang (Alasdair Gray himself, of course); one of these portrays Bella as 'Bella Caledonia' – no qualifiers attach to any of the other 'portraits' in the book. Full-lipped, full-bosomed, with shoulder-length black hair she looks confidently out of her frame, leaning as on a window-ledge, on the legend of her Scottishness. She is wearing an eighteenth-century slightly shepherdessy hat crowned with thistles and a rose, over one shoulder she wears a plaid. Behind her is an intermittently recognizable backdrop of Scotland: it is possible to distinguish the Forth Bridge, the Wallace, Monument, the Edinburgh Observatory, industrial installations, sea and hills. Here, evidently, is the spirit of Scotland. Reinforcing this is the secret message concealed under the dust-jacket of the book: 'Work as if you live in the early days of a better nation', a message that will be discovered sooner or later depending on how one reads.

If we attend to the reading that such clues would seem to demand, then what sort of nation do we find? Well, first of all it is a nation that has to be invented, it will not simply evolve in the natural way of things and when it is invented it will be a monster; it will contain but may have forgotten its own history; it will combine the perceptions of innocence with the power of experience. And it must be prepared to 'marry' its vigour to the decently worthy, however dull it may appear. The results for the novel, of course, are hilarious as Bella scythes her way through the conventions, restrictions, oppressions and hypocrisies of Victorian Europe. Alasdair Gray takes the optimistic view that innocence and compassion are coextensive – Bella's nascent linguistic skills disintegrate under the pressure of observing extreme poverty and suffering in Alexandria. It may or may not be true that compassion is more 'natural' than cruelty, but in the novel it goes without question.

Alasdair Gray then gives monstrosity a good name: Bella Baxter is a show and a showcase of what might be possible, if Scotland could come to believe that the conjunctions that pessimists despair of might miraculously produce a version of Scotland that can look the world in the eye and spit in it, if necessary. Sceptics need not worry, however, for Alasdair Gray, as might be expected, deconstructs his own creation. Partly this proceeds out of a kind of self-deprecation, for Bella herself is the creation of the quintessential liberal humanist, Godwin Baxter, whose grotesque weary face, which bears some resemblance to Alasdair's own, gazes out of the dust-jacket, while his arm embraces the 'poor things', Archibald and Bella, creatures of his own dream. One man may make a book but he cannot quite dream a nation. And so McCandless's memoirs are followed by a letter to posterity from Victoria McCandless MD. In her letter she disclaims – but she would, of course – the miraculous nature of her birth. She comes quite simply from a Manchester slum and through a series of extraordinary but natural events, including vain attempts to seduce Gordon Baxter, ends up the wife and doctor that McCandless describes. Victoria McCandless's noble illusory beliefs are first in International Socialism and, after the corruption of that ideal in Germany, in the British Labour Party. In his concluding 'Notes Historical and Critical' Gray produces an alleged letter from Victoria to MacDiarmid. It is written shortly before her death in 1946, the year of Labour victory; she writes ecstatically:

> Britain is suddenly an exciting country. The anti-trade-union laws of
> 1927 are being repealed and it seems we WILL get social welfare and
> national health care for all, and Fuel and Power and Transport and
> Iron and Steel WILL become Public Property! As public as
> broadcasting, telephones, tap-water and the air we breathe! . . . It
> seems John Maclean was wrong. A workers' co-operative nation will
> be created from London, without an independent Scotland showing
> the way. (*Poor Things*, p.316)

With the ironic placing of this letter in the now of 1992, Gray drives
his readers back to desire for a story of monstrous promise.

Like *Poor Things*, Iain Banks's *Crow Road* is a bourgeois fiction
and Banks claims that vantage point so that he can look both up and
down the Scottish class spectrum, and, like Gray's novel, *The Crow
Road* is generically promiscuous. As Douglas Gifford remarks, it 'can
be read as family chronicle, thriller, *bildungsroman* or spiritual
journey';[16] it can be read too as Banks's first big attempt to grapple
with the idea of the nation, an idea which in any case rises predictably
out of the family. Alasdair Gray's literary avatars are those novelists,
European, British and American, from Cervantes and Sterne to Barth
and Fowles, that we used to call ludic; Iain Banks, a younger man,
claims kinship with the magic realists, paying explicit homage to
Rushdie's lonely penance. His west coast town, Gallanach, and its
surroundings are a mixture of the invented and the real, like the
Macondo of García Márques's *One Hundred Years of Solitude*.

In Gallanach he places three generations of the McHoan family,
moving the narrative among them, in a series of temporal dislocations
and fragmentations, again reminiscent of Marquez, from Grandma
Margot, who explodes in the book's first sentence (because her
pacemaker has not been removed before the cremation of her body) to
her grandson Prentice, whose name signifies his narrative function.
Prentice, from child to not very successful student at Glasgow
University, provides the principal focus on events, but his father
Kenneth also acts as a focal centre. Kenneth is a schoolmaster, but
more importantly he is a teller of stories. Both Banks and Rushdie feel
the significance in the making of meanings and the forming of values,
of a father telling stories to his sons. Kenneth's stories are microcosms
of the whole novel whose eclectic mixture of the traditional and the
up-to-date, tends towards, yet finally refuses, parable. Thus passages
on the pre-history of the land, references to folk myth and custom
crowd together with the whatever was all the rage from the fifties to the
nineties. The challenge of the novel, like the challenge of national
formation, is to make some sense out of this gallimaufry.

Prentice progresses through the normal rites of passage of a typical comic hero, he grows up with a group of friends and relatives, male and female, nice and nasty, high and low; he loses Verity, the impossible object of his desire, to his alternative comedian elder brother. He loves his grandmother and his mother, is alternately amused and embarrassed by the more eccentric members of his family, loves his father intensely, manages to fall out with him and fails to effect a reconciliation before his death. Prentice's quarrel with his father is about his rejection of his father's lack of faith. Kenneth believes in the efficacy of story and refuses what he sees as the spurious comfort of faith. Prentice cannot believe that history can have a meaning without something outside history:

> But didn't there have to be something out there, just to witness, just to *know*? Hell, it didn't even have to do anything; it didn't have to act on prayers or have us singled out as a special species, or play any part in our history and development; it didn't even necessarily have to have created us, or created anything, all it had to do was exist and have existed and go on existing, to record, to *encompass*. (*The Crow Road*, p.217)

Prentice is scarcely more than an adolescent, but it is not only adolescents who have found the void intolerable to contemplate and the stories of fathers a relatively flimsy bulwark against it. Kenneth dies ludicrously. After a drunken argument with his religious brother, Hamish, Kenneth shouts, 'All the gods are false. Faith itself is idolatry', and defiantly begins climbing what turns out to be the lightning conductor of the Shore Street Church in Gallanach. He is struck down by an outrageous cliché – a flash of lightning blows him off the conductor, smashing him on the stone below. Prentice wins through to harmony of sorts, to a probable future union with Ashley, his childhood friend from the wrong side of the tracks, to completing his degree and to a perception of death not as cessation and nothingness but as change and continuity:

> We continue in our children, and in our works and in the memories of others; we continue in our dust and ash. To want more was not just childish, but cowardly, and somehow constipatory, too. Death was change; it led to new chances, new vacancies, new niches and opportunities; it was not all loss. (p.484)

But if the only real unity is mortality, where does that leave the nation? Well, it leaves it in this novel as brittle and as resilient as glass, the making of which substance forms the sub-plot of *The Crow Road* and provides a number of its organizing motifs. For Gallanach has an ancient glass-works, owned by the Urvill family, whose present head, Fergus, the Urvill of Urvill, is Prentice's uncle by marriage, his Uncle

Hamish being the works manager. Glass wonderfully figures the unity in diversity to which the idea of the nation aspires. It is a compound of disparate naturally occurring substances which behaves as a solid though it has many of the properties of a liquid. Anyone who has visited a glass-works can testify to the various ways in which glass production seems magical, the creation of beauty and purity out of the wholly unremarkable. The end product may shatter at a sound, yet another version of it may provide the material for the nose-cone of a rocket. Fergus Urvill, the aristocratic inheritor of the Gallanach Glass Works has been capable of the poetic gesture of presenting a necklace made of the remarkable natural glass, fulgurite, to his new-born niece, Verity, but he is also the villain of the piece, who murders his wife and her brother and his friend, Rory, who has worked out his guilty secret.

Fergus and glass and guilt are thus inextricably linked in *The Crow Road*. And the guilt is in some ways a class guilt which in its turn figures the burden of a guilty past. As a boy Fergus was responsible for the accident which deprived Lachlan Watt of his eye. Lachlan is the gallus scion of a deprived home who taunts Fergus about the authenticity of the objects in the wealthy boy's glass museum cabinet; Fergus, enraged, pushes Lachlan's face through the glass. He loses his eye and the Gallanach Glass Works, Ornaments Division, makes him a glass replacement. This does not, however, wholly disadvantage Lachlan, for many years later as a returned merchant seaman, he is able to couple with Fergus's wife after a party which has left Fergus in a drunken stupor. But Fergus, using a secret entrance through his observatory, becomes an unwilling and unknown witness of the act. He confides this secret to Rory, Prentice's wandering, travel-writer uncle and when Rory guesses that the death of his sister in a car crash was engineered by Fergus, Fergus kills him too, and sinks his body and his motor cycle in a loch.

This guilty secret is hidden in a cryptic manuscript, 'The Crow Road', left by Rory with his former lover Janet in her flat in Glasgow's actual Crow Road. The allusion in Rory's title is, however, to his mother's saying, 'He's awa' the crow road', meaning 'he has died', has made that last of all journeys. Prentice carelessly loses the manuscript, but, this being a post-technology novel, there are copies on floppies and Prentice is ultimately able to crack the code with the aid of a computer buff friend of Ashley's. He endangers his own life when he insinuates his discovery to Fergus, but beats off Fergus's attack with a computer keyboard. Fergus at last does the decent thing and crashes his plane into the Atlantic: he bequeaths Prentice his Bentley Eight with the glass paperweight that killed Rory in the dashboard. Prentice throws the paperweight into the sea and sells the Bentley.

Well, this is all rollicking, adolescent stuff, but I think it is how

Iain Banks had to do it. His choice of a callow, well-meaning lad as central consciousness, as pivot of his generation, is courageously right, for how are the naïve questions to get asked, if novels are too sophisticated to ask them, and how is guilt and complicity to be discovered if there is no bothersome boy detective with nothing material to gain, to ferret them out. Aristocratic guilt is not, however, wholly purged at the end of *The Crow Road*. Fergus's daughters are modern girls but their continuance as happy girls depends on their ignorance of their father's guilt. And Ashley Watt is educated and middle-classed before she and Prentice come together. The class problem remains to unsettle visions of harmony, whatever the claims for the democratic spirit of the Scottish people.

It seems proper then to consider the view from above, not from an aeroplane but from the vantage point of the last of the lairds. David Gilmour is a historian and the son of the Conservative ex-minister Sir Ian Gilmour, one of the last of the Tory gentlemen. He is also author of a biography of Lampedusa, the Sicilian aristocrat and author of *The Leopard*. David Gilmour's *The Hungry Generations*[17] seems to offer to do for the Scottish Lowland aristocracy what Lampedusa's novel, set in Napoleonic Sicily, did for its supplanted nobility. It is beautifully written, elegiacally evocative and wholly biased in a way that its model *The Leopard* is not, for Lampedusa is more appreciative of the robust materialism which replaces the noble houses than David Gilmour can bring himself to be about whatever it is that will fill the void left by the vacillating and insecure inheritor of Starne, the great Borders house that claims 'Young Lochinvar' as one of its more colourful ancestors.

Hugh Gordon of Starne has never in any real sense inherited Starne. Guiltily in flight from the obligations of the Big House, he has an unsatisfactory marriage to a politically correct American, Ellen. He grows his hair and involves himself in well-meaning causes, discovering too late his commitment to Starne, a commitment which he himself recognizes as a deep nostalgia not for his own past but for earlier, seemingly more organic days. The whole novel is informed by this rather Yeatsian poetic and this is an unkind poetic for the notion of Scotland in the twentieth century. All authoritative statement about the states of the nation, past and present, are given to Hugh's grandfather and father. Hugh's father is allowed a devastating and completely persuasive routing of Ellen's naïve Marxism:

> She had somehow acquired muddled and naïve ideas about Scottish nationalism. Scotland was a nation, she appeared to believe, which had been conquered and exploited by England and was now justifiably demanding its independence. She even talked about the

'national struggle' as if Scotland were a Third World colony and the SNP a liberation movement like Frelimo.

'But they've been fighting for centuries for their independence,' she claimed.

'They fought several hundred years ago, not in recent centuries.'

'What about those Jacobite people?'

'The Jacobites aspired to change the king in London. They were not Scottish nationalists and in 1745 they did not have the support of a single great chieftain in the Highlands.'

(*The Hungry Generations*, pp.90–1)

And so it goes on: 'Scotland became a wealthy nation in the eighteenth century following the union with England'; the Clearance landlords were Scottish and in any case 'the great majority left because they did not want to starve. Furthermore, at the end of the so-called Clearances there were more people living in the Highlands than at the beginning.' And furthermore 'the real Scotland had been Anglo-Norman since at least the twelfth century and . . . Gaelic was a useless language incapable of modern adaptation. Like Welsh and Basque.' Ellen's last stand for the Soviet Union is similarly wiped out: her defence of that state is like Plato's of Sparta, admiration for a totalitarian state which would have denied the freedoms that enabled that admiration (pp.91–5).

Ellen is generally too unsympathetically presented to allow readers that 'but wait a minute' that they might otherwise have supplied. The marriage finally collapses when Ellen admits that their son is the result of a careless adultery. Here, although Hugh has all the speeches, Ellen begins by her very reticence to occupy the moral high ground. Hugh's defence of the double standard in adultery, because of the threat that female infidelity posed to family life, is careless of Ellen's need to love and protect her child in the present, as well as slipping over the likely number of secret bastards in the houses of the old Scottish gentry.

After an abortive love affair with his cousin and sharer of his childhood, Hugh is at last left alone with his unreachable past as poor consolation. He goes, true to the Modernist origins of Gilmour's discourse, 'not with a bang but a whimper':

We should have gone long ago, I thought, a useless class in a world we neither liked nor understood. Better to have extinguished ourselves in a brief period of consuming decadence – after the last waltz, the guttering candles, the empty bottles of port on the green baize card-tables, the florid figures sprawled in leather arm-chairs waiting for the dawn footmen to remove them. Better to have disappeared in the carts of the Terror or to have danced ourselves to death under the gaze of an emperor with a death wish. Better by far to have gone quickly with a final, hopeless, absurd flourish of bravado than to survive slightly, complacent and useless, without style, without wisdom, even without comprehension. (pp.193–4)

Hugh's rhetoric, for all its plangent appeal, is self-addressed: no one is listening.

All the versions of Scottishness I have discussed so far are by men; they are also clearly gendered versions. As a possible figure for the nation Bella Caledonia may have little appeal for female readers; her joyful sexuality, her location of the salvation of humanity in the 'cuddle' smacks rather of male wish-fulfilment. Indeed, a number of Scottish male writers are keen on the 'cuddle' as panacea, a phenomenon which may surprise the mothers of young boys: no doubt the 'cuddle' seems more desirable when you are thirty-eight than when you are eight. Bella certainly is an unconventional mother, but Prentice's mother in *The Crow Road* fills the expected spot in the desirable warm family: the father tells the stories and the mother is always lovingly there. Are these roles that women imagine for themselves within a Scottish economy?

Elspeth Barker's *O Caledonia*[18] shares stylistic miscegenation with the male writers. It is, as it were, *The Mill on the Floss* written by Edgar Allan Poe with debts to Keats and others. The novel begins by recording with a peculiar unsentimental lyricism the 'bloody, murderous death' of sixteen-year-old Janet in her home, the Scottish Gothic castle of Auchnasaugh: thus Janet's life is read in the light of her bizarre end. She lies in death beneath a stained glass window depicting a white cockatoo, his breast transfixed by an arrow, swooning in death: 'at night when the moon is high it beams through the dying cockatoo and casts his blood drops in a chain of rubies on to the flagstones of the hall.' (p.1) She is clearly marked as sacrificial victim, victim, as the title signals, of the country that bore her and of the times, from the middle of the war to the late fifties, she lived through. Douglas Gifford is unhappy about this: 'I don't', he says 'recognise Scotland here.'[19] Perhaps Elspeth Barker has an answer for him from within the novel. Janet's Grandpa is a parrot-keeping man who speaks of the memories of long-lived parrots:

There must be a fair number of such long-lived birds in Scotland – even perhaps in England – and it would be a fine thing to have them all gathered in a great dining hall, invoking ghostly midshipmen and dragoons, violent drinkers and merry rhymesters, perhaps even occasionally an elderly lady of refinement. This, he said, would afford a historical experience of rare value; indeed, ancient parrots should be feted and cultivated as true archivists. (pp.14–15)

But the past offered by the parrot is unshaped by the imagination; if what it offers are truths, then they are truths that humans would not recognize. Elspeth Barker's Caledonia is not parroted – it is fully and freshly imagined. I would also contend – and I am the age that Janet would have been, although I was brought up in a council house, and am without experience of Gothic castles fifty miles from Aberdeen – that there are sufficient intersections with my own memories of childhood and adolescent joys and miseries, not least Startright shoes, Celanese knickers, 'The Grand Old Duke of York' in the Church Hall, and a habitual oscillation between arrogance and low self-esteem. If it is not Scotland's fault, whose is it?

Elspeth Barker's imagining of the life of the developing individual consciousness within the nation, focuses on the two basic parameters: places and people. Places seldom fail Janet, people always do. She is the eldest of a family of four girls and a boy; she disappoints her father by not being a boy and her appalling mother by not being a sufficiently feminine girl. She is a disaster at games, wholly unclubbable at her Anglicized boarding school, and makes the mistake of being genuinely devoted to the books she reads instead of merely accepting reading as the done thing. As child and adolescent Janet has no place to locate the love that burns within her, fuelled by her experience of nature and of poetry. Her complacent, snobbish, materialistic parents do not want it, her grotesque alcoholic cousin Lila is beyond appreciating it, only at last her pet jackdaw receives her gift of love. When she is dead 'in desolation, like a tiny kamikaze pilot, he [flies] straight into the massive walls of Auchnasaugh and [kills] himself'. (p.109) He is the only real mourner. Janet is murdered by Jim, the hunchbacked gardener of dubious sexual proclivities, but he merely strikes the blow; Janet and her needs have been dead things to those around her for most of her life.

It is the writing of Janet's passionate affair with place that is the splendour of the book. Auchnasaugh, which Janet's father Hector inherits from a cousin, is in many ways unwelcoming. The house is freezing in winter, the garden contains a grove of poisonous Heracleum and resists all Vera's attempts at southern prettification. But here, amid 'the haunting wind of dawn . . . a wind thrilling and melancholy, tender and cruel, a wind of beginning and ending' (p.109), Janet imagines her spirit set free. Here, too, she has a series of visionary moments, often triggered by birds, a fulmar or a kingfisher, incommunicable to her family, whose impatience or cynicism with her effusions constrain but never obliterate their authenticity.

How is all this to be read? Clearly the lyrical intensity of Janet's perceptions has a power hugely in excess of the forces which squash them. Early in the book Elspeth Barker provides a brilliant, grotesque figure for the impotent oppression of the exhausted past on the imagination of the young. Janet is a child at a party in the village hall; tea is being served in two sittings; the elder of two Miss Pettigrews returns from the first sitting:

> Very old Miss Pettigrew came trembling up, leaning on her stick. 'Here you are then, Annie,' she said to her sister. Her jaw dropped loose, her mouth hung limp and open; in went her black-veined claw; out came a set of pinkly glistening false teeth. Her sister grabbed them; with no ado she popped them into her own mouth. She paused for a moment, sucking noisily. 'Macaroons!' she cried, 'Och, that's braw!' She and Nanny headed briskly for the tea table. Janet and the ancient sat silent together, both dribbling a little. (p.14)

The teeth of the mean-spirited are false, they do not even have uninterrupted possession of them, but they can still chomp their way through a scone or two. But perhaps Elspeth Barker should mind more about this. If Caledonia is merely, for the passionate female imagination, a place fit to die in, should not outrage overpower lament?

A. L. Kennedy, like Iain Banks, is one of *Granta*'s 'Best of Young British Novelists'. At first it seems that her study of young Margaret Hamilton's search for self-coherence in *Looking for the Possible Dance*[20] is as far as it could be from Iain Banks's sprawling family saga. But it becomes apparent that they are close kin, with A. L. Kennedy's novel providing female gendered versions of Banks's historicized modernity; and her specifically female understanding of family complementing his masculine presentation. Like Banks, Kennedy employs time shift and fragmentation to indicate the tangled relationship of the past with contemporary experience. Linear history of the individual and the country is impossible, but they may just be caught in the gaps of time.

Margaret is born in Glasgow; she suffers the Scottish educational system of the sixties and seventies which, Kennedy tartly says, has as its fourth commandment that 'the chosen and male shall go forth unto professions while the chosen and female shall be homely, fecund, docile and slightly artistic'. (p.15) It is a system which engenders a peculiarly female guilt; Margaret is always apologizing, 'she had only ever been rebellious as an infant'. She studies English Literature in an English university where she meets Colin McCoan. Her fluctuating relationship with Colin, lived out in fragments during journeys between England and Scotland, forms the fitfully organizing strand of the novel.

But the central love affair of Margaret Hamilton's life is her passionate attachment to her father and, given the almost overwhelming masculinity of the Scottish cultural tradition at least in the Lowlands, it is A. L. Kennedy's immense contribution to the idea of the family that this love is enabling not crippling. And the proper physicality of the love between father ('daddy') and daughter is conveyed without embarrassment or excess:

> He came over gently to let his weight tug down one side of the bed. She didn't move, didn't open her eyes, knowing that he wanted her to be there, but nothing else. That was nice in a way; not as good as talking but nice. (p.102)

I have nowhere else encountered a touch like this; I do not think a man could do it.

Margaret scarcely remembers her mother who may have died or may have been a faithless slut. Beyond one brief burst of anger her father never speaks ill of her, but for Margaret she simply does not count. When Margaret is still little more than a child her father takes her to a dance in a Methodist Church Hall; outside the hall while they take a breather in the moonlight her father tells her that simply being alive is important: 'Everything else is a waste of time.' But finding 'a possible dance', a possible way to *be* alive, is not so easy for Margaret.

The Scotland, more specifically the Glasgow, that she must be attached to, if she is attached to any place, is in many ways horrible. After graduation she works in a community centre, ironically dubbed the Fun Factory by its *habitués*. Her work is socially worthwhile but constantly threatened by the centre's lecherous director who engineers Margaret's dismissal after she has rejected his advances and witnessed his humiliation at the hands of his alcoholic wife. This, however, is nothing compared with the 'lesson' that Colin receives as a punishment for interfering with the activities of the loan sharks who prey upon the poor. He is beaten up and nailed to a floor. After such a lesson what forgiveness, what trust, what 'possible dance'?

A. L. Kennedy takes on, in the least sensational way possible, the worst that can be told about this country, does not push the responsibility elsewhere, and pulls out of it all a low-key triumph of love and trust. Margaret is able at last to commit herself to her damaged lover and her crippled country because she has reached through her love of her father a new sense of the family as interiorized within the individual conscience. In a dream of her now dead father she comes to understand that they occupy forever the same space: 'under the sadness she felt a flicker of peace at that; she was sure she would always be family now, even if nobody else ever knew.' (p.155) Colin is worthy of her love, of her family; Scotland is probably not, but it gets into her heart anyway, because it must. Margaret is journeying south for the last time and on a return ticket:

> The walls by the side of the track are very strange now, grey brick and black brick and honey brick. Margaret has entered a foreign country. She remembers seeing waxwings searching the grass when she was at university and suddenly feeling homesick because they were not Scottish birds. There was something a little impossible about them. And that was all it took to make you miss things, a mild impossibility, a sight difference of birds. (p.236)

From everything that has gone before it would seem that stable, empowering national allegory and myth in the contemporary Scottish novel are as unwritable as they are unreadable; yet the need to write it into fiction and read it out of fiction is inescapable. It partakes thus of the Beckettian paradox of the necessity of expression without its means. Why not simply say then that the notion of Scotland is rendered post-modern in a series of post-modern novels? Is that not, after all, what we should expect from a period which has learned to reflect in its writings the dissolution of any universal system of meaning or any one privileged discourse? And, indeed, given the self-consciousness of the fictions I have been describing, their use of pastiche, of literary and other nostalgia, their throwing together of disparate discourses and value systems, surely the label is earned? Perhaps, but will it take the enquiry to any recognizable destination?

In the first place, to label these novels post-modern seems dangerously close to explaining away one series of bewilderments by invoking another. Besides, Alasdair Gray and Iain Banks have already anticipated and undermined the label. In the 'Blurb for a High Class Hardback' on the dust-jacket of *Poor Things* Alasdair Gray is described as having 'at last shrugged off his post-modernist label and written an up-to-date nineteenth century novel'. Iain Banks gives Prentice's alternative comedian brother a satirical 'faux-naïve spiel about post-isms' which Prentice's flat mate, Gav, finds 'a little bewildering' (*The Crow Road*, 115); other such jokes are easily found. This is either post-post-modernism or a proper sense that the struggle with the 'now' cannot be post anything because what has gone before cannot be put behind.

Nor does literary label account for the obligation and desire to encounter the nation and fiction. There is a residue of passionate enquiry in these novels that cannot be subsumed under style. They do not have to do it, these writers; they could fly the nets of family and country simply by changing the places of their fictions; some of them have shown, indeed, that they can do this if they want to. Yet that 'slight difference of birds' seems to pull them back.

Carl MacDougall, whose recent *The Lights Below*,[21] is yet another contribution to the idea of the nation, speaks in a review of Iain Crichton Smith's *Thoughts of Murdo* of the 'search for personal and national identity' at the base not only of Smith's fiction but of Scottish visual art as well. 'As a nation,' he says, 'we don't know who we are.'[22] Well, maybe not, but we know we want to keep on enquiring and we know at least some of the places to look for the materials to invent ourselves: indeed, we will soon surely find new and exciting places to look when 'the New Scots'[23] from other ethnic origins take up the novel. It may be that after all the nation is legitimized by desire rather than by conviction. Bewilderment has its uses.

References

[1] Henry James, Preface to *The Princess Casamassima* (1886).

[2] Benedict Arnold, *Imagined Communities*, 2nd edn. (London, Verso, 1991), p.xi.

[3] Ibid., p.xi.

[4] Tom Nairn, *The Break-up of Britain* (London, New Left Books, 1977).

[5] Idem, 'Demonising nationalism', *The London Review of Books*, 25 February 1993, p.3.

[6] Timothy Brennan, 'The national longing for form', in Homi K. Bhabha (ed.), *Nation and Narration* (London, Routledge, 1990), pp.44–70 (p.49).

[7] Andrew Greig, *Electric Brae* (Edinburgh, Canongate, 1992), fly leaf and p.161.

[8] 'Andrew Greig talking to Rory Watson', *Verse*, Vol. 10, No. 1 (Spring 1993), pp.44–53 (p.52).

[9] Alan Spence, *The Magic Flute* (Edinburgh, Canongate, 1990).

[10] James Kelman, *A Disaffection* (London, Secker & Warburg, 1989).

[11] Jean Franco, 'The nation as imagined community', in H. Aram Veeser (ed.), *The New Historicism* (London, Routledge, 1989), pp.204–12 (p.207).

[12] Brennan, op. cit., p.63.

[13] Alasdair Gray, *Poor Things* (London, Bloomsbury, 1992).

[14] Iain Banks, *The Crow Road* (London, Scribners, 1992).

[15] Alasdair Gray, *Independence: Why Scots Should Rule Scotland* (Edinburgh, Canongate, 1992).

[16] Douglas Gifford, 'Raven's Way and Crow's Road', *Books In Scotland*, No. 43 (1992), pp.11–16 (p.12).

[17] David Gilmour, *The Hungry Generations* (London, Sinclair-Stevenson, 1991).

[18] Elspeth Barker, *O Caledonia* (London, Hamish Hamilton, 1991).

[19] Douglas Gifford, 'Honour where it's due', *Books in Scotland*, No. 41 (1992), pp.7–16 (p.11).

[20] A. L. Kennedy, *Looking for the Possible Dance* (London, Secker & Warburg, 1993).

[21] Carl MacDougall, *The Lights Below* (London, Secker & Warburg, 1993).

[22] Idem, 'At once the author's most hilarious and horrifying work', *The Herald*, 29 May 1993, p.19.

[23] See Bashir Maan, *The New Scots: The Story of Asians in Scotland* (Edinburgh, Edinburgh University Press, 1992).

Not changing the world

A. L. KENNEDY

I have a problem.

I am a woman, I am heterosexual, I am more Scottish than any-thing else and I write. But I don't know how these things interrelate.

I believe that writing can have a spiritually nourishing dimension, I am an emotional anarchist, I dislike racisms and bigotry. Still, I cannot predict how this will affect my work.

I enjoy dialogue, I have quite a well-developed sense of smell, I love the taste of language in and for itself – sometimes irrespective of its meaning. Yet while I work I am almost completely unaware even of these elements which are certainly obvious in what and how I write.

So here is my problem. I have been asked for a personal response on my writing, Scottishness in literature and Scottishness in my work, but my whole understanding of writing and my method of making it does not stem from literary or national forms and traditions.

If I am completely honest I will always describe writing as a sensual rather than an intellectual process. When I write, my aim is to communicate, person to person. I am a human being telling another human being a story which may or may not be true, but which hopefully has a life and truth and logic of its own. This process of telling must above all feel right – if the words don't feel right I will change them. I can translate this process into a literary terminology, but that will be for the benefit of an observer, it will have nothing to do with the work.

Now it is, of course, embarrassing to have to say all this. Goodness knows, I don't want to appear pseudo-mystical and airy-fairy. Particularly not about the only way I know how to earn a living. I don't want to dispel what meagre intellectual kudos being a writer can earn me, by saying that all I do is tell stories. A lot of what I do is about appearing to be in unquestionable control of a complex web of incident, character, themes, leitmotifs, symbolism and perhaps a dash or two of fashionable psychology. And now here I am saying that's all just telling the story, too – if I keep my unconscious nicely stoked it will come up with the goods, pretty much without me. (Freud didn't invent Freudian symbolism, for example – we were all dreaming in it without his analysis for lifetimes, thank you very much.)

But let's get practical and perhaps even moral. I don't believe I have the right to lecture you on what I am, or what you are. I wouldn't accost a friend or someone I respect (and I always try to respect my reader) with my pet theory on any kind of -ism or -ness. If I tried to, you wouldn't listen to me, you wouldn't read on. If I can't engage your attention, keep you interested, make that contract of mutual respect and define the truth we will be working with, then I fail as a writer. In other words, if I do not say what I want to the limit of my ability, I rob myself of any chance I might have to develop my craft and I fail as a writer. If you don't read me, I fail as a writer. I don't get to say anything, or if I do, you won't be listening. So person to person is the only way I know to make fiction work. It solves a complicated problem, very simply.

So does this mean I think we are all – readers and writers – helpless, isolated individuals, driven by subconscious clockwork. No. That truth I was talking about, that world I will always be trying to define well enough for you as a reader to move in and believe – that's where identification comes in.

And with identification? There we find the moral, political, sexual, etc. meat of any piece of work. I, as one person, tell you about part of my reality. If I'm writing about (for example) love, murder, being a Scot and, if I am any good at it, I will redefine those things in my terms as I make my fiction. I will be telling whatever lies are necessary to give some appreciation of what my truth is. What you do with my perception of the world is none of my business and, as I have said, should I start to hector, lecture, deviate from the parameters of the truth we have agreed, or just be tedious, then you will be quite right in having nothing more to do with me. Believe me, no one dislikes being bored more than I do. I write fiction, fiction must be interesting and believable, that's what I try to make it.

When I talk about identification, I really become an honorary reader and can talk about the moment when a piece of fiction can release me from the limitations of my isolated individual reality. This is where reading becomes a mammoth, communal experience. (I don't know if my work does this for anyone else, it would be nice to think so, but to investigate the matter more than that would go beyond my remit as an author).

I can't tell you how exciting it was to read *Lanark* and recognize the atmosphere of a country I knew. A whole part of my life became three-, if not four-dimensional. When I saw the dialogue in *The Dear Green Place* I was delighted to find the humour and rhythm of something I heard around me. Part of my definition of myself and elements of my identity like nationality comes from the media. I believe writing is the most intimate of the media. I believe that fiction with a thread of Scottishness in its truth has helped me to know how to be myself as a Scot. I knew there were other Scots like me out there – I was no longer alone. Equally Mona Simpson reinforced how I felt about being a daughter in *The Lost Father*. Anything by Kurt Vonnegut or André Brink, among a thousand or so others, makes me simultaneously proud and ashamed to be a member of the human race. Writing can give me a sense of power within my own identity, a permission to be myself and a message from the world beyond me that there are other people who feel the way I do.

Which brings me back to writing as a complex sensual and spiritual experience of enormous power. I think it is a wonderful and important thing for an author to legitimize a marginal experience. I look forward to a time when a book from a Scottish experience will be no more remarkable than a book from an American experience, a Russian experience. Slowly, female truths are coming to be examined more and more as literature rather than publishing aberrations. Homosexual experiences of humanity are becoming more and more another part of a rich appreciation of reality.

If I respect my reader and am willing to enter into a relationship of trust, if not love, with them, I would prefer not be labelled and categorized in return. For my part I am a writer, speaking for myself and for my reader.

I am a full human being with a dignity and identity drawn from many sources, both empirical and theoretical. My nationality is beaten together from a mongrel mix of Scots, Welsh, Scots-Irish and Midland English. Because I love Scotland I will always seek to write about it as enough of an outsider to see it clearly. By sharing my intimate, individual humanity – Scottishness included – I hope to communicate a truth beyond poisonous nationalism or bigotry. By communicating, a good writer invites identification – not exactly changing the world, but certainly part of the personal change which I feel is at the root of any wider positive social or national alteration. I am a happy writer because I love what I do. I hope to be a good writer. To say more than that is none of my business.

6

Remembered poverty:
the North-East of England

PENNY SMITH

In his foreword to the 1989 reprint of Sid Chaplin's *Sam in the Morning*, Alan Plater (*Z Cars*, the *Beiderbecke* series) accuses both academics and reviewers of not being able to deal with a writer like Chaplin: 'The term "regional novelist" tumbles out, at best patronisingly, at worst as a pejorative. The critical sloppiness of this approach has many mansions.'[1] Chaplin himself attempted to shrug off the label, arguing that:

> The regional label is a comparatively new departure, the result of increasing centralization of outlook – who are the metropolitans anyway but re-settled provincials? There is no such thing as a regional writer . . .
> All writers go to the same market with their wares, and that market is increasingly international as well as national, to such an extent are we becoming a global village.[3]

Maybe there had been a time when things seemed to be heading that way – according to Stan Barstow, Chaplin's fiction was 'a shining light for a younger generation of would-be novelists from the industrial regions of England who, in the 1950s, wanted to write about working-class life from the inside'.[3] But Chaplin's own novels were not swept along by the critical enthusiasm that met the work of these younger writers and his obituary in a Newcastle paper in 1986 paid scant attention to his novels and collections of short stories: the regional tag had been firmly attached and as often as not this tag brings with it the probability of a short – sometimes astonishingly short – shelf-life. Chaplin was aware of this, although in the obituary he wrote for Jack Common in 1968 he puts Common's failure to win critical acclaim, or even the barest of financial rewards, down to: 'Typically "kiddar's luck" . . . the firm that published both Jack's books folded up before there was time even to reprint, and no paperback publisher has ever had wit enough to make a very good buy.'[4] In 'Born-Again Geordies' Robert Colls identifies the regional label itself as the source of this bad luck, pointing out that Common's novels were

> bracketed in the vaguely northern, curiously simple, lyrically poor-but-happy genre. Within this code, 'northern' meant regional, regional meant working-class and, for the working-class author or painter . . . this meant someone who inevitably looked back, back at what he had been but no longer was.[5]

The reviewers were unable to cope with the true nature of Common's work and so 'missed the measure of Common's achievement. Especially they missed its life and universality.'[6]

Almost fifty years on, the North-East nourishes a cluster of literary journals with international reputations, including *Stand*, *Writing Women*, *Iron* and *Panurge*. On Tyneside the Modern Tower poetry readings have become a local institution – it was here that Basil Bunting first read *Briggflats* (1966) – and Newcastle is not only the home base for Britain's best-known theatre-poet, Tony Harrison, but also for the cannily successful publisher of poetry, Bloodaxe. Despite this, however, since Common and Chaplin the regional novel has not thrived. Some of the reasons for this are common to anywhere at any distance from London and the large publishing houses. Other reasons are no doubt to do with outside perceptions of what constitutes North-Eastern identity: as far as a television audience goes there appears to be a steady demand for grainy depictions of Geordies, dourly wise-cracking against a backdrop of back-to-back housing and decaying docklands. Whether this has anything to do with reality, however, is a different matter.

But what I am most concerned with here is the post-war North-Eastern novel as a region in itself. What does this region, the region of the novel, look like? What is its landscape? And what future routes and directions does this landscape suggest, not only for readers with an interest in things regional, but also for the region's writers?

The contemporary North-Eastern novel begins with Jack Common – although this is not strictly true because before Common there was A. J. Cronin's *The Stars Look Down* (1935), set in a Durham mining village, as well as non-fictional works like Ellen Wilkinson's *The Town that was Murdered* (1939). However, Common's published novels do in actuality mark the beginning of the region's fiction. Common was born in Heaton, then a working-class suburb of Newcastle, in 1903. His father worked on the railway and Jack attended school until he was fourteen, when he entered a commercial college. He went on to become a solicitor's clerk before being sacked ('as a scapegoat'[7]) and thrown onto the dole for three years. After being 'given the assault of the Means Test'[8] he moved to London in 1928. In London he was picked up by the editor of *The Adelphi*, Middleton Murry, and after starting off as a circulation man he became assistant editor and was, temporarily, acting editor. He was befriended by George Orwell and during the 1930s produced numerous political essays. Common turned to fiction after leaving *The Adelphi* and his two novels, *Kiddar's Luck* (1951) and *The Ampersand* (1954) were written in dire circumstances, with the writer supporting his family by working as a manual labourer from seven to five, producing reports on film scripts from seven to ten in the evening, then working on his own books on Saturday and Sunday afternoons.[9]

Kiddar's Luck and *The Ampersand* are autobiographical novels in that they fairly closely follow Common's history on Tyneside. *Kiddar's Luck*, in particular, has the feel of autobiography, but this is definitely fictionalized autobiography; that it reads with the conviction of social history is a measure of Common's novel-writing achievement. Common's first novel was out of print until 1975, and then again until Bloodaxe reprinted it in 1990 as 'a classic work in modern English fiction'.[10] (How many undergraduate courses, one wonders, is it taught on?) Only one academic article has appeared on Common's work; in this, Michael Pickering and Kevin Robins point to the way in which Common

> succeeds in fashioning a particularly sensitive working-class vision within the autobiographical mode. What Common does is to marry literary technique and style . . . with certain qualities and features of popular oral cultural expression, ranging from the commonplace but localized traditions of repartee and kidding, through the idiomatic narratives of the raconteur and folk-tale teller, to the more formal characteristics of monologue recitation and stand-up comic turns.[11]

The influence of music-hall is emphasized by the title and epigraph: 'Hallo, kidders! How's yor luck? (Jimmy Learmouth at the Newcastle Hippodrome).' Kiddar is Geordie for brother, or mate, and is also the surname of our hero, Will Kiddar, whose story this is from conception to age fourteen. On one level this is a celebration of a working-class, North-Eastern boyhood: as Sid Chaplin points out, the first four chapters, dealing with life before the age of five, are 'a miracle of total recall, including a description of how it feels to be a bairn in a pram with the sun kissing your face, or crawling and registering every detail of the furniture'.[12] But although our kiddar's experience of a child's streetlife is one of blissful belonging – 'The street was my second home' (p.16) – underlying this sense of community is a chafing dissatisfaction:

> There were plenty of golden opportunities going that night. In palace and mansion flat, in hall and manor and new central-heated 'Cottage', the wealthy, talented, and beautiful lay coupled – welcome wombs were ten-a-penny, must have been. What do you think I picked on, me and my genes that is? Missing lush Sussex, the Surrey soft spots, affluent Mayfair and gold-filled Golder's Green, fat Norfolk rectories, the Dukeries, and many a solid Yorkshire village . . . I came upon the frost-rimed roofs of a working-class suburb in Newcastle-upon-Tyne . . . (p.5)

This is 'kiddar's luck', although in this first novel the full implications of this are not evident beyond a jocular self-deprecation; community wins out here and the real cause of anguish is not the limitations of Kiddar's aspirations by class but the deterioration of his parents' marriage, and in particular the alcoholic decline of his mother:

> I am hungry, but mother lies helpless in the armchair: I pester her and she answers with an incoherent snore of broken words; I climb on a chair and get a tin of condensed milk from the table, take it to her; her hand grips it clumsily, she looks at it, and seems to listen to me now; her eyes close and she tilts the tin, slowly the thick condensed milk runs down the blue velvet over her breast, a great cream snot on the lovely deep-blue softness I loved so much. I am heart-broken. (p.22)

And then father comes home . . . Will's father's concern is that his son should behave responsibly and, as Pickering and Robins have shown, for a working-class lad, responsible behaviour involves a transition from time experienced organically in childhood to the mechanical time-keeping of adulthood. Both patriarchy and capitalism rely on the fact that at the end of childhood there looms 'the oncoming express-train of work'.[13]

An inability to cope with things as they really are is the root cause of the predicament of Will's mother, and the truth is simply stated in the novel's first sentence: 'She was a fool, my mother.' Her mother told her as much when she married a handsome railway man totally unsuited to her, and her mother knew where foolishness could lead because although her front door 'looked out on a row of freshly-whitened doorsteps and well-polished door-handles', there lurked behind 'the middens of the Oystershell Lane slum'. (p.1) Will's mother's drinking, and his father's philandering, lead to scenes of domestic disharmony and chaos, and to something more serious when she collapses in the street and narrowly avoids finishing up in gaol. In *Kiddar's Luck* this is cause for a child's bewilderment and excruciating embarrassment; however when *Kiddar's Luck* is read in conjunction with its sequel, *The Ampersand*, the mother–son alliance becomes more ominous because if Mrs Kiddar is a fool, so is her son, and her fall from grace presages his own.

Robert Colls says that the reviewers (and the Left who, 'waiting for something else, for The Great Proletarian Novel . . . did not recognise *Kiddar* when it came') failed to see how Common was not offering a slice of social history, 'regionality . . . as a static thing', but was depicting a living, changing community.[14] This is true of both novels, although it also has to be acknowledged that while the region's culture might be changing and moving in one direction, the hero is moving in another.

To go straight from *Kiddar's Luck* to *The Ampersand* is to experience a strong dislocation. For a start, *The Ampersand* is in the third person, the emphasis on the fictionalized rather than the autobiographical self. And this self has changed surnames – Will is still Will but the Kiddars are now Clarts. Not only has there been a name change between texts but Will Clarts's identity is made even more elusive because of the different ways in which he is referred to throughout the narrative: he is William, Will, Willie, Bill. This shifting identity is foregrounded by the case of mistaken identity which begins the book, when young Will comes close to an ignominious end: 'He nearly shot you . . . thought you was a rabbit.' (p.150) The rabbiters ask if he is a runaway from the reformatory and are informed, untruthfully, that he is Tom Kennedy, forced to leave home because of a hostile stepmother.

We are then told Will's story in retrospect, but what has already been established is that he has left family and community behind and is experimenting with a new, created sense of self. Will's story picks up where *Kiddar's Luck* leaves off, with the school-leaver in search of work. Will Clarts is a step ahead of Will Kiddar, however, in that he has had a revelation, an epiphanic insight into the way in which the world of commerce is 'built around a glorious fiction', the ampersand. The world of the ampersands, 'Somebody & Co.', is a 'phantasmagoria' (p.154) and Will is optimistic that through it there runs a path leading to a place where Will can be that 'Somebody', to 'new countries – the Amazon'. (p.175) This venture into the shifting realm of the ampersand is, naturally, doomed. In the employ of a firm of solicitors, Messrs. Mealing and Dillop, Will Clarts lingers over errands and falls into elaborate fantasies in which he is a notable. Fantasy and reality then merge with the help of some blank cheques left in his charge by his drunken, dishonest employer. Watching his master fiddle the books, Will convinces himself that he has been given an implicit *carte blanche* to do the same, not realizing that he has been set up to provide the perfect scapegoat.

When Will's avid reading brings him to 'Property is theft' his mates can only agree: 'they appreciated that as practically a corner-lad's motto, neatly put, true, but a bit scandalous that it should get into books'. (p.188) But the cheques are a different matter; these represent serious crime while the way in which Will spends the money – buying expensive seats at the theatre, lording it over his friends – sets him apart and his old gang formally drops him: 'We do not wish to have any more to do with you.' (p.295) When the discrepancies at work are discovered there is only one avenue left open – flight to London. 'Clarts's name was mud, always had been.' (p.304) Clarts is Geordie for mud or muck and Will's downfall is pre-ordained.

Will Kiddar/Clarts has hit rock-bottom, but we are well aware that this is a *künstlerroman*, that Will's lies will evolve into fictions and that it as a writer that he is remaking himself. In his handling of reality Will has followed his mother rather than his father and the result is that he leaves both class and region behind. *Kiddar's Luck* might be 'the seminal text of Geordie culture'[15] but in conjunction with *The Ampersand* it is about not being sure of who you are, and about not belonging. The 'front-rimed roofs of a working-class suburb in Newcastle-upon-Tyne' were the wrong place, at the wrong time.

Unlike Common, Sid Chaplin spent only five years away from the North-East. Chaplin was born in Shildon, a mining village in County Durham, in 1916. He was apprenticed at fourteen as a colliery blacksmith and then won a year's scholarship to the Fircroft Workingmen's College in Birmingham. He returned to the Durham area and the mines but began writing poetry and short stories. Encouraged by the editor of *Penguin New Writing*, John Lehmann, he won the Atlantic Award for his short stories in *The Leaping Lad* (1946). In 1950 he became a reporter for the trade magazine *Coal*, and spent five years criss-crossing Britain, and visiting the United States, but with his home base in London. In 1957 he returned to the North-East, living in Newcastle and working as a public relations officer for the Coal Board.[16]

Chaplin's first novel, *My Fate Cries Out* (1949), is set around Durham in the eighteenth century and, as a historical romance, is a far cry from the *The Day of the Sardine* (1961) and *The Watchers and the Watched* (1962). Nominally these later novels are set in Newcastle, in the suburbs of Byker, a stone's throw away from Jack Common's

Heaton, and Elswick, a working-class suburb to the west of the city. But the time is the 1950s and the blurbs for both novels do not specify Newcastle but 'a northern industrial city': North, but not necessarily North-East.

In 'Region and class: an introduction to Sid Chaplin (1916–86)', Peter Lewis argues that Chaplin needs to be read in terms of region rather than class:

> Critics who concentrate on the issue of class in Chaplin's writings almost invariably do so at the expense of region. For Marxists, 'class' obviously takes precedence over 'regionalism', but to ignore or play down the crucial experience of the North-East in Chaplin's work is totally misguided. Working-class life was an inspiration to him, but it was working-class life in a very specific area with its own special history, and Chaplin's allegiance was primarily to his own region, not to a theoretical abstraction such as 'the industrial proletariat'.[17]

Chaplin's commitment to the region is much in evidence in his early short stories, and in the articles he wrote for *The Guardian* and other papers and journals. But in his two 'Newcastle' novels there is a television in the corner of nearly every working-class home, and the old sense of community has fragmented with the physical fragmentation of the cityscape. In *The Day of the Sardine* the local streets are the site of 'the wreck of an historic village' and further violation has become part of the scenery:

> Every now and then some tired types come along, strip a roof or two, then smoke a tab and drink tea while a bull-dozer has fun. Result: plenty of open spaces, some as big as a football pitch, and ideal for stacking old beds, decrepit settees, ancient prams, buckets, tin cans, dust-bins, and sometimes the odd body . . . Then there are abandoned streets and jagged ends where they've stopped demolishing. You'd laugh when they evacuate such a street. Soon as it's dark the place is alive with characters that fancy the odd door or a dozen or two window panes – ideal for greenhouses.[18]

This could be any working-class area, in any city, after the war. Writing in 1969, Chaplin says that Newcastle's quandary 'is that, without any reserves and with the paydirt running out, we have to find a new substance to live for, not off, a new *raison d'être*. In this respect, of course, Newcastle is Britain; only more so.'[19]

Where Jack Common's street boys engaged in minor pilfering, the gangs in *The Day of the Sardine* carry knuckledusters and knives, and the central character, Arthur Haggerston, grows up under the influence of street violence, television and the *Beano*. He has left school and is having to cope with the pain of an adult world in which the Old Lady has treacherously fallen for the Lodger and where, between the ages of sixteen and seventeen, he is to suffer

> . . . the slow torture of six dead-end jobs. Dead-end is right. Everybody down there, heaving coal, running errands, carrying meat, watching a machine, walking about or sitting on his backside, matterless what, is either dead or dying. (p.28)

Faced yet again with unemployment, Arthur and his mother reluctantly turn to Uncle George, from the more affluent side of the family. Uncle George is a Labour man, a magistrate and ex-mayor who is on the fiddle, like nearly everyone else. When Arthur discovers this he is out of a job, with no support from the union who are also part of that merry band, 'the forty thieves'. (p.219) 'Don't be a sardine. Navigate yourself,' the Lodger tells him. (p.22) A woman is murdered and Arthur, who is frightened but does not want to inform, runs away. But, where Will Clarts did not look back, Arthur returns, although well aware that he does not really fit:

> . . . I'm the crazy one . . . odd boy out . . . Brother, sometimes I feel that if some character walked up to me and gave me the nod I'd follow on. And never mind the suitcase with the spare shirt and socks. (p.286)

In *The Watchers and the Watched*, Tiger (Timothy) Mason is about to go through the next rite required of a young working-class male – marriage. This, although inevitable, threatens masculine independence. 'Ah'm ganna be boss, see?' he assures his friends, 'Ah'll treat her proper . . . but Ah'm ganna' be the boss.'[20] Newly-married, however, Tiger is at a loss as to the direction his life is to take, and for a while can do nothing but follow in his father's footsteps, which lead to an allotment and the mysteries of competitive vegetable-growing. But Tiger will never produce a prize leek and his new hobby is short-lived: '. . . the garden was only an excuse. He realised that now. What he was after was the secret spring in the old man, the meaning of that old lost life.' The secret, his father tells him, is discipline. 'Discipline's the key, kiddar . . . Get discipline an' there's nothin' ye can't set your mind to!' (p.104)

Tiger's father believes that his class is losing its pride and independence while George, Tiger's student brother-in-law, says they are like men in gaol: 'These streets an' these bloody awful shops, an' the muck an' filth an' everythin' second best because folk know nothin' better. An' the entire derelict bloody city an' all.' (p.103)

For Peter Lewis, 'to describe Chaplin as an elegist for a dying working-class culture . . . as is often done, is to ignore the positive sense that something new will emerge from the death of the old – a kind of resurrection. This becomes clearer if the critical emphasis is switched from "class" to "place".'[21] Even with this switch, however, it is difficult to see any resurrection beyond that of the individual's sense of self. Thus, by the end of *The Watchers and the Watched*, Tiger has found a purpose for his own life, taking a lone stand in front of a violent mob as it attacks the homes of Asian immigrants. But although Tiger's future will be assured through independent action, the future of his class, and his region, is bleak. Socialism offers no organized resistance to the fragmentation of the community, the unions and the Labour Party being seen as ineffective or corrupt or both. And, at the same time, place offers no security either: the city is being ripped apart and the cultural boundaries of the North-East, discernible in Common's novels, are here already blurred into a larger Northernness which is itself little more than the blandness of post-war society.

Where Common's Will left the region, Chaplin's protagonists do stay, although at a psychological and emotional distance from their community. As Philip Dodd says in 'Lowryscapes: recent writings about "the North"', this is a region which seems 'all past . . . no future . . . In so much writing "the North" is a place one leaves behind.'[22] And part of the reason for this must be that in fiction the North is synonymous with working-class, and working-class is synonymous with realism. At the beginning of his writing career, in *The Thin Seam* (1949), a short novel set in a Durham County mine, Chaplin's experimentation with dialect and form suggests a possible pushing out of realism's boundaries. But, although he later said he liked this approach, 'clipped, elliptical writing – because that's pretty near working-class speech', he also felt it was too uncompromising, 'it makes no concessions'.[23] Thereafter Chaplin did not experiment further, even though *The Thin Seam* was '*read* by the lads . . . One miner wrote to me and said that he'd worn seven copies out!'[24] The question then is, who found it too uncompromising? For whom did it make no concessions? And the answer must be a middle-class readership who expected Standard English for a start, and who had also come to expect 'straightforward' realist depictions of working-class life. The writer who leaves a traditional realism behind must also, according to these expectations, leave the working class behind.

Faced with this choice, Chaplin eventually abandoned the novel altogether and in *Sam in the Morning* (1965), the work which follows *The Watchers and the Watched*, it is possible to see this happening. Here we have a middle-class Geordie character, Sam Rowlands, coping with the power struggles of big business. However, with its London setting verging on the surreal, its sixties sexuality and sharp one-liners, this reads less like a novel than a prospective television script. Looking back over Common's thwarted career, Chaplin concluded: 'Jack

Common . . . should have made a play but never did.'[25] And this seems to have been a conclusion at which others in the North-East have also arrived for, while the region's novelists have not, on the whole, thrived, playwrights and scriptwriters have fared better.[26] With the help of Alan Plater and Alex Glasgow, *The Thin Seam* became *Close the Coalhouse Door*, televised on the BBC in 1969,[27] and although in 1970 it was possible to claim Chaplin as 'one of the most important contemporary English novelists',[28] by the time of his death in 1986 he was known, even on Tyneside, not for his novels but for his television writing, and in particular for his 'contributions towards BBC's When the Boat Comes In.'[29] The small screen had provided a market which the regional novel, as it was then, had not been able to come up with.

In an article in *The Newcastle Journal* in 1967 a local reporter cites: 'Quite an impressive list of recent books which are either the work of regional writers or of authors who have taken the North-East for their subject.' With no mention of Jack Common at all the question is: 'Are these the first of the regional writers?' The final prognosis, however, is gloomy: only Sid Chaplin and Catherine Cookson can really be described as established regional novelists and Jon Silkin, the editor of *Stand*, says that he for one is highly doubtful about a new regional consciousness having much foundation in reality. The conclusion is that:

> While the North-East has its own individuality, it is certainly difficult to maintain that it possesses an immediately identifiable culture . . . While there are probably more North-Eastern writers getting into print . . . there is little sign of the sort of regional consciousness people have talked about.[30]

In 'Born-Again Geordies' Robert Colls says that it was in the late nineteenth century that the North first developed a distinctive sense of self: 'Prompted by national re-evaluations of what it was to be "English", the regional intelligentsia struggled to establish their "northernness". "Northernness" was not the same as Englishness.' By 1919, the North-East was identifying itself 'as a place of power and personality . . . Reborn by 1919, dead by 1934, the region was reborn again after 1945 – spectacularly so in Labour politician T. Dan Smith's planning hopes for a Newcastle as "the Brasilia of the North".'[31]

But by the late sixties and seventies, large and somewhat ominous question marks were forming over the area's post-war identity. And, with the plan for 'Brasilia' going badly awry, the tendency was to turn to the past rather than an unknowable future. Thus, in the wake of Common and Chaplin, regional working-class autobiography continued in works like James Kirkup's *The Only Child* (1957) and *Sorrows, Passions and Alarms* (1959), and *Pit-Yacker* (1962) by George

Hitchin. Frederick Grice's *The Bonny Pit Laddie* (1960) is a fictional account of a Durham mining village not dissimilar to the one in which Grice had grown up, while David Bean, a journalist originally from London, followed on from A. J. Cronin, depicting the effects of industrial decline on the area's mining and fishing communities in *The Day of the Bugles* (1964), *Waster's Sabbath* (1965) and *The Big Meeting* (1967). This sort of writing resulted in a steady trickle of regional fiction, but no one could match, in popularity or output, the work that has made one local writer an international best seller: this is, after all, Catherine Cookson Country.

Catherine Cookson was born as Katie McMullen in Jarrow in 1906. Looking back on her childhood she says she was the only child 'who, as I remember, went on the slacks – the Jarrow slacks where the tide brought up the refuse, all the stuff from the boats . . . I was the only child who followed the coke carts'.[32] As far as the North-East is concerned, Cookson is 'Our Kate', the writer who has put the 'North on the map'.[33] Although Cookson left Tyneside when she was twenty-two, not to return to live here until 1976, nearly all of her novels are set here and she considers them to be social histories.[34] This is a point others debate. For Robert Colls, Cookson is a paradox: 'a woman whose name is synonymous with the region itself, yet she is not a regional writer. Her stories are set in the North-East, but it is not the region that matters; they could be just about anywhere.'[35] It seems slightly fairer to say that Cookson's settings are a generic North, although Bridget Fowler insists that there does run throughout 'a concern with the North-East as a region', her writing being

> grounded in certain structural features of the region: especially the widespread nature of domestic service for women, the hostility of the agrarian ruling class to popular education, the coercive structures behind *noblesse oblige* and the array of repressive punishments meted out to the working class.[36]

Despite Cookson's success only two academic discussions of her writing have been attempted,[37] and it might be that this particular *œuvre* is best understood as constituting a region in itself. As far as the evolution of the North-Eastern novel goes, however, what is significant is the way in which a blend of region, realism and romance has made available to Cookson an area that Common and Chaplin explored, but finally felt unable to inhabit. This is the area of gender relations, the site of family. It is here that both Common and Chaplin are actually at their strongest, as can be seen in the mother–son relationships in *Kiddar's Luck* and *The Day of the Sardine*. But, where Cookson has been able to utilize this space over and over, Common and Chaplin were creating masculine fictions in which the masculine trajectory is outward, a movement which almost inevitably leads away not only from relationships and family but also from class and region. *The Ampersand* begins with Will's lie about his past, in which he says his mother has died. In his fantasizing Will is his mother's son but while he can escape, she is trapped. Similarly, in *The Watchers and the Watched*, Tiger's wife, Jean, has dreams and aspirations far beyond those of Tiger (p.56) but at the end of the novel it is Tiger who, with Jean's encouragement, will venture out into a wider world of experience while she can only wait, 'knowing he was away but confident he would return'. (p.320)

Another writer who sometimes frequents a similar terrain to that of Cookson, albeit devoid of the romance, is Pat Barker. While Catherine Cookson is the North-East's best-known 'popular' writer, Pat Barker is its most-acclaimed 'serious' novelist. Born in Thornaby-on-Tees in 1943, Barker is one of a generation of working-class writers who went from grammar school to higher education. She studied history, politics and economics at the London School of Economics and later taught history at a further education college in the area. Her first four novels are set in the region (ostensibly Teesside but, once again, more North than North-East), and in the first two of these, *Union Street* (1982) and *Blow Your House Down* (1984), her subject matter – working-class women's lives and issues like rape, abortion, and prostitution – succeeds, as Philip Dodd has observed, in making central what has hitherto 'been on the periphery of the "Northern" work as we understand it'.[38]

Barker also breaks from previous patterns in that her early texts focus on women and their importance is seen in relation to the whole: instead of an inexorable drift away, we remain within a working-class community which is seen to be an organic entity. Thus, in *Union Street*, realism is combined with 'a stream of consciousness or dream-narrative technique' which allows the experience of seven working-class women of different ages to blend into a composite life.[39]

Union Street won Barker instant recognition; she was a joint winner of the Fawcett Prize for Fiction, a runner-up for the Guardian Fiction Prize, and was chosen as one of the twenty 'Best of Young British Novelists'. However while critics like Lyn Pykett praise her 'feel for the gritty realities of female working-class experience',[40] Philip Dodd is disquieted by the physical descriptions of her working-class characters, noting 'an appalled fascination with the women she depicts'.[41] Smeared mouths, veined legs, dropped wombs: as Dodd further observes, this is hardly a new departure – its antecedents go back to earlier twentieth-century fictional depictions of northern working-class men by southern, middle-class observers, and to 'the late-nineteenth-century reports of middle-class observers of working-class life, and to their sibling, literary naturalism.'[42]

And with this is in mind it is worth taking a closer look at Barker's depiction of women in relation to an organic community. In *Union Street* and in *Blow Your House Down* it is the focus on women which keeps the focus on the community: just as in Common and Chaplin, women do not leave. But in Barker's later novels her attention turns to male characters and the powerful tug away from community is felt again. Thus, in *The Century's Daughter* (1986), Liza Jarrett's life story is embedded in the story of her family, class and community while Stephen, the young social worker to whom she tells her story, is set at a distance by his education and homosexuality. By the end of the novel, 'Stephen has become Liza's inheritor: privileged by the knowledge he has acquired of his relation to his own past and by being the empathic recipient of Liza's story'.[43] Liza enables Stephen to move forward into his own future – just as Mrs Clarts enables Will in *The Ampersand*, and Tiger is enabled by Jean in *The Watchers and the Watched*.

In Barker's next novel, *The Man Who Wasn't There* (1988), we can see a gradual turning away not only from the depiction of women, but also from the depiction of the working class. Colin, the twelve-year-old at the centre of the novel, is being brought up in a working-class community; but in his fantasies he inhabits a glamorous world in which he is a heroic, classless (or middle-class) figure, fighting his own war in occupied France. Barker's following novels, *Regeneration* (1991) and its sequel *The Eye in the Door* (1993), are about the effects of the First World War on two young soldiers, the upper-middle-class Siegfried Sassoon and the working-class Billy Prior. Through Prior, Barker's latest text maintains contact with working-class experience, but her prime concern is now with individual male characters rather than the community, and her main site of interest is no longer the North-East, or even the North.

For Linda Anderson, Barker's endeavour to weave an apparently seamless history of women–men, past–present, results in a failure substantially to challenge realism and its 'ideological legacy',[44] while for Philip Dodd her texts represent an example of how 'the "North" of the present continues to be haunted by an earlier "North" which it cannot escape'. Northern writing, he contends, is trapped by its own past, having failed to 'engage with and contest available representations'. What about the North in the post-sixties period? What about T. Dan Smith? And cosmopolitanism, and popular music? Why, he laments, 'is this "other" North absent?'[45] The answer to this, for the North-East at any rate, is that it is not entirely absent, just a mite unexpected.

'It used to be a hard land,' Jan says in Mark Adelard's *Multiface* (1975). 'Even the country houses were like forts.'[46] This is the North-East, Teesside to be precise, in the twenty-first century and things are still fairly rocky. Teesside is the site of a vital, large-scale industry but the latest technology is out of control and chaos threatens. *Multiface* is the last of a trilogy which includes *Interface* (1971) and *Volteface* (1972). Genre writing, in the form of science fiction, thrillers, psycho-thrillers, supernatural thrillers and supernatural horror, has taken up residency in the region with writers like Adelard, Chaz Brenchley and Daniel Easterman. It is true that Adelard's North-Eastern novels do not happily fit into the regional category as defined so far – in fact most of the local landmarks have all but disappeared under a warren of space-age tunnels and accompanying infrastructure. However, the fact that a brand of regional science fiction can be supported by the landscape is encouraging, especially if Alasdair Gray's *Lanark* (1985), one of the most challenging regional works to have been produced in recent years, is kept in mind. Adelard's trilogy does not do for Teesside what *Lanark* does for Glasgow, but it does bring with it intriguing possibilities.

Other new areas are also suggested by Daniel Easterman in his thriller, *The Ninth Buddha* (1988), which begins in Hexham, albeit swiftly moving to dark deeds in Tibet. Easterman writes supernatural thrillers under the name Jonathan Aycliffe, and the latest of these, *Whispers in the Dark* (1992) is set in Northumberland. *The Samaritan* (1988) and *The Garden* (1990) by Chaz Brenchley are psycho-thrillers set in Newcastle: like Easterman, Brenchley is an immigrant to the North-East and as such feels he has 'a different perspective from local-born writers. I see the city darker, more dangerous, and it's the threat implicit in that darkness that informs my books.'[47]

Another newcomer to Newcastle is Margaret Wilkinson, whose experimental writing in *Ocean Avenue* (1991) is probably best described as a brand of domestic magic realism. Confronted by a carton of Brillo pads bouncing off the back of an unmarked van, Ida Manpearl knows a miracle when she sees one.[48] In the late 1980s the memory of this story can turn a Scottish sky the colour of steel wool for Ida's granddaughter, Minna Carp, despite the incident having taken place during the Second World War, in the Bronx. Memories become family stories and blur the past into the present; Poland becomes the United States becomes the North-East of England. For Minna, marriage to George offers escape from the grinding dullness of the New World. And for a Jewish New Yorker a long way from home, George's mother's stories bring with them a certain romance of their own:

116

After dinner, George's mother told a story about the time she found a horse in her own kitchen. She remembered Sunderland when it was a wilderness of smoke-filled huts littered with proggie mats and poss tubs. She remembered the old wash house where clothes were beaten with sticks. Where she paid at the door for hot water. And when she was finished, wheeled her clothes home wet, in an old pram. (p.210)

This is the remembered poverty that comprises much of the regionalism of Common, Chaplin, Cookson and Barker. Here, however, it becomes something else, refracted through an outsider's eyes it offers a touchstone for the present rather than the past, although the past of her own family is something Minna cannot transform as easily:

George was taking me to meet his mother in England. At last. I moved close and squeezed his hand. 'Blame me,' I told him. But the train was not crowded. No one would see. A secret motion lifted my skirt. Right there on the train. My face flushed like a woman sitting in front of an opened oven door. 'Shh,' George covered my mouth.

Scratched on the seat-back in front of us was a swastika and the message: 'Death to all Jews.' (p.203)

Talking about working-class writing and the restrictions of realism, Ken Worpole notes:

Since we live in a new era of cultural displacement and migration (both within and between countries) we shall have to find the appropriate literary forms and styles which can explore and reflect these shifts and changes in people's lives and their material circumstances.[49]

A novel obsessed with Wilhelm Reich, Auschwitz and chicken soup might seem an unexpected source for new directions in the North-East of England, but it is writing like this, writing that is not afraid to experiment, which is needed in the creation of a new regionalism.

There are other writers working in the area whose novels do have Northern settings: Carol Clewlow's best-selling *A Woman's Guide to Adultery* (1989) exposes infidelity as it is practised in the English Department of a Northern university, while Brigid Murray's *Figures in a Landscape* (1991) begins outside Durham. These are not, however, regional in the same way as the works of Stephen Laws, a writer of supernatural horror whom I have kept until last as a possibly surprising successor to Jack Common and Sid Chaplin. Laws has written six novels, *Ghost Train* (1985), *Spectre* (1986), *The Wyrm* (1987), *The Frighteners* (1990), *Dark Fall* (1992) and *Gideon* (1993), all of which, except for *The Frighteners*, are set in the North-East. In these novels a strong sense of region gives the supernatural a firm grounding in reality; more than this, however, Laws weaves region and plot together so that the former does not function merely as background but becomes part of the narrative.

Born in Byker, Laws says that he grew up wanting to write for television, *à la* Alan Plater: television seemed an accessible aspiration for a boy from the working class whereas novel-writing was serious, in other words middle-class, and effeminate.[50] Here there are similarities of experience with Sid Chaplin, who reminisced that in a Durham pit village oral story-telling was a recognized masculine activity, whereas 'writing was very effeminate so I said nothing about it'.[51] And in fact it was Chaplin who helped Laws begin his career when in 1981 he chaired a panel that awarded Laws first, second and third, prize in a short-story competition run by *The Sunday Sun*. Horror writing usually presents as a masculine domain but Laws attempts to challenge this with strong female, and gay, characters, and it is noticeable that in his works the masculine movement is not outward from community: in order to survive his characters need to return to their roots. Thus, in *Spectre* (which Laws describes as 'Industrial Gothic'), the haunting of a group of friends who grew up in Byker results in the re-establishing of old, class-based relationships. In order to discover what the horror is that is pursuing them, and why, they must go back to a working-class suburb which has had the heart ripped out of it:

> Designated a slum area, the old Byker had been cleared and demolished and a new housing development, the Byker wall, had emerged, a concrete barrier against motor-way noise for a by-pass that never existed.[52]

Laws does not confine himself to an urban environment. *The Wyrm* makes good use of a North-Eastern rural setting ('Shillingham' is Hexham), but his natural affinity is with the city and his sketches of Newcastle are as recognizable as those of Jack Common. Byker has always been haunted by spectres of one sort or another, as often as not by 'The Spectre of Unemployment'. (*Spectre*, p.35) And when the Devil's representative finally makes an appearance it is clear straight off that he is not a Geordie:

> '. . . he's not a Byker lad . . . Nor Newcastle either. Strange kind of accent. Kinda southern, like.' (p.211)

For Sid Chaplin, the real pity was that the North-East had once been the nerve centre: 'the model and matrix of the modern world. It had been, if not all-exclusively, the "brain-tank" of the nation during a great period of flowering which lasted roughly from 1800 to the early 1900s.'[53] In the late twentieth century the region has seen massive industrial decline, large-scale unemployment, riots and areas of urban hopelessness reminiscent of the inter-war period. The shipbuilding, and the coal, gone; where does that leave the North-East? A long way from the better-off South, that is clear, but not quite Scotland: the North-East is the region of Other.

Despite the economic and social problems, however, there is little of the political urgency that can be sensed in parts of Scotland and Wales, and which informs some of the more powerful writing of the contemporary period. Without this political edge it is doubtful that a strong regional culture will flourish in the near future; but in the mean time regional fiction does exist, although the regional label might not always be accommodating enough to include it. As Alan Plater says, 'regional novelist' can be a critically sloppy term, either patronizing or pejorative. It is also a term which can be too narrow, too rooted in the mainstream and removed from the challenges of the remoter corners of the literary landscape.

References

1 Alan Plater, 'Foreword' to Sid Chaplin, *Sam in the Morning* (Buckhurst Hill, Scorpion, 1989, 1st edn. 1965), p.6.
2 Sid Chaplin, 'Walking the bounds', in *The Smell of Sunday Dinner* (Newcastle upon Tyne, Frank Graham, 1971), p.8.
3 Stan Barstow, 'Foreword' to Sid Chaplin, *The Watchers and the Watched* (Buckhurst Hill, Scorpion, 1989, 1st edn. 1962), p.5.
4 Sid Chaplin, 'A prince from the Tyne', in *The Smell of Sunday Dinner*, op. cit., p.62.
5 Robert Colls, 'Born-again Geordies', in Robert Colls and Bill Lancaster (eds.), *Geordies: Roots of Regionalism* (Edinburgh, Edinburgh University Press, 1992), p.17.
6 Ibid.
7 Huw Benyon and Colin Hutchinson (eds.), 'Introduction' in *Jack Common's Revolt Against an 'Age of Plenty'* (Rochdale, Rochdale's Alternative Press, 1980), p.8.
8 Ibid.
9 Lyall Wilkes, 'Introduction' in Jack Common, *Kiddar's Luck* and *The Ampersand* (Newcastle upon Tyne, Frank Graham, 1975, 1st edn. 1951, 1954), p.v. All references to these novels are to this edition.
10 Neil Astley, quoted in 'The Common Touch', *Northern Echo*, 11 July 1990.
11 Michael Pickering and Kevin Robins, '"A revolutionary materialist with a leg free": the autobiographical novels of Jack Common', in Jeremy Hawthorn (ed.), *The British Working-class Novel in the Twentieth Century* (London, Edward Arnold, 1984), p.79.

12 Sid Chaplin, 'A prince from the Tyne', op. cit., p.63.
13 Michael Pickering and Kevin Robins, ' "A revolutionary materialist" ', op. cit., p.82.
14 Robert Colls, 'Born-again Geordies', op. cit., pp.18, 17.
15 Robert Colls and Bill Lancaster, 'Guide to further reading', in *Geordies*, op. cit., p.185.
16 See Peter Lewis, 'Region and class: an introduction to Sid Chaplin (1916–86)', in *Durham University Journal*, Vol. LXXXV, No. 1 (January 1993), pp.105–9.
17 Ibid., p.106.
18 Sid Chaplin, *The Day of the Sardine* (London, Eyre & Spottiswoode, 1961), pp. 16–17. All further references to the novel are to this edition.
19 Sid Chaplin, 'The busted empire', in *The Smell of Sunday Dinner*, op. cit., p.124.
20 Sid Chaplin, *The Watchers and the Watched* (London, Eyre & Spottiswoode, 1962), p.21. All further references to the novel are to this edition.
21 Peter Lewis, 'Region and class', op. cit., p.108.
22 Philip Dodd, 'Lowryscapes: recent writings about "the North" ', in *Critical Quarterly*, Vol. 32, No. 2 (Summer 1990), p.18.
23 Michael Pickering and Kevin Robins, 'The making of a working-class writer: an interview with Sid Chaplin', in *The British Working-class Novel of the Twentieth Century*, op. cit., pp.149, 150.
24 Ibid., p.149.
25 Sid Chaplin, 'A theatre for the Tyne', in *The Smell of Sunday Dinner*, op. cit., p.22.
26 See Alan Plater, 'The drama of the North-east', in *Geordies*, op. cit., pp.71–84.
27 Ibid., p.75.
28 Geoffrey Halson (ed.), 'Introduction', in Sid Chaplin, *The Leaping Lad and Other Stories* (London, Longman, 1970), p.vi.
29 'Sid Chaplin dies, 69', in *The Evening Chronicle*, 13 January 1986.
30 David Tattersall, 'Are these the first of the regional writers?', in *The Newcastle Journal Weekend Review*, 27 May 1967.
31 'Born-again Geordies', op. cit., pp. 3, 6, 7.
32 *Daily Express*, 21 April 1973.
33 *The Newcastle Journal*, 12 February 1958.
34 *The Newcastle Journal*, 2 October 1985.
35 Robert Coll, 'Born-again Geordies', op. cit., p.30.
36 Bridget Fowler, *The Alienated Reader: Women and Popular Romantic Literature in the Twentieth Century* (London, Harvester Wheatsheaf, 1991), p.87.
37 See also J. Batsleer et al., *Rewriting English* (London, Methuen, 1985).
38 Philip Dodd, 'Lowryscapes', op. cit., p.25.
39 Lyn Pykett, 'The century's daughters: recent women's fiction and history', in *Critical Quarterly*, Vol. 29, No. 3 (Autumn 1987), p.72.
40 Loc. cit.
41 Philip Dodd, 'Lowryscapes', op. cit., p.26.

[42] Ibid., pp. 25, 26.

[43] Linda Anderson (ed.), 'The re-imagining of history in contemporary women's fiction', in *Plotting Change: Contemporary Women's Fiction* (London, Edward Arnold, 1990), p.133.

[44] Ibid., p.132.

[45] Philip Dodd, 'Lowryscapes', op. cit., p.27.

[46] Mark Adelard, *Multiface* (London, Sidgwick and Jackson, 1975), p.18.

[47] Mid Northumberland Arts Group, *The Directory of Northern Writers* (Ashington, MidNAG and Northumberland County Library, 1991), p.81.

[48] Margaret Wilkinson, *Ocean Avenue* (London, Serpent's Tail, 1991), p.15. All further references to the novel are to this edition.

[49] Ken Worpole, *Dockers and Detectives* (London, Verso, 1983), p.93.

[50] Information about Laws's work from an interview with the author, 20 September 1993.

[51] Michael Pickering and Kevin Robins, 'The making of a working-class writer', op. cit., pp. 141, 143.

[52] Stephen Laws, *Spectre* (London, Sphere, 1988, 1st edn. 1986), p.23. All further references to the novel are to this edition.

[53] Sid Chaplin, 'An Empire such as we have never known', in *The Smell of Sunday Dinner*, p.14.

Writing in the dark

MARGARET WILKINSON

My own personal image of writing in the North-East of England is of writing with my eyes closed. Not looking. Writing with my left hand. Trying to connect my hand directly to my brain. Writing in the middle of the night. Writing quickly. Trying to capture, rather than record, a vision.

I was born and raised in New York City; when I first came to England I expected quaint villages, Miss Marples, Beefeaters and woollens. In my mind, England was synonymous with these things. England was London, perhaps Oxford. I do not believe I'd ever heard of the city of Newcastle-upon-Tyne previous to my arrival in 1980. Newcastle was outside my vision of England. Where were the thatched cottages? I couldn't understand it. England was elsewhere. Someone pointed south. 'Look in that direction,' they said. I experienced an odd sense of voyeurism. Maybe I needed to have my eyes tested. A cold wind blew off the North Sea, a stiff wind. The place I'd expected was another, interior England. Newcastle-upon-Tyne, by comparison, was exterior, the dark pavement beyond the window of England. I was uncomfortable, but I profited from this sense of dislocation. For a writer, a degree of otherness, of being on the outside looking in, is a good, not a bad, thing. It confirms the position of the writer as witness.

I was already an outsider. I was Jewish. Outside New York City I never fit into mainstream American culture. Why was it, in the North-East of England where I was most foreign, I soon felt at home? It's a region strong in spirit and warmth, with no lack of identity; however there's a feeling, in the North-East, of everything happening elsewhere. The region stands alone. For this reason, my own sense of otherness, foreignness and isolation seemed poignantly shared. Newcastle can't offer the diversity of London or New York City. It positions the writer in an exterior relationship to much contemporary imagery. The position of looking on, rather than being in, is crucial. It is like existing in the margin, the blank edge on the page of a book. New York City, on the other hand, was an assemblage of exotic characters, interesting dialogue, and images that were already stories – images that didn't have to be constructed, only recorded. Nothing had to be imagined or laboriously scraped together. Nothing was ordinary. In New York City, the Naked City, one extraordinary thing I observed seemed as important as another. Moreover, each extraordinary thing was illuminated and complete. There was nothing to process, shape, develop, or change. I couldn't make it better, more exciting, more interesting than it already was. 'There are a million stories in the naked city,' the narrator of a television programme I loved as a child used to cry each week. I was thrilled, sitting in the glare of the cathode ray. But it didn't last.

There are probably a million stories in Newcastle upon Tyne, but they are hidden. First you have to find them, then you have to develop them, complete them, imagine their details as if half-seeing in the dark. Fascinated with eyes and vision, like a blind woman in collision with the environment, I feel my way around. There are no distractions in the North-East of England. There is stimulation and energy, but for me it's a non-eventful place. In the North-East of England where not much happens, images are not disposable. They are hoarded and reworked. This seems to reflect the culture, not of excess, but of insufficiency. With a paucity of imagery, adventure and occasion, I have to look harder, imagine more. For the writing I think this is a blessing in disguise. It's like trying to work under a low-wattage bulb, you strain closer to the page.

When I teach creative writing classes in Newcastle I often use this idea as a starting point: Write not only what you know, but value and develop what you know. Don't sentimentalize, but prize your personal experience, your vision, your thoughts, dreams, daily observations, your background, your family, history, memories – however ordinary, sparse, provincial – as special, interesting, unique and worth writing about. The result, although based on realism, has little in common with the gritty style often associated with the region. Valuing everyday life gives everyday life a magical quality. A frugality of imagery can be seen as a gift rather than a handicap. Making the ordinary world glow with meaning, mystery, menace, beauty, develops writing skills. The need to pay attention to detail, to sharpen the senses, is also crucial when you are not overwhelmed with material.

And then there's memory. When life is not particularly exciting, the role of memory is intensified. What we think we remember of the past seems especially rich and promising. Because memory is not exact, because it needs to be enhanced by the imagination, it is of particular value to the writer. For me the process of writing and the process of remembering, filling the void with detail, gesture, words, are synonymous. In Newcastle nothing is wasted. Here's an example of a half-remembered fragment from my own life, an ordinary errand with my uncle, that I've improved with imagination, and tried to ignite with a little mystery, humour and consequence:

> When I got up in the morning, two tufts of hair dangling in front of my ears, my uncle Raymond was at the kitchen table drinking coffee without milk. 'How about a jelly doughnut?' my father's beard burnt my cheek. I walked around the table. 'Oh yeah?' I looked under the table.
>
> 'I don't see any jelly doughnuts either!' my mother opened and closed the kitchen cabinets. 'Do you?'
>
> My father bustled to the door. He undid the double locks and peered into the gloomy corridor beyond our small apartment. He was dressed in a bathrobe. Velvet slippers flopped off his feet. 'Ya wanna take ya Uncle to the bakery?' he asked the floor tiles.
>
> In front of a mirror that hung behind the hall closet, my uncle put on his overcoat. As he lifted his steep collar and smoothed his lapels, I jumped up too. My legs were like pea stems. Recently, my hair had been cut over my forehead in a stiff little row of short and wirey curls, with two awkward sideburns left hanging on each pale cheek. My mother called these 'payees', like the long earlocks worn by yeshiva boys. 'Comb ya payees,' she slammed the kitchen hatch while Raymond handed me my coat which was made out of a coarse alpaca, and hung down to my ankles.
>
>
> In a bakery with the name TOWN AND ROSE painted above its front windows, Raymond and I bought six jelly doughnuts in a white cardboard box fastened with a string. Behind the counter they ladled milk into pitchers. I watched without comprehension. Ten times over I read the words TOWN AND ROSE, on the windows, wondering what they meant. As we exited I saw my face reflected on the plate glass, Uncle Raymond at my side. I blew myself a kiss.
>
> 'Can I hold the jelly doughnuts?' I began pestering Raymond as soon as we walked back through the gates of Stuyvesant Town. I was only a little girl. I had little hands. 'I wanna hold the box.'
>
> 'Ya wanna hold the box,' Raymond squinted above the smoke of his cigarette. Can anyone be called handsome that squints? I squirmed.
>
> 'Don't hold it by the string.'
>
> I was usually all elbows, and had a problem with my posture. But my handsome uncle was very self-possessed and brought out the best in me, posture-wise. At first I held the bakery box as he

instructed with both hands cradled against my chest. But I couldn't resist. Like the toads and princesses of fairy tales, I ignored warnings. Soon I was holding the box by the string. I held the string delicately. 'Whaddya think of Adlai Stevenson?' Raymond swung his feet forward. A car slushed past.

Turning over and over like rolling wheels, our jelly doughnuts accelerated towards a distant vanishing point, when the string I was holding suddenly broke. 'Catch em,' Raymond waved. Crazily I noticed the buildings lining the pavement were purple and pink. 'Over there. Behind you.' I felt a motor whirring inside me. My shoes clacked on the cobbles.

A jelly doughnut covered with powdered sugar bumped down a broad flight of concrete stairs. Another curled under a parked car. I chased a third into a recessed doorway. When I looked up I could see cracks in the wooden doorframe, and a small hole made by insects. I started to cry. A figure, leaning out of an upper window in her nightgown, watched me. She held a jug with a handle and a long spout.

'This isn't coffee,' I thought I heard my father complain through the open casement.

'It's coffee,' my mother cried.

I sat on a car hood with Raymond outside my apartment building. I didn't care if I ever went home. We'd found all the jelly doughnuts, although some looked battered, and some, laced delicately with mud and street hair, inedible. Nevertheless we placed them carefully back in the box under a wrapper of waxed paper. The box looked normal. I licked my fingertips. The sky, in my memory, was blue and flat, the pavement, closer to my face than it would be nowadays.

'Ya hungry?' Raymond winked one eye rimmed with powdered sugar. He was my idol. Where sunlight shone, even in the gutter, I cast a squat morning shadow on the pavement at his side.

When I came to the North-East of England and began writing seriously and for the first time about my Jewish background, I thought it was a coincidence. I thought because I'd left New York City and was homesick for my place, the images of my past were especially potent. To an extent I still believe this to be true, but I also think my experience was metaphorical. It stood for the experience of writing in the North-East of England. The North-East is every writer's foreign country. Perhaps the region isolates native writers too, isolating in the sense of grounding, focusing, and placing apart. In this way, the North-East throws you back upon yourself, throws you into darkness. The dark is not only formless, it is secret and deep.

What I'd experienced elsewhere seemed suddenly very important in Newcastle. What I saw each day, living and working in the North-East, seemed to require unfolding. A crumb became a kernel. 'Is this real life?' I tortured myself. Maybe there was no real life in the North-East of England. Real life was what happened elsewhere, or happened here once upon a time. But here is where writers can find their own portion of space, I thought. Finding your writing space is like finding your writing voice.

I work very hard in Newcastle because I feel isolated here. Far from a London-based literary establishment, in a region that's associated with workers and physical labour, my labour has become obsessive. I am obsessed with contrast and opposition. I exist in a state of creative friction with my particular surroundings. Perhaps all writers living here feel this way. I work in the margins. I work harder in the shadows, in the dark part of the picture. My own voice, an unreal thing in this landscape, becomes clearer. My position, outside the factories, the dole queues, the fish quays, the pubs, becomes more defined. My own sense of dislocation defines me. My work now reflects this tension.

I'm currently writing an historical novel, *The Tales of Gittel Crank*, in a distinctly modern voice. The style conflicts overtly with the subject matter, because I'm fascinated with dissonance. I live dissonance. While attempting, in the novel, to recreate the past, I also try to banish it, with a detached voice, absurd dialogue, irony and gaps. Perhaps I could not be writing this unlikely book anywhere but here. Do the contractions my writing now seems to embrace have anything to do with my position, my place in the North-East? I press one force against another. I face and resist, like a thumb to the other fingers. People in conflict with their environment become my natural territory. Gittel Crank, for instance, the central character in my new novel, resembles a wise-cracking New Yorker. But she's locked in a culture that endorses arranged marriages, denies women an education and values only their ability to bear a child. Portraying scenes from her traditional life in a modern idiom, I'm engaging opposition, light and shade:

> The entire house consisted of one large room with a sagging floor in which the furniture undulated, as on the sea after a shipwreck. It was damp in the old Jewish Pale of Settlement and they knew nothing of insulation. The warped floor curved in segments. One segment was a place to rest, a tousy platform of rocking mattresses filled with ropes of twisted straw that smelled of footsteps and feet. The kitchen segment contained a bed with a headboard rimmed in brass, a ladder, and a large cookstove with an open grate. In front of the grate stood a chair on cement blocks where Meyer Crank sat toasting his feet.
>
> Meyer Crank was a shoemaker, a *shuster*. Normally at this time of day he was at his stall, a board on two trestles, in the marketplace grinding boots. But not this morning. He peered down at his second wife.

Gittel knelt on the floor below him with a bucket of water and a tin of *Amhoorets* foaming soda, her dress rucked at her armpits. In the two years since they had been married Gittel had grown stout. 'Pfoo,' she said. The baby squelched under her feet.

In the middle of the room there was a great table, buoyant as gopher wood, upon which papers and clothes were heaped. A smaller table flanked by narrow benches and kitchen stools was used for meals. 'Where's my scrap?' Gittel patted the floor behind her ample buttocks. At foot level it was smoky and dark. The windows seemed to cast their light upwards illuminating only Meyer's great chair. In a shiny black coat, waistcoat and trousers, he idled with his back to the room.

'Have ya seen my scrap?' Gittel asked Meyer.

'Stop fardling around,' her husband replied, turning to face the untidy chamber. 'Passover's coming. Pick up ya feet,' he pointed to the unwashed floor. 'Ya feet.'

A large saucepan of tea towels boiled on the hob.

Gittel ignored his shouting. Behind his lofty chair she fardled to the table and back to the door, lifting her shoes in an exaggerated impression of forward motion. With a long handled broom she swept a carrot top, a rotting turnip and a chicken bone into a pile.

'Ya fardler,' Meyer pushed away the chipped breakfast plate he held on his knee. 'Get busy.' He clapped his hands above his head. 'Have ya starched the tablecloth? Ya hafta finish before sundown.' He turned his back on the half-opened drawers, the heaped bedclothes, the upturned buckets, and stared into the fire.

7

Fiction in conflict:
Northern Ireland's prodigal novelists

EVE PATTEN

TROUBLES WRITER: A known subspecies in the North, almost always of foreign extraction. Compulsively Romeo-and-Juliets his characters across the sectarian divide. Arrives in two varieties: the Weekend Troubles Writer will typically fly into Belfast for a few days to suss out his setting, return home, and get everything wrong. Type two, the Infatuated Troubles Writer, will stay for much longer, and often returns more than once. Embraces his new home Where Everyone Is So Alive with embarrassing enthusiasm. Will often remain in the North well beyond the point where everyone is quite bored with him. Frequently composes his Serious Novel in situ. Prefers Yeats in the title. Gets everything wrong with feeling.[1]

Since the beginning of the current phase of conflict in Northern Ireland in 1969 fiction set in the Troubles has become one of the region's few growth industries. With an element of tongue-in-cheek, Belfast's Linenhall library devotes an entire section to what has become a cult phenomenon in which hardened terrorists race across flat-roofed buildings and blow up sidewalks, misguided idealists die for Erin and lovers are caught in the crossfire. The authors vary as widely as the quality. Amongst those who have staked their claim on this fertile territory, shelved alongside professional thriller writers such as Jack Higgins (*A Prayer for the Dying*, 1975) and Tom Clancy (*Patriot Games*, 1987), are politicians from both sides of the debate (Douglas Hurd's *Vote to Kill*, 1975, and Danny Morrison's *West Belfast*, 1989), journalists (Alan Judd's *A Breed of Heroes*, 1981; Gerald Seymour's *Harry's Game*, 1975) and the occasional academic opportunist, as represented by Valerie Miner's hideously misinformed but politically correct emigrant lesbian feminist thriller of Republican heroics in London, *Blood Sisters* (1981).[2]

While the sprawl of Troubles-trash appears in some respects as a literature appropriate to a situation of political sterility and rampant exploitation, it begs a number of questions concerning the way in which Northern Ireland is represented in works of fiction. Other than that of the pulp-merchants, no characteristic school has emerged here to compare with Glasgow's urban chroniclers or Dublin's new 'dirty realists', but if it is accepted in critical terms at least that some sense of a creative separatism governs literary sensibility in this part of the world, then can an authentic fictional response to the Troubles be demarcated from the sensationalist narratives which have dominated the field? In what register does the novelist address political and social conflict without succumbing to platitude, and is it still possible to produce fresh images of the situation in a medium impoverished by cliché and overkill? Finally, how does material alluding to the Troubles endorse or contest received images of Northern Irish society from British, Irish or American sources, without reverting to provincial whimsy?

Fiction in the North of Ireland has a relatively strong, if low-profile pedigree. A twentieth-century inheritance spanning the Ulster pastoral of Michael McLaverty, the Northern Gothic of Sam Hanna Bell and Janet McNeill, the post-Catholic malaise of Brian Moore's 1950s Belfast and Maurice Leitch's speculations on sectarianism and sexuality in the 1960s offered later writers a basis for the elevation of the parochial into the viable art form.[3] Religious affiliation, cultural identity, repressive ideology, taut family relationships and sexual constraint merged in a thematic paradigm which established the rudiments of a self-conscious regional critique. Since the early 1970s, however, 'serious' fiction in Northern Ireland (a category which admittedly leaks into popular genres of thriller and romance) has been subjected to pressures which have fractured its relationship to issues of region, ideology, culture and language. Skilled writers such as Jennifer Johnston and Bernard MacLaverty have been highly acclaimed for their work but more, one suspects, because they reinforce for an international readership a compulsive literary stereotype – that of the Irish writer defiantly extracting the lyrical moment from tragic inevitability – than for their ability to engage with a multi-textured and abstruse society.

In recent years, however, fiction from Northern Ireland has begun to change dramatically. This is a manifestation, firstly, of the emergence of a new generation of writers who have come of age since the beginning of the Troubles and whose reconstructions of childhood experience effectively undercut the moral baggage and creative paralysis of their predecessors. Secondly, it marks the overdue exploitation of literary strategies such as perspectivism, ambiguity and displacement which, though categorically post-modern, may also be perceived as attributes of a sustained constitutional and psychological identity crisis germane to any representations of a contemporary Northern Irish self-image.[4] At a time when regional definition has become a priority in European political currency, concepts of identity in Northern Ireland have already reached saturation point in terms of determination and parody. To an even greater extent than other regions in Ireland, which are similarly depicted in romanticized and essentialist terms, the North is, in the phrase of writer Gerald Dawe, a 'proverbially congested space' which provokes in its artists the urge either to leave or to rebel against the status quo.[5] But the resultant congestion offers a site ripe for ironic exploitation, an incentive towards double-think predominantly visible in the work of younger poets from the North but beginning to surface in prose.

Three novelists in particular have sought to capitalize on the ambiguous parameters of communal, regional and national affiliation in Northern Ireland. In the writing of Frances Molloy and Robert McLiam Wilson a pervasive irony provides an enabling distance from which to survey and destabilize the configurations of home. Glenn Patterson has likewise assimilated in his fiction the process of ironic displacement but purposefully transcends it in order to address issues of identity through a restorative fictional anthropology. Highly conscious of the charged political context from which they emerge and of the received patterns of writing with which their own texts engage, each of these writers has subjected the heavy contingency of Northern Irish literature to a series of rearguard tactics, in order to renegotiate its terms of representation.

In Ireland, traditional perceptions of the writer as responsible for the registration of public sensibility have long been a source of poetic capital. The literary community continues to prioritize its poets as the primary agents of articulation and critique, a tendency which has been linked both to the legacy of a bardic past and to the twentieth-century inheritance of a Yeatsian aesthetic grounded in the creative tension between commitment and artistic independence.[6] The personality cult of Seamus Heaney and the critical energy devoted to an Ulster poetic renaissance – Derek Mahon and Michael Longley, Paul Muldoon and Medbh McGuckian – have meanwhile served to maintain poetry's monopoly on literary/political exchange in a series of landmark volumes such as Heaney's allegorical *North* (1975) and Muldoon's offbeat *Mules* (1977).

Inevitably, perhaps, during the early years of the Troubles expectations were extended from a poetic tradition to an indigenous prose which would, it was envisaged, produce a counterpart, a fiction adequate to deal with the provocative and disturbing events of the time. J. W. Foster, in his major study *Forces and Themes in Ulster Fiction*, established the rich genealogy from which the new generation would emerge to confront the obligatory Ulster agenda of 'sex, violence and sectarianism'. The critic Richard Deutsch anticipated a similar evolution from 'the more established Irish writers who have not yet tackled the present Ulster question', his phraseology assuming on behalf of Maurice Leitch, Brian Moore, Edna O'Brien and John McGahern that such an engagement was necessity rather than choice.[7] Demands on the prose writer have persisted on a muted level into the present decade and were expressed recently by the thriller writer Ronan Bennett who, condemning the inhibitions of contemporary Irish writers in comparison to their counterparts in South Africa, argued that 'in countries which have experienced similar social and political fragmentation, violence and death – and, the other side of the coin, heroism, idealism and sacrifice – novelists would find it inconceivable not to portray the strife raging round them'.[8]

The representational onus has arguably exacerbated two limiting trends in Northern Irish fiction. The first is the continued grip of a realist mode, a characteristic of Irish writing in general which despite the aberrations of Flann O'Brien, John Banville and a succession of fabulists, has continued to prize a skeletal (and necessary bleak) realism as the most appropriate means of national self-critique. Novels set in the North have frequently expanded the realist brief into documentary, however; a result on one hand of the desire for legitimate or authentic representation distinguishable from the mass of pulp sensationalism and on the other, of Irish fiction's close proximity to journalism and sociology.[9] From early novels such as Menna Gaillie's ambiguously titled *You're Welcome to Ulster* (1970) which documents Catholic grievances at the time of the Civil Rights campaign to *Give Them Stones* (1987), Mary Beckett's pseudo-autobiographical narrative similarly cemented to the 'rites-of-passage' of the early Troubles, the use of the novel as a personal auxiliary to public history has been a recurrent trend, while journalistic fervour in recent books such as Lionel Shriver's information-laden *Ordinary Decent Criminals* (1992) has demonstrated the continued susceptibility of Northern Ireland to foreign faction-junkies.

The second and parallel trend in Northern Irish writing has been a novelistic obligation to offer a consensual (and usually apolitical) liberal humanist comment on the predicament. A series of slim novels set against the violence of the seventies and early eighties established a determinist formula which repeatedly located a well-meaning individual within a debilitating and ultimately damaging political context. In fiction the Troubles thus represent, as critic Joe McMinn explains, 'a separate but proximate world which impinges on the preference for a private order . . . The preference is that of a search for belonging, for self-expression and self-fulfilment, with the war as a reminder of the uselessness of most such searches'.[10] The conflict of innocence and involvement – the latter always victorious – and of wistful relationships swamped and severed by a faceless paramilitary machine serves as a means of assimilating and dealing with the Northern Irish situation in reductionist terms, retrieving the *condition humaine* from a complex, impersonal reality.

The reliance of novelists on this fictional essentialism is by no means surprising and a number of eloquent and well-executed novels have emerged as a result, in which the conflict of interests is typically resolved through the closure of bomb, bullet, prison or exile. Among the best known as a result of its screen adaptation is Bernard MacLaverty's *Cal* (1983), which dramatizes the story of a youth who, despite being coerced into terrorism, manages to conduct a rueful affair with a police widow until the security forces catch up with him. In Jennifer Johnston's *Shadows on Our Skins* (1977) the relationship between a young boy and a schoolteacher in Derry is destroyed when she is tarred and feathered because of her engagement to a British soldier. Johnston's *The Railway Station Man* (1984) cuts short the emergent love affair between a Troubles widow and an English railway enthusiast with a premature IRA explosion. Brian Moore tests the integrity of a Belfast hotelier against terrorist thugs holding his wife to ransom in his weak 1990 thriller *Lies of Silence*, and most recently in David Park's *The Healing* (1992), an elderly man's tentative friendship with a schoolboy traumatized by his father's murder is threatened when the man discovers his own son's paramilitary affiliations.

The ruling dichotomy of innocence and complicity and the tragedy which results from the clash between the two have thus become standardized as the hallmarks of this category of writing about the North, and as a result fiction which has supposedly addressed the situation has, almost to the same extent as the romantic thriller, effectively bypassed it. Recourse to the juxtaposition of vulnerable individuals with an amorphous and superficially drawn terrorist presence has supplanted the novel's function of critique with a kind of literary compensation: consolatory images which provide for an unreflective but consensual response have obliterated the need to examine the complexity and ambiguity of social conflict, while the elevation of individual sufferings has largely obscured the exploration of community, identity and motivation charted by a previous generation of writers. Fraught with responsibility, the 'serious' Troubles novel has tended to universalize rather than particularize the situation, circumnavigating the Ulster condition through one-dimensional narrative and thematic limitation.

Paradoxically then, the surfeit of fiction published in relation to Northern Ireland since 1969 has failed to provide a credible regional voice or to analyse in any depth the social environment from which it emanates. Recently, however, this ingrained sterility has been challenged by contemporary writers who have developed various means of overcoming the multiple straitjacket of literary insularity, narrative realism and ideological responsibility. Novelists who have rejected the alienating burden of a national literary tradition described by the critic Seamus Deane as 'the mystique of Irishness' are beginning to employ techniques which destabilize previous conceptions of Northern Ireland and, simultaneously, previous conceptions of the Northern Irish novel.[11] The introduction of an ironic purchase on the fictional representation of identity and of a bifocal vision, a narrative voice combining internal experience with externalized critique, have rekindled the literature of the region.

Significant fissures in the liberal humanist aesthetic appear in Frances Molloy's novel, *No Mate for the Magpie* (1985), a portrait of the artist which picks up on the imaginative anarchy of Flann O'Brien rather than the formalized iconoclasm of Joyce. Written in the first person, the narrative also employs regional dialect, a manoeuvre surprisingly rare in Northern Irish fiction and one which enables the author to circumnavigate the stylistic complacency in which others had become trapped. A rich black comedy, the novel launches an attack on the corrupt and bizarre institutions of Northern Ireland through the eyes of its protagonist Ann McGlone, a Catholic from a working-class family living outside Belfast up to and during the era of the Civil Rights campaign. Molloy's heavy colloquialism proves an effective medium for what, in many respects, consists of politically sensitive material. Her technique is deflationary, dramatizing Irish social conflict in the microcosm of the McGlone family's embroilment in a series of battles with the neighbours, the nuns, the council and the police. She refuses the potential romanticism of her subject: sectarianism is encountered as a bitter exchange over the trimming of a garden hedge, prejudice as a gaggle of workplace bullies with a cigarette-lighter. The family tragedy of Ann's father, interned for four years on a Catch 22 legal technicality, is presented in the same dead-pan register as an attack by the housing estate's Catholic matriarchs on a local breadman who has allegedly cursed the pope. This characteristic substitution of burlesque for piety comprises the author's primary means of assault on sacrosanct perceptions of identity and affiliation. In one typical scene Molloy highlights the absurdities of religious segregation when Ann, who has naïvely accepted a job in a Protestant-dominated factory, is obliged to disguise her background from her colleagues for an entire day:

> To begin way, a had te be very careful not te say the wrong thing in
> case they twigged on that a was a catholic, so a limited mesel' te
> repeatin' verbatim what the dreadful catholics from our town said
> about us protestants, an' only repeatin' some of the better known
> anti-catholic slogans, but as me confidence increased, a got to enjoy
> the part a was playin' so much, that a become more excessive an'
> outspoken that any of the others in me scathin' criticism an'
> condemnation of fuckin' popish scum. (God was a glad that me ma
> was outa ear-shot.) (p.108)

Through the satirical undertow to the narrative levity here and
elsewhere in the novel, Molloy challenges the sanctimony with which
other writers had approached aspects of life in Northern Ireland.
Despite veering in this way from tragicomedy into slapstick, however,
No Mate For the Magpie stops short of trivializing the issues and
attempts a serious critique of national identity by contextualizing the
North's degeneracy within that of Ireland as a whole. Ann's escape
across the Irish border in the wake of the Civil Rights marches in
Derry completes her passage to disillusionment as she confronts in
Dublin a fossilized iconography and the ascendancy of opportunism
and emotional repression. Her eventual flight from Ireland caricatures
Joyce's Stephen Dedalus and at the same time occasions a series of
leave-taking vignettes which epitomize the imaginative and moral
bankruptcy of the nation:

> A mother fingerin' prayer beads in hir pocket on hir way home from
> the pawn shop. A child smacked hard across the face for handlin'
> toys in a supermarket. 'Please give generously an' god will reward
> you' boxes shoved under noses, by well-fed, well-dressed, well-past
> middle-age ladies. Punch-ups about places in a bus queue.
> Invitations to walk roun' stores with no obligation. Why not visit
> oour movin' crib? – bring all the family – great reductions. A black
> english student cryin' on the doorstep of a boardin' house because
> the lan'lady didn't like the colour of hir skin, a mean-mouthed
> woman dressin' down a teenage girl for wearin' a maxi-length coat. A
> hungry youth oglin' cream buns in a baker's window. A mother
> stoppin' traffic on O'Connell Street because hir toddler was missin'.
> The vacant eyes of a young drug addict who'd got lost forever on a
> bad trip. And the people with the answers to all the problems of the
> land, toutin' their propaganda sheets for nine pence a copy outside
> the historic General Post Office. (p.170)

In this comparative light, corruption in the North is identified with an
ideological decay rife throughout the island as a whole, as Molloy
replaces a Northern Irish identity based on historical obsession and
localized tribal warfare with that of a contemporary, national
dysfunctionalism. Having struck out at the travesties of British state

control, therefore, her deceptively picaresque novel subsequently turns on the redundancy of claims for Irish nationhood.

No Mate for the Magpie thus fractured the respectable veneer of contemporary Northern Irish fiction in its decidedly political confrontation with history as far as 1970. Since that date a generation has experienced the Troubles as the norm rather than the exception, a fact which does nothing to dull the impact of violence but which has continued to widen the range of strategies available to the writer. Two younger novelists have followed Molloy in seeking to expand the linear determinism of previous narratives into a conglomerate image of the region within its 'parent' environment – this time taken as the UK – in order to place its idiosyncrasies in context. The connections are on one level personal and stylistic: both Robert McLiam Wilson and Glenn Patterson are participants in Northern Ireland's 'brain-drain' to English universities and each reflects the influence of a British school of fiction, Wilson showing his debt to the Martin Amis of the *Rachel Papers* era and Patterson emerging from the Malcolm Bradbury school of creative writing at East Anglia. More than this, however, the development of perspective in their novels relates to the spin which both writers have put on the Irish fetish of literary exile.

Displacement is predominant first of all in the construction of plot. In Wilson's *Ripley Bogle* a Belfast-born tramp recalls experiences of his native city from the poverty of the London underworld, while Patterson's second novel *Fat Lad* centres on a Northern Irish emigré in a state of suspended animation between Belfast and Manchester. But it is also pertinent to the way in which each writer addresses his material from a consciously dislocated vantage point, occupying a position similar to that which Aritha Van Herk has termed in relation to Australian and Canadian fiction, the 'prodigal':

> To be of the colony but far beyond it, part of the family but happily renegade has been the chief incitement for the post-modern, post-colonial text to pretend to itself that it is homesick for homesickness, at the same time as it revels in the juicy ambiguity of its literary languishment. The prodigal has a good time before he goes home, and these prodigal novels linger over their reflections from home at the same time as they textually announce that they will never return.[12]

While it is problematic to locate literature from Northern Ireland within a post-colonial discourse, Van Herk's terminology is useful in drawing attention to the full effects of an intermediary status on the writer and in highlighting the resources which the resultant cultural, psychological and literary discrepancies provide for a new dialogue between region and nation. Liberated through their ambiguous 'prodigal' status, Patterson and Wilson use England not as a means of resolution through exile but as an active accomplice with Northern Ireland in a mutual and continuing process of self-definition.

The 'aegis of irony' under which any kind of commitment to constructed identities must be experienced is key to the register adopted by Robert Wilson in his debut novel, *Ripley Bogle* (1989).[13] The eponymous Bogle, born to a Welsh-Irish family of low repute in the Republican Turf Lodge area of West Belfast, explains how on his first day at school he was introduced to the conundrum of constitutional loyalties. Belfast, his fervently nationalist schoolmistress insists, is in Ireland, and her pupils' names will therefore always remain Irish. Confused, the narrator describes how he immediately dubbed himself 'Ripley Irish Bogle':

> This temporary solution was, however, shattered when little Miss Trotsky herself told us that the occasional Misguided Soul would try to call us British, but that of all the wrong things to call us – this was the wrongest. No matter how the misguided souls cajoled, insisted or pleaded, our names would remain Irish to the core, whatever that meant.
>
> Well, as you can imagine, this buggered me up no end. I was dazed and anxious. I was worried and confused. But with a precociously fine critical instinct and a juvenile distrust of pedagogical fervour, I decided to consult the maternal oracle upon my return home. In the meantime, in the spirit of compromise (ever with me even then), I dubbed myself 'Ripley Irish British Bogle'. (p.14)

The passage has been used by the critic Edna Longley to illustrate the 'anorexic' condition of Ireland's withering ideologies, but it introduces at the same time the level of satirical duplicity though which the narrative voice will operate throughout the novel, the *faux naif* as central persona immediately foregrounding the discursive schizophrenia with which Wilson seeks to deflect the possibility of consensual or unilateral response.[14]

The use of a childhood perspective – the streetwise kid who combines innocence and experience – becomes the primary means in the novel of usurping previous compensatory readings of the North. What Bogle describes as the 'telescoped' nature of his development in witnessing adult conflict at close quarters – 'You zip along to cynicism – blink and you'd miss it' – paradoxically allows a completely unpremeditated perspective on violent acts which are defamiliarized by Wilson's worm's-eye-view technique. The stoning of army vehicles is experienced as schoolboy entertainment long before it is perceived as political activity. Set-piece descriptions of a soldier being shot by a sniper and of a local girl tarred and feathered for consorting with British soldiers are presented in vivid cinematic detail, but in the context of childhood horror and voyeurism rather than adult condemnation. Bogle's memory of Internment Night (on which British soldiers rounded up and imprisoned members of the Catholic community without charge) is politically irreverent and irrelevant in its particular slant. Waking up in the dark to the sight of a tall West Indian corporal brandishing his automatic rifle, Bogle's excitement knows no bounds:

> My untutored blood raced with elation. I had never seen a real black man before and now I had one standing, albeit rather sheepishly, in my own tiny and familiar bedroom. Boy, was I chuffed or what! He brought a breath of exotic and dangerous glamour to me. The man remained motionless and embarrassed for some moments while I felt my eyes grow moist with love. Uncertain, he tried a feeble wink and his teeth smiled whitely in his tactile, ebony face before he abruptly disappeared from view. (p.27)

The combination of narratorial experience with an ingenuous consciousness is disarming, allowing Wilson to reappropriate such incidents on a fresh level of perception and to undermine at the same time the formulaic management of 'Troubles' material pervasive in earlier works of Northern Irish fiction. What becomes evident, however, is the extent to which domestic experience is shaped by the presence and expectations of a foreign audience, a feature of Wilson's writing which tacitly situates England as the voyeuristic correspondent of the Irish situation. This is not simply a result of the novel having been published by a mainland UK publisher; rather it comprises part of an internal commentary through which Bogle/Wilson acknowledges the contrivance of his narrative, his 'albumfodder', in relation to an implied consumer:

> Oh yes, those Troubles! Those nasty Irish things! The Northern Irish conflict certainly did its bit for the decoration of my early years. I made damned sure I got a good seat. I needed the material and it came to me early and gratis (mostly). They served it up to me and I fell to it with a will and a half. (pp.26–7)

The elicitation of Irish identity by an external audience is itself part of an acknowledged literary convention in which English readers sought Irishness as exotica, and Wilson's allusion to the process reinforces, albeit ironically, his 'prodigal' status. In a discourse defined by the critic J. T. Leerssen in terms of nineteenth-century Irish fiction as 'exotericism', the Irish author is paradoxically dissociated from an Irish subject: 'the destinatory vector towards an English audience is so strong that the author no longer identifies with the country which is represented, but becomes an intermediary, an exteriorised, detached observer.'[15] Wilson's adoption of this strategic position in relation to his material is part, therefore, of a self-conscious allusion to the way in which an Irish literary identity has been formed, and part also of an attempt to detach himself further from subjective identification with Northern Ireland in order to indulge in parody and caricature. His authorial dislocation appears to work in two ways, however. As an intermediary, he is able to juxtapose hackneyed versions of Ireland with equally contrived accounts of England, illustrating not only the Celtic periphery but the heart of the Empire as party to a duplicitous confederacy. On one hand there is easy rebellion against the pretensions and trappings of home:

> O yes, begorrah! Belfastard! Cities to use with our voicey badges of accent unIrish. Ulstermen speak in tones Scottish. Little Irish about them. My landkin's voice is pigstick to me. Their shared badge of country. All that old Irishness crap promoted by Americans and professors of English literature. Menace and cupidity. All balls. (p.160)

But simultaneously England as the stable centre in terms of which an entire history of Irish 'otherness' has been defined is now fissured, impoverished and insecure. Bogle as Orwellian *clochard* at large in London is suitably located to deconstruct its myth of integrity. A self-styled Mick who can no longer feel happily foreign in a city of ethnic flux, he sees Englishness in collapse all around him. Civility breaks down with a knife-fight in Hyde Park; culture is now the mindless mid-Atlantic drivel of a commercial radio deejay which cuts across a cricket game. At Cambridge, last bastion of the kind of Anglo-Saxon superiority against which Bogle can play the 'working-class-Paddy-cum-clown', the English mystique is suddenly gross and transparent:

> These people were almost indistinguishable, one from the other. The nebulous impalpability of ideas and trends was preferred at all times to the brute empiricism of humanity. The tricky area of personality was treated with some trepidation and individuality was rare and largely ignored. The feared human, interior congress. They disliked the notion of people differing from themselves. In one of my epic, universal moments, I concluded with rare intelligence that an Englishman's lack of interest in himself naturally precludes any interest in others. Remote, impersonal, disengaged. Easy pickings for the dark, concocted vitality of the Celt (i.e. me). (p.171)

Englishness, too, has become a contrived identity prey to caricature and manipulation, and the England which Bogle had imagined through his childhood reading of Dickens is now a site of spectacular decomposition against which his own constructed Irishness is thrown into a peculiarly reassuring relief.

The author of *Ripley Bogle* flirts with a post-modern eccentricity in order to criticize the competing cultures from which he has emerged. In the composition of the novel, too, he relies on stylistic *bricolage* as a means of incorporating and defusing elements of his supposed literary inheritance. Joyce remains the dominant target, the obvious model of Bogle's graphic birth scene which opens the novel and later of his burlesque encounter with three Irish brothers and a prostitute in a Kilburn pub, presented by Wilson as a vaudeville extravaganza in ironic deference to the 'Nighttown' episode in *Ulysses*. Additionally, Wilson seeks to foreground and deflate the more immediate heritage of the Troubles novel, incorporating within his story both a send-up of a love-across-the-barricades tale and a sub-plot covering the fate of a friend engaged in paramilitary activity. Positioning each between bathos and outright parody, he successfully undermines the two dominant conventions of Northern Irish fiction as part of his overall pattern of subversion.

As his contemporary Glenn Patterson has observed, Wilson broke with allegiance in many ways in *Ripley Bogle*, radically altering the image of the Northern Irish Catholic writer: 'He refused the limits of his past, and those borders. He was very revolutionary in that sense, very iconoclastic and swiped at the romantic nationalism expected of previous generations of Irish writers.'[16] The novel is effective, too, in its negation of the critical and social responsibility shouldered by its author's predecessors; but what is the overall achievement of writing which hinges almost entirely on pastiche, ironic deflation, caricature and subversion? The resultant material is flashy but insubstantial, and Wilson's attempt to portray the 'midnight's children' of the Northern Irish Troubles succeeds chiefly as a comic study of contemporary alienation. While bringing a welcome deflation to the pieties and clichés of Northern Irish fiction, therefore, his method of contesting the status quo runs the risk of indulging in a warped folklore and producing in the end a neo-provincialism based entirely on oppositional cynicism and ironic excess.

An alternative to this abrasive self-consciousness is presented by Glenn Patterson in two novels set in Northern Ireland. Patterson emerged from the same generation as Wilson but from a Protestant unionist working-class background upon which he drew extensively in his debut novel *Burning Your Own* (1988).[17] As with Wilson, much of his material is autobiographical, reliant on the fresh perspectives of childhood experience for its effect. Tracing the events of the summer of 1969 through the eyes of Mal, a ten-year-old boy on a Protestant housing estate, he seeks to expose the manner in which concepts of community and identity are pressurized and manipulated in the escalation of sectarianism and public anxiety. Where Wilson deflated his origins through hyperbole and satire, Patterson recreates them in a detailed realism which pre-empts a media image exploring one representative segment of the Protestant community as a signified which has slipped from a superimposed political sign.

The central image of the book relates to the building of the celebratory twelfth of July bonfire on the estate, an event which Patterson uses to redefine an obscured community. The bonfire, now readily associated with sectarian aggravation, is experienced from Mal's perspective as a social occasion on which the local residents who form the corporate identity of the neighbourhood are suddenly and painstakingly illuminated in their individuality:

> As sticks with petrol-soaked rags wrapped around them were driven in at points around the base of the bonfire, people converged on it from all sides: the Bells, the McMinns, the McMahons and the Crosiers, Tommy Duncan and his family, the Smyllie twins with their wives, the Garritys, the Presses, the Kerrs and the Boyles, the Sinclairs, the Hughes, the Jamisons and Stinsons, Mrs Clark and old Mr Parker, the Hemmings, the Taggarts, the Greys, the Whites, all of the Campbells except for the father, the Tookeys, the Cleareys, the Kellys and Craigs, McClures, Milligans, Hawthorns and O'Days, the Wheatcrofts, the McDevitts, the Viles, wee Ernie Buchanan with his Bible-tract sandwich boards. More faces in the end than Mal could identify. And when everything was in place, Andy lit a final torch and touched off all the others. The bonfire had begun. (p.91)

The precise, almost pedantic, process of naming here is characteristic of the manner in which Patterson seeks to establish an authenticity which has been erased in other readings of Northern Irish society. The community which is elsewhere perceived as ideologically and culturally homogenous is renegotiated as a conglomeration of distinct personalities. With a similar positioning of the concrete above the symbolic, Patterson attends closely to details of the urban geography of his environment, listing the names of greater Belfast districts, tracing the topographical spread of urban housing estates across a rural terrain and marking the progress of an encroaching Catholic ghetto. The territorial theme which is played out in miniature through Mal's friend Francy, a Catholic who has taken over the local dump, is replayed throughout the city as established neighbourhoods find themselves squeezed between urban planners and demographic shifts. *Burning Your Own* draws constantly on a heavy materiality to illustrate social negotiations over territory, identity and exclusion as part of an ongoing process rather than a fixed matrix of terms. Localities distanced by the television screen are suddenly proximate: Catholic Derrybeg expands to threaten Protestant Larkview, Larkview paints its pavements red, white and blue to ward off outsiders, sectarian graffiti begins to mark the limits of each vicinity.

The meticulousness of Patterson's local detail represents the reclamation of what critic Terence Brown has identified as distinctly Joycean realism, under-exploited in Irish prose generally but valuable in 'its capacity to suggest the density and complexity of human consciousness in its material contexts'.[18] More than simply an aspect of Joycean technique, Brown continues, it is a matter of world view – a psychological transition from local to universal which Patterson exploits as a thematic motif in his novel. The process of naming, appropriating and identifying through which Mal experiences the territorial insecurity of his own community is emphasized by the external events to which the narrative makes systematic reference. Woken in the middle of the night by his parents to watch the televised broadcast of the moon landing, Mal comprehends the scene as one implicitly connected to his own experience. On screen, the astronaut waves at the camera:

> In his visor was reflected the capsule, the capsule whose camera filmed him. Waving reflecting. Encapsulated within the television set, which Mal's mother, uncle, aunt, cousins watched. Which Mal watched. (p.128)

Patterson displays in this novel a particular brand of duality, an instinct for individualism or dissent which is balanced by a sympathy for the defensive strategies and contrived political solidarity of the wider community. The subtlety with which he approaches such issues contrasts sharply with Wilson's assault on Ireland's sacred cows. Patterson uses fiction not to challenge orthodoxies outright but as a forum within which tokens, concepts and ideologies in general may be exposed as vulnerable to new readings and contradictory perceptions. Mal's childhood confrontation with adult definitions highlights repeatedly the many discrepancies between metaphors or signs and real experience. This emphasis is crystallized in one scene of a family dinner-party during which Mal's older cousin makes shapes out of ice-cream spilled on the table-cloth:

> 'That another world-map?' Mal asked her.
> 'No', she said, 'it's Ireland.'
> Ireland; the world: Alex's maps were pretty much of a piece to Mal's eyes: none of them bore the slightest resemblance to what they claimed to be. He watched as she continued her moody scratchings. 'Looks more like a pig if you ask me.'
> 'Slow, slow, quick quick, slow,' Alex loured. 'That's what it's meant to be: "the old sow that eats her farrow".'

Mal scraped the gateau off the fork with his teeth. She'd lost him totally.
'What's a farrow when it's at home, then?'
'Baby pigs,' Alex lashed at him, letting fall her spoon. 'Fat, slimy, baby pigs.'
The sponge disintegrated in Mal's mouth. His tongue melted through the air-dried outer coating of cream to the sugary soft centre. He pushed the side-plate into the middle of the table and in an instant all eyes were on him.
'What's the matter? Bite off more than you could chew?' (p.149)

The careful positioning of childhood repulsion to an image reconceived in its graphic visual and sensory reality rather than as a stale Joycean aphorism is at the heart of the way in which the book cautiously but systematically readdresses an inherited system of perception. Like *Ripley Bogle* and *No Mate for the Magpie*, therefore, *Burning Your Own* is a classic Northern Irish *Bildungsroman*, but one in which the author uses to maximum extent the education and disillusionment of its central character as a means of exposing redundant or pernicious aspects of his society's cultural conventions.

The intensity of local detail incorporated in Patterson's writing disguises the extent to which he, like Wilson, depends upon a 'prodigal' vantage point. In an interview in 1992 he emphasized the sense of nostalgic displacement which governs his material as an Irish writer living in England: 'I see someone in the street and I don't know where they're coming from. All my fiction is written from within that Unionist, Protestant community back home. It's been a working out of how to respond to the events there.'[19] The ambiguity which has resulted from his decision to live in England has been an enabling feature of his work, however, and the tension between opposing locations provides the psychological focus of his second level. In *Fat Lad* (1992)[20] he attempts once again to excavate the historical individuality and identity of his home community but this time through its contemporary image of anonymous European commercialism and short-term prosperity. Drew Linden returns unwillingly from Manchester to Belfast to take up a managerial post in 'Bookstore', part of an international chain of identikit bookshops which recreate themselves with 'historical' façades in the midst of every major city. At the same time, Drew's return brings him into conflict with a genuine past; his own troubled childhood and complex family relations which now claim his reluctant attention through the presence of his dying father.

The novel is an ambitious one, reaching from its contemporary setting into the history of Belfast from the Second World War to the early phase of the Troubles, a sweep which includes Drew's childhood

memories of the 1970s. Again like Wilson, he seeks to assimilate and
thereby negate conventions of the Northern Irish novel, including both
a cross-the-barricades love story and the fate of an involved acquaintance as sub-plots within the main narrative. The result is somewhat
unwieldy and *Fat Lad* lacks the thematic clarity of *Burning Your Own*,
but its points of reference in the relentless detailing of changes in
urban topography and social history are similar:

> The Belfast he left, the Belfast the ex-Pats forswore, was a city dying
> on its feet: cratered sites and hunger-strikes; atrophied, self-abused.
> But the Belfast he had heard reports of this past while, the Belfast he
> had seen with his own eyes last month, was a city in the process of
> recasting itself entirely. The army had long since departed from the
> Grand Central Hotel, on whose levelled remains an even grander
> shopping complex was now nearing completion. Restaurants, bars
> and takeaways proliferated along the lately coined Golden Mile,
> running south from the refurbished Opera House, and new names
> had appeared in the shopping streets: Next, Body Shop, Tie Rack,
> Principles. And his own firm, of course, Bookstore. (p.4)

Patterson's portrait of Belfast as a huge contemporary UK shopping-
centre serves a dual function: the documentation of faceless anonymity
to which 'identity' has been reduced and the erosion of the familiar
fictional image of a blasted city upon which a previous generation
relied with a kind of perverse romanticism. Having cut himself off in
this way from the tropes of an inherited tradition of fiction, how does
he sustain commitment to the illustration of a regional image? His
response to the issue is noticeably cautious, in that he resists the
temptation to reclaim his native city through a nostalgic array of
colloquial exotica marking its difference from 'the mainland'. Rather it
is through the heightened sensitivity of the returning exile that he is
able to mark the discrete points of resistance which disrupt a
superimposed anonymity. As Drew waits for the airport transport bus
to take him into the centre of Belfast, for example, he notes the
particularity of a fellow passenger's remark:

> 'Imagine sending a Flexibus' the woman behind Drew said, making
> Flexi rhyme with taxi, so that Drew wondered whether
> subconsciously she had established some analogy between function
> and pronunciation. (p.5)

Identity becomes an ironic contest between such latent, understated
idiosyncrasies and the enforced facelessness of contemporary
metropolitanism. The recognition of a regional character based on
barely perceptible, sub-political remnants of language, attitude and

custom is sustained in this way throughout the novel as a gesture towards a distinction which can no longer be taken for granted.

Meanwhile the increasing insecurity of an established Northern Irish self-image is emphasized by the way in which Patterson reveals, just as he did in *Burning Your Own*, gaps between received metaphors or folklore and new perceptions, represented once again in terms of a childhood clash with adult terms of reference. The book's title derives from the letters scratched by Drew's older sister Ellen on her school ruler, the initials of the six Northern counties – Fermanagh, Armagh, Tyrone, Londonderry, Antrim and Down – 'carved there like the name of his sister's favourite pop star, her idol, her crush: Fat Lad' (p.229). The political significance of the mnemonic in its reference to the separation of Northern Ireland from the Republic is outplayed by the value of the item as a comical image or a linguistic plaything which the pupils learn alongside 'Richard Of York Gave Battle in Vain'. A similar slippage between perceived affiliations and reality is exposed in Drew's memory of a rainy day-trip to the seaside. As the family sit marooned in the car, his grandmother unexpectedly recalls an incident from her own past:

- Just here's where your grandpa helped bring the guns ashore.
- What guns, granny? Ellen asked.
- The UVF [Ulster Volunteer Force] guns.
- *The* UVF?
- Not that UVF, her father said. The real UVF. The men of 1914, Lord Carson's UVF.
- I suppose that makes it all right then, Ellen sarked. Her father rounded on her.
- The guns that were landed that night, he said, his false teeth clacking in advance of his words, (so that he seemed to be delivering a telegraph message rather than speaking for himself), were what kept Ulster British.
  Ellen looked out her rain-slurred window at the dismal little seaside town.
- I'm sure the British were delighted, she said. (p.238)

Finally, in conjunction with these adjustments to existing readings Patterson seeks new images of Northern Irish society which allow for complex rather than essentialist representation. From a detailed realism and period exactitude he ventures towards imagism in the book's circular motifs – a goldfish endlessly swimming round its bowl, the disconnected wheel of an army vehicle spinning into a bar, the psychedelic, concentric rings which appear at the end of a TV 'Loony-Tunes' cartoon. These might be understood as emblematic of Ireland's historical cul-de-sac, but the author's consistent pressure against such meta-narratives mitigates against this reading. They highlight instead the organic concept of identity which his writing endorses, the hidden networks which he perceives as the fabric of his society. In one of the most striking passages of the novel, the unseen connections of his environment are represented in a single sentence which carries the reader through a chain of images, the sensational fusing with the defiantly mundane:

> In the early hours of the morning of the second Saturday in August 1971, a sniper operating from the darkened window of a terraced house in an estate on the foothills of the Antrim Plateau discharged a rifle for the second and last time in his life, sending a single high-velocity bullet flashing down into the Lagan valley, evading the soft exposed parts of a platoon of soldiers pinned down behind a hedge a block away, evading chimney-pots, treetops, road signs, traffic lights, advertising hoardings, lampposts, church spires, flagpoles (an inordinate number of church spires and flagpoles), and all make and manner of buildings besides, till, closing in on the darkened window of another house on another estate two miles to the south-east, it drilled a perfect hot-poker hole in the glass, puncturing with ease the roll blind, the drapes, the kitchen's boast door, and the chipboard wall of the larder, where it entered and exited in turn a box of Kellogg's cornflakes, a packet of Polson's cornflour, a packet of Atora suet, a box each of Whitworth's sultanas and raisins, a tin of Campbell's cream of tomato soup; entered, finally, a full bag of Tate & Lyle sugar (annihilating the craggy sugar-cube gladiator), but, encountering solid brick on the far side, did not exit and came instead to a stunned halt deep in the granular belly of the bag. (pp.119–20)

The extract illustrates the density and exactitude in Patterson's technique, his use of the commonplace in the list of product names offering an ironic reduction of Troubles heroism and his neo-realism bordering on aspects of contemporary Northern Irish poetry.[21] Throughout *Fat Lad* appeals to an epic or romanticized heritage are similarly underwritten by prosaic commentary, shattering the conceit of ingrained tragedy with fresh and ambiguous perspectives. Patterson exposes a communal identity in a state of flux, therefore, informed on one hand by contemporary tensions and dislocations, negotiating on the other a network of historical detail and experience, as the Belfast which has redesigned itself in plate-glass and post-modern commercialism is exposed as a façade for the Belfast which built the Titanic. The quest for a self-image is a quest for some means of continuity between the two, and the negative capability which the author pits against a range of intervening political, economic and sectarian definitions becomes the psychological catalyst of the novel.

Recent writers of fiction have, therefore, succeeded to some extent in countering or adjusting the sterile images produced by mainstream Northern Irish writers during the Troubles. Molloy, Wilson and Patterson have managed to combine strategies of irony and dislocation with fresh approaches to realism in order to contest established readings of their situation without imposing new stereotypes. Their self-conscious relationship to an exhausted literary inheritance and to the pitfalls of provincial cliché has been an enabling feature of their writing while the tactics they have developed, from dialect to pastiche and satire to historicity, have helped to expose images of Northern Irish society which disrupt pietistic or complacent narratives. Perhaps the most significant breakthrough of a new generation, however, has been the refusal of regional limits, or in other words the rejection of a literary convention which pandered to the isolation of Northern Ireland as a stagnant and erratic phenomenon. Each of the writers examined has in some way broken with the concept of their disturbed environment as autogenous in its political and social perversions, by bringing into focus its relationship with or reflection of its constitutional neighbours. For Wilson and Patterson in particular, interaction – personal, literary or imaginative – with the rest of the UK has informed and contextualized their visions of home. Their exploitation of a post-modern 'prodigalism' not only in stylistic aspect but in terms of a dual, ambiguous perspective has relieved the intense concentration on Northern Ireland as the province of doom in an otherwise normal world, and as a result their writing has moved well beyond the straitened territory of the traditional Troubles novel.

The production of a prose literature appropriate to contemporary Northern Ireland remains, however, a struggle to intercept the pull of familiar or perceived characteristics. As Edna Longley has noted, 'Ulster people hug wonderfully "fossilised" versions of their own or someone else's Irishness/Britishness; which retards newer definitions in the Republic and Britain.'[22] The susceptibility of identity to political schemata will ensure that synthetic constructions persist, a process which renders the Northern Irish writer's relationship to the field of image and representation even more oblique than in other regions of the UK or the Irish Republic. In this respect a diverse, metamorphic fiction is undoubtedly more useful than any standardized, definitive mode of writing. Desirable as a characteristic regional voice may seem, its ability to encompass a society which already relies too heavily on fixed perceptions and definitions is probably outplayed by the sporadic challenge of discrete and individual imaginations.

References

1 Lionel Shriver, 'Glossary of troublesome terms', *Ordinary Decent Criminals*, originally published in New York as *The Bleeding Heart* (1990), (London, HarperCollins, 1992), pp.425–6.

2 For differing studies of the phenomenon see J. Bowyer-Bell, 'The troubles as trash', *Hibernia*, 20 January 1978, p.22, and Bill Rolston, 'Mothers, whores and villains: images of women in novels of the Northern Irish conflict', *Race and Class* 31, No. 1 (1989), pp. 41–57.

3 Anthony Bradley expands on these categories in 'Literature and culture in the North of Ireland', in Michael Kenneally (ed.), *Cultural Contexts and Literary Idioms in Contemporary Irish Literature* (Gerrards Cross, Colin Smythe, 1988). The most complete study of pre-Troubles novelists remains J. W. Foster's *Forces and Themes in Ulster Fiction* (Dublin, Gill & Macmillan, 1974).

4 I am indebted to Linda Hutcheon's discussion of irony and perspectivism in relation to Canadian fiction in her essay 'Circling the downspout of Empire', in Ian Adam and Helen Tiffin (eds.), *Past the Last Post: Theorising Post-Colonialism Post-Modernism* (Hemel Hempstead, Harvester Wheatsheaf, 1991), pp.167–89.

5 Gerald Dawe, 'Breaking camp: notes on a Belfast upbringing', *Eire–Ireland* (Winter 1991), p.11.

6 For discussions of this issue see Edna Longley's essay, 'Poetry and politics in Northern Ireland', *Crane Bag*, Vol. 9, No. 1 (Dublin, 1985), pp.26–40, reprinted in *Poetry in the Wars* (Newcastle upon Tyne, Bloodaxe, 1986), and Daphne B. Watson, 'The Cross of St George: the burden of contemporary Irish literature', in Robert Giddings (ed.), *Literature and Imperialism* (London, Macmillan, 1991), pp.25–43.

7 J. W. Foster, op. cit., p.254; Richard Deutsch, '"Within two shadows": the Troubles in Northern Ireland', in Patrick Rafroidi and Maurice Harmon (eds.), *The Irish Novel in Our Time* (Lille, Publications de l'Université de Lille (CERUIL), Nos. 4–5, Cahiers Irlandaises, 1975–6), p.151.

8 'Politics is another country', *Guardian*, 20 June 1992, p.29.

9 See J. M. Cahalan, *The Irish Novel: A Critical History* (Dublin, Gill & Macmillan, 1988), p.294. Seamus Deane comments at length on the substitution of Irish literature for sociology in his essay 'Mary Lavin', in T. Brown and P. Rafroidi (eds.), *The Irish Short Story* (Gerrards Cross, Colin Smythe, 1979), p.244.

10 'Contemporary novels on the Troubles', *Etudes Irlandaises*, No. 5 (1980), pp.113–21; p.120.

11 Seamus Deane, 'Heroic styles: the tradition of an idea', *Ireland's Field Day* (Hutchinson Field Day Theatre Company, 1986), p.57.

12 Aritha Van Herk, 'Post-modernism: homesick for homesickness', in Bruce King (ed.), *The Commonwealth Novel since 1960* (London, Macmillan, 1991), p.218.

13 Robert Wilson, *Ripley Bogle* (Dundonald, Blackstaff, 1989) (published

in England by André Deutsch, 1989). All references are to the Blackstaff edition. See Seamus Deane's introduction to Terry Eagleton, 'Nationalism, irony and commitment' (1988), in Terry Eagleton, Frederic Jameson and Edward W. Said (eds.), *Nationalism, Colonialism and Literature* (Hutchinson Field Day Theatre Company, 1990), p.4.

14 Edna Longley, 'From Cathleen to anorexia: the breakdown of Irelands', LIP Pamphlet Series (Dublin, Attic Press, 1990), pp.5–6.

15 J. T. Leerssen, 'On the treatment of Irishness in romantic Anglo-Irish fiction', *Irish University Review* (Autumn, 1990), p.258.

16 Glenn Patterson in interview with Candida Crewe, 'Belfast slabbers pave a literary way', *Guardian*, 18 February 1992, p.32. See also Wilson's comments on the redundancy of the novelist in Northern Ireland in his article 'Cities at war', *Irish Review* No. 10 (Spring 1991), pp.95–8.

17 Glenn Patterson, *Burning Your Own* (London, Chatto & Windus, 1988).

18 Terence Brown, 'Redeeming the time: the novels of John McGahern and John Banville', in James Acheson (ed.), *The British and Irish Novel since 1960* (New York, St Martin's Press, 1991), p.159.

19 'Belfast slabbers . . .', op. cit.

20 Glenn Patterson, *Fat Lad* (London, Chatto & Windus, 1992).

21 I refer in particular to the poetry of Ciaron Carson whose collection *Belfast Confetti* (Oldcastle, Gallery Press, 1989) documents the imagery and hidden history of Belfast as a city in transition.

22 'Poetry and politics . . .', op. cit., pp.33–4.

I am a Northern Irish novelist

GLENN PATTERSON

I grew up in a house with a bookcase at the top of the stairs. The bookcase measured three feet by two and a half feet; it has sliding doors to protect the books and a shelf at the top for ornaments. The bookcase and the books inside it had been bought from the Readers' Digest when my parents were first married. In all the years of my childhood I cannot recall a single instance when I opened the doors with the intention of taking one of these books out to read. My curiosity extended no further than the gold lettering on the spines. The names of the authors – Chandler, Kipling, Mitchell – were all one to me, dead behind the glass.

This museum image of literature held even after I began to explore the shelves of the local library. The books I found there contained nothing that spoke to me of my own world. Nor did I expect them to. Instead I wrote stories in imitation of *their* world, about a Norwegian boy detective evacuated to an English castle during the Second World War. I christened him Nnelg Nosrettap, myself translated, smuggled back-to-front into the place and time where fiction happened.

My first Irish writer, a year into secondary school, was Frank O'Connor. (James Joyce's *A Portrait of the Artist* was already a familiar name from an older brother's reading list, but, since it was on the O level curriculum, I took its author for English like all the others: Austen, Golding, Dickens, Waugh.) It was not until I was sixteen that I finally heard my own city evoked in literature, at a reading by the Belfast poet Frank Ormsby.

These things I say by way of preface to what was to have been my opening line: I am a Northern Irish novelist. The fact that I feel the need to preface it at all (and there are days – tomorrow might be one

149

of them – when I would be damned if I would) expresses something of my concern that in our Anglo-, or should I say *London*-centric culture, regional identity is often used to confine rather than define us as writers. If a novel can be neatly labelled 'Northern Irish' (or 'Scottish', or 'Welsh'; only the inverted commas are important) then it can, to an extent, be marginalized, or even, on occasion, neutralized completely.

And yet there is no denying the Northern Irish content of my own fiction. My first novel, *Burning Your Own*, published in 1988, was set in Northern Ireland in 1969. Ending on the day that British troops arrived on the streets of Belfast, it charted the disintegration into violence of a community at the physical limit of the city's optimistic 1960s expansion. *Burning Your Own* was in part an exploration of how individuals – and their communities – react when the assumptions on which they have based their lives are undermined or fail them. The characters in the book, working people, will blame themselves, becoming self-destructive, or blame other working people, creating social unrest, rather than accept that the assumptions themselves are at fault. To my mind, however, the novel was at least as much concerned with events in the rest of the United Kingdom in the years leading up to its writing in the late 1980s as it was with Northern Ireland in 1969. It was as if, living in England, observing at close quarters the traumatizing effects of the miners' strike, mass unemployment, the depredations of local democracy – the gamut of the conservative government's politics of confrontation – I was given an insight into the tensions which surfaced in Northern Ireland when I was a child of eight. By the same token, I hoped that by exploring in novel form territory that existed at a historical and geographical remove I might be able to find new perspectives from which to view events that were, in 1986–7, in every sense much closer to home.

This is, of course, hardly a radical ambition. It is, after all, in the nature of the novel, indeed of all art, that it speaks outside the specificity of its author's own experience (otherwise you would write, paint, compose, for an audience, ultimately, of one: yourself) *and* outside the surface particulars of its setting. As I have already suggested, I did not come to novel-writing through Northern Irish, or any other kind of Irish (or, for that matter, English) writers. Instead my gradual recognition that this was the form that offered me most freedom as a writer came through my reading of American and European novelists. Here were people writing out of demonstrably different cultures yet addressing issues and concerns that were deeply familiar to me; certainly more familiar than the often sterile and unimaginative fictional representations of my own country. I took as my text at this time a formulation of American novelist Robert Coover:

Fiction, myth, these are necessary things: I doubt if any of us could exist in the world without inventing a name, or names, that allow us to operate in it. But the world changes, or our perceptions of it, or our needs in it change, and new fictions come from it. Fiction then . . . has, as I see it a double purpose. On the one hand it draws into itself what seem to be the truths of the world at any given moment, and on the other it struggles against falsehood, dogmas and confusions, *all the old debris of the dead fictions.* (My emphasis)

I heard strong echoes of Coover in the work of Salman Rushdie. Reading *Midnight's Children*, indeed, was perhaps the single most important factor in my decision, not so much to adopt the novel as a form, but, having adopted it, to turn to Northern Ireland for my subject matter. Rushdie's treatment of countries as collective fictions (willed or imposed) and as significant *characters* in their inhabitants' lives accorded perfectly with my own ideas of how to begin reimagining Northern Ireland.

I had grown up in a society characterized – in fiction as in everyday speech – as morbidly immutable; yet there was another equally valid reading which said that, quite the reverse, change was in fact the society's only constant. Even as children, I remember, we took a great interest in politics, keeping a close watch on political shifts and realignments. Small movements in these circles, we knew (the shaking of hands, the easy flow of a pen across a page, the lifting of a telephone), could lead to enormous upheavals on our streets. The order to introduce Internment, for instance, on 9 August 1971 (my own tenth birthday) ended with 1 per cent of the population of Belfast on the move, at that time the largest displacement in Europe since the Second World War. The city was changing day by day, its buildings were being erased, its roads rerouted, its territorial boundaries redrawn. While there can be no ignoring the destabilizing effects, social and psychological, of all this (I choose the words deliberately) deconstruction and revision, it nevertheless contains within it a certain liberating potential. In particular it resists the closure of traditional interpretations in which one unchanging territory is endlessly contested by two mutually exclusive tribes: the old politics of one thing or the other. Identity becomes dynamic rather than birth-given and static. Concepts like flux and exchange replace the language or original states.

Even before the disaster of former Yugoslavia, it seemed to me that these were issues of wider, international moment. (And not just to me, for independently of one another several writers with a Northern Irish background had begun to develop similar themes in fiction and poetry. Again, there is no mystery in this, for every era, I believe, provides the writer with the specific means, and the metaphors, to describe it.) Paradoxically perhaps, when I came to write *Fat Lad*, a novel which tried to give fictional form to much of this thinking, I was keen, in a way I had not been with *Burning Your Own*, to play up the novel's focus on Northern Ireland. I hoped, however, to do it in a manner which stressed its connection to other regions and countries rather than its isolation from them. I had in mind when I started an image of jet streams as threads binding disparate land masses together; cumulatively, in their comings and goings, the characters in *Fat Lad* were intended to weave a complex pattern of external relationships, to give human expression to historical context.

Perhaps I am saying no more at the end of this argument than I was at the beginning. The act of writing, like the act of reading, is the making of connections, the negotiation of the space between the particular and the general. As the traffic in ideas between cultures accelerates it is harder than ever to confuse mere setting with subject or significance. What the writer's sense of place does give (allied of course to the complexities of personal biography) is a way of seeing that at once says something about the particular society of which she/he is a product and about the wider world in which that society exists. Robert McLiam Wilson's second novel, for instance, *Manfred's Pain*, whose central character is an ageing London Jew, is as interesting from the point of view of its author's Northern Irish background as *Ripley Bogle*.

As writers we are often pulled in seemingly contrary directions, looking inwards and appealing outwards. In reality, though, there need be no contradiction, for (and here I speak as a reader, grateful to the many authors whose work has reached out to me) in trying to understand one place very well it might just be possible to understand many other places at least in part.

The passionate periphery: Cornwall and romantic fiction

ELLA WESTLAND

In *The Saffron Eaters*, a novel written in the early 1970s, Roy Phillips laments a Cornwall nearly lost, not a remote realm of Celtic legend or landed gentry, but the place the author calls the 'real Cornwall'.[1] This reality resides in the daily life of a twentieth-century fishing community before the postwar invasion of 'emmets' (a local word for ants or tourists). The novel records how an unnamed town (the writer's native St Ives) has been 'commercialized and degraded, and the people corrupted by greed' (p.36), as locals leave their old ways to exploit a picture-postcard image of Cornwall that draws in visitors and raises property prices, participating in the commodification of their own way of life.

Traditional Cornish values are carried into the 1960s by the book's fisherman hero Steve Trevorrow, but even he cannot resist the invaders. It is not just a matter of compromising commercially during the season, using his boat for trips across the bay and his home for bed and breakfast. He experiences a more insidious transformation than that wrought by greed, as the unromantic wooing and wedding customs of a small community are disrupted by the force of modern romantic love. Across the Tamar comes the irresistible Cleo, blonde, blue-eyed, bra-less and bohemian: a character from another place, another class, another genre. She undermines the fictional conventions of social realism which the novel has carefully established, by seducing Steve into a relationship defined in romantic terms. This is an encounter between strangers, under the spell of a sexual power they cannot control. Their passion is physical, bringing two beautiful bodies together to swim naked in the sea and make love on the cliff-top; it is also imbued with the spiritual aura prescribed by romance, upholding the lovers as soul mates and affording Cleo the greatest compliment that a Cornishman can bestow, apotheosis into an honorary Celt.

However, there is ultimately no place for Cleo in the 'real Cornwall' of *The Saffron Eaters*. Romance opens up the possibility of lovers being each other's all in a strange land, but since Steve's identity is bound up with his community, fleeing together across the Tamar is not an available option. This affair is bound to end in separation, and it is Cleo the incomer who must leave. But elsewhere Cleos and Cornwall have a happier fate. In the domain of romance, a deep affinity is assumed between beautiful women, dark Cornishmen, craggy cliffs and sensuous seas, and Cleos find a natural home in the passionate periphery.

Love meets landscape: the history of the Cornish romance

One story of the contemporary Cornish romance began some two hundred years ago, far from the south-western peninsula, when love and landscape became simultaneously and inextricably transformed by the shift in European sensibility known as the Romantic Movement. By the 1790s, it was no longer necessary to leave Britain in search of a rugged landscape which would inspire ecstasy, tranquillity, sweet melancholy or Gothic horror, since artists had prepared enthusiasts to experience the serene and sublime in regions like the Lake District, the Scottish Highlands, the Wye Valley and the Isle of Wight. The transformation of Cornwall in the English imagination depended on rocky shores and surging seas taking their place with dark forests and snowy summits as approved sites for romantic sublimity, and literary evidence suggests this had been achieved before 1800. When Goethe's *Werther* reads his translation of Ossian's songs to Charlotte in 1774, he ends on a maritime note: 'When the storms aloft arise, when the north wind lifts the wave on high, I sit by the sounding shore, and look on the fatal rock'.[2] Twenty years later, towards the end of *The Mysteries of Udolpho* (1794), Ann Radcliffe selected a shipwreck for a melodramatic set piece, and having landed her heroine safely, permitted her to frequent a lonely promontory overlooking the sea. Here Emily regularly leaned against the broken walls of a ruined watch-tower to think of her lover Valancourt, 'and, in melancholy dejection, watched the waves, half-hidden in vapour, as they came rolling towards the shore, and threw up their light spray around the rocks below'.[3] (IV, vii, p.558). Twenty years later again, Jane Austen did not think it necessary to leave the shores of England to find a romantic coastal landscape. In *Persuasion* (1818), she sang the praises of the Lyme Regis area, with its 'sweet retired bay, backed by dark cliffs' and 'green chasms between romantic rocks', comparing the scenery favourably with 'the far-famed Isle of Wight'. Her young people were 'wild to see Lyme', lingering on the shore 'as all must linger and gaze on a first return to the sea, who ever deserve to look on it at all', and leaving the modern reader in no doubt that for this generation a feeling for the sea – experienced from the safety of the cliffs – was a sign of the finest sensibility.[4]

At the turn of the eighteenth century, the Land's End was less accessible than Lyme Regis as a target for this 'romancing' process. It was difficult to reach over land, and the traveller who chose to enter the county by road, crossing the Tamar from the lushness of Devon, initially encountered uncongenial scenery. William Gilpin, who is credited with creating the romantic image of regions like the Highlands and the Wye Valley, came to Cornwall in the 1790s in search of picturesque scenes to paint and turned back bored at Bodmin.[5] Indeed at this stage Cornwall's image in the eyes of the rest of Britain was more likely to have been formed by ideas about maritime activity and the mining industry than by any notions of glorious solitude. William Wordsworth's 'Old Man Travelling' in *Lyrical Ballads* (1798) is going to Cornwall not to admire the sea views but to visit his dying son, 'Who from a sea-fight has been brought to Falmouth/And there is dying in an hospital'. William Beckford, who spent a week in Falmouth in 1787 waiting for a boat to leave for Lisbon, described the surrounding Gwennap mining area as 'a bleak desert, rendered still more doleful by the unhealthy appearance of its inhabitants'.[6] Although some remnant lingered of Cornwall's eighteenth-century reputation as 'West Barbary', a land of half-savage wreckers and rioters, by the early 1800s Cornwall was more likely to be associated in the national imagination with the arrival of packet boats and warships in the busy port of Falmouth, the development of steam power for the tin and copper mines, and the respectable attractions of towns like Truro and Penzance, rather than with quaint fishing craft and craggy grandeur.[7]

Later, as dangerous coastlines and stormy seas became the rage – and as Cornwall's economic and naval importance declined – the county at the Land's End became a repository for romantic images. The county began unpromisingly by offering itself as a temperate resort for gentlefolk in a delicate state of health, and larger towns like Falmouth and Penzance began to represent themselves as spa-style holiday resorts. But a local newspaper description of 1806, while stressing the county's 'salutary effect . . . on the delicate constitution of valetudinarians', also referred to its 'romantic and ever-varying view'[8] and an early tourist guide, Stockdale's *Excursions* (1824), expressed Cornwall's romantic attractions in terms that might well have appealed to Jane Austen's young people. Stockdale introduced Mevagissey, for example, as the foremost fishing village in the county, but he went on to draw attention to its 'romantic appearance when viewed from the neighbouring heights, with the beautiful mansion and plantations of Heligan forming the background' (p.50). It is a view from a distance, such as a judicious artist might have selected. By 1848, the Revd Johns was addressing his *Week at the Lizard* to 'tourists who visit Cornwall in search of the picturesque',[9] and taking pains to ensure that visitors did not repeat Gilpin's disappointing experience by directing them to the 'loftier cliffs', 'deep ravines', 'romantic little coves' and 'picturesque rocks' of spectacular spots like Kynance Cove.[10]

The lure of the Lizard and the Land's End became irresistible to Victorians. They came to the wildest places they could find to ramble, scramble and swim, to sketch and botanize, to fall into raptures and to fall in love. In her *Unsentimental Journey Through Cornwall* (1884) Mrs Craik saw the cliffs at the Lizard as the natural place for a pair of lovers:

> The usual place where the sun dropped into the sea, just beyond the point of the Land's End, was all a golden mist. I hastened west, climbing one intervening cliff after another . . . and there I saw – Actually, two human beings! Lovers of course . . . They sat, quite absorbed in one another, hand in hand, looking quietly seaward, their faces bathed in the rosy sunset . . .[11]

But Dinah Craik had come to Cornwall in search of something more complicated than landscape and lovers. Her account of a brief fortnight's holiday recognizes that 'It is not the things we see, but the mind we see them with, which makes the real interest of travelling' (p.1), and admits that her own urge to come to Cornwall had grown from a lifetime of literary expectations:

> This desire had existed ever since, at five years old, I made acquaintance with Jack the Giantkiller, and afterwards, at fifteen or so, fell in love with my life's one hero, King Arthur.[12]

She and her nieces brought with them on their Cornish trip Malory's medieval *Morte d'Arthur* and Tennyson's medievalizing *Idylls of the King* to read on rainy days. Not surprisingly, they found Arthurian influence everywhere, even in the dignified bearing of their fisherman guide.[13] This affords an excellent illustration of another tale that can be told about the emergence of romantic writing in Cornwall. For, interwoven with the dominant narrative of post-Romanticism, foregrounding scenery, run the colourful threads of the ancient Celts and the Court of King Arthur. Swinburne, who knew Tintagel and the North Cornwall coast well, painted a stirring word picture in his long poem *Tristram of Lyonesse*, where Queen Iseult prayed in agony alone in her room at Tintagel:

And the night spake, and thundered on the sea,
Ravening aloud for ruin of lives: and all
The bastions of the main cliff's northward wall
Rang response out from all their deepening length.[14]

Cornwall was lightly touched by the first Celtic revival of the mid-1800s through the work of William Borlase (1754); a century later, visitors were combining their passion for romantic landscape with the mid-Victorian rage for antiquities. J. T. Blight's *A Week at the Land's End* (1861) promised to deal with the region's 'romantic scenery, its natural productions, and its ancient legends', expecting readers to be equally impressed by the region's 'bold, magnificent cliffs', its variety of wild life, and those 'hoary monuments of ages past . . . surrounded by a deep halo of mystery, which the speculations of the antiquary can scarcely penetrate'.[15]

Craik's childhood hero, Jack the Giantkiller, is a reminder of another strand of Cornish storytelling that is still with us: the boy's adventure novel. In the later nineteenth century, the period of Ballantyne and Stevenson, 'West Barbary' offered itself as an ideal land for exciting tales of wrecking, smuggling and danger at sea. It was also mysterious and spooky; the earliest recollections of Joseph Hocking (born in 1860), the younger of the prolific Hocking brothers, were of 'sitting in the old chimney corner, with a log on the fire, and my mother telling me ancient Cornish stories of wizards, wreckers, ghosts, and haunted houses'.[16] Silas Hocking's *Sea-Waif: A Tale of the Cornish Cliffs* (1882) opens characteristically with: 'A wild night on a wild coast',[17] swiftly followed by a shipwreck off Mount's Bay, and the rescue of a child washed up in a basket by a brave fisherman's wife. Cornish novels in a similar mode poured from the pens of Sabine Baring-Gould and Sir Arthur Quiller-Couch. Evangelical authors used the form to produce Sunday school prize books, like Cobb's *The Watchers on the Longships* (1878) and Moore's *Tre, Pol, and Pen* (1887). Unlike many Sunday school prizes, copies found today in second-hand bookshops bear the marks of having been much read, an indication of their power to enter children's imaginative worlds and colour their mental pictures of the Cornish coast. Crosby Garstin's 'Penhales' trilogy, published in the 1920s, is an adult variant of this adventure genre, which continues to influence images of Cornwall.

In the early twentieth century, Cornwall increasingly capitalized on its romantic aura. The tourist trade continued to recommend its mild climate and warm beaches, promoting it as the 'Cornish Riviera' (remarkably similar to Italy, one railway poster claimed), ideal for convalescents. But visitor's guidebooks and Great Western Railway posters never abandoned romantic views of salty fishermen and cliff walks, and paintings produced in the artists' colonies at Newlyn, Lamorna and St Ives from the 1880s onwards gave currency to similar images in higher social circles. The Victorian brew of literature and legend acted as a heady stimulant on later visitors, and the 1920s marked 'the highpoint of Arthurian fever' at Tintagel.[18] The second Celtic revival, which began in the late nineteenth century, resulted in the establishment of Cowethas Kelto-Kernuak (The Celtic Cornish Society) in 1901; during the 1920s a large network of Old Cornwall Societies was set up, and 1928 saw the staging of the first Cornish Gorsedd festival. In the 1990s, Old Cornwall Societies are still going strong; New Age interests have encouraged the further development of 'mystical tourism', bringing visitors to wonder at the stone circles, tie a token by the holy well at Madron, or test the healing properties of the Men-an-Tol stone; and people continue to migrate here under the influence of the Celtic myth, believing they can find a meaningful alternative lifestyle that is of course entirely alien to the actual culture of local Cornish communities. Today it looks as if the romantics have conclusively won the battle for the periphery.

Cornwall can bear the weight of all these romantic associations because it is a mentally manageable region. Tapering off into the Atlantic, it promises an agreeable wildness and remoteness. Cut off by the Tamar from England, it claims an independent history and tradition, offering Celtic depth without inconvenient breadth. Its industrial history presents stark and simple contrasts between poor miners and rich capitalists; there are none of the obvious problems of comprehension posed by large cities with their complex past and continuing industrial present. The mining era in Cornwall is fixed in time, represented by ruined chimneys and engine-houses in areas now recovered by moorland. Paradoxically, more distant peoples seem palpably close; the untrained eye sees traces of Iron Age farms in the fields and weekend hikers walk the ramparts of Castle Dor. These romantic images are powerful enough to obliterate whole tracts of scrubby countryside; with little imaginative effort, the peninsula can be casually unpeopled and culturally redeveloped – not only in fiction, but as a matter of fact.

For, like the native 'saffron eaters' of Roy Phillips's St Ives, the Cornish and their councils have to collude in this romancing process, prostituting an economically weak county to bring in the summer trade. The tourist industry depends on displacing Cornwall's past social history and present social condition in favour of a cluster of easily manipulated signs (Celts, cliffs, mines, wrecks) that stand for Cornwall. Visitors who spend their time eating cream teas, sitting on the beach and spending money in theme parks, are persuaded by these prompts that they are having an authentic Cornish experience. But their idea of Cornwall, brought in their holiday luggage, is predominantly an urban invention. In *Englishness: Politics and Culture 1880–1920*, Philip Dodd has insisted that such manipulation of Cornwall's identity is inherently colonial:

> The fate of Cornwall at the hands of the colonists may be taken as a metaphor for the general relationship between the Celts and the English. The Celts are licensed their unique contribution to and place in the national culture: the cost is that they know their peripheral place as the subject of the metropolitan centre.[19]

Dodd's model, which exposes the power relationship between the dependent periphery and a London-centred England, offers a partial explanation of Cornish romantic fiction. Though some of its writers are indigenous to Cornwall, the genre can still be cynically defined as written by incomers for emmets. The books package selected locations for tourist consumption, trivializing and further peripheralizing the 'real Cornwall'. But this colonial model works on only one level; it does not provide a three-dimensional view of why these books are written and read. To understand the phenomenon more fully, we need to turn to romance writers and readers, and to the Cornish novels on the bookstands.

Passion, place and permanence: the pleasures of the romantic text

'By Tre-, Pol- and Pen-/ They will know Cornish men', according to the rhyme, and the same can be said of Cornish novels. The names Tregaran and Tregallis, Poldark and Pengarron, Pendorric and Penmarric (in the titles of novels by Mary Lide, Mary Williams, Winston Graham, Gloria Cook, Victoria Holt and Susan Howatch), are the badges of a distinctive kind of writing, where the super-imposition of romantic love on romantic landscape promises all the multiple pleasures of the genre. Beside these chunky regional romances, slim Mills and Boon novels seem insubstantial; Cornish fiction lies at the other end of the spectrum to, say, the new Mills and Boon 'Euro-romance' series, where Portugal and Paris are as indistinguishable as their airport lounges. If the label 'Cornish romantic novel' has any meaning as a sub-genre, it must depend on the uses the books make of this craggy periphery. Passion and place are interdependent, bearing Cornwall along on two centuries of the Romantic reconstruction of love and landscape.

Certain novels are instantly recognizable as conforming to the modern mainstream of the genre, with titles, cover illustrations and advertising blurbs raising highly specific expectations in browsing readers. The back cover of *Trenhawk* by Mary Williams (1980) gives this appetizing plot summary:

> Rugged, craggy and vast, the granite-faced mansion of Trenhawk looms over the fiery young life of Adelaide Hawksley. Cruelly widowed in the Crimean War, she turns her back on her suitors and the elegant London salons to claim her husband David's ancestral home on the storm-tossed Cornish moors. But Trenhawk has a rival heir, the stubborn and domineering Rupert Hawksley . . . Torn between the golden memory of David and her yearning for the sweeping thrill of love, Adelaide must face her dark inheritance – and the turmoil of her wilfully passionate heart.

On the front cover stands a gypsy-like heroine with long wind-blown hair and an unlikely white dress (in appearance not much resembling the heroine of the text), standing in front of a phallic mine chimney and holding two red roses. The image is both knowable and mystifying. My analysis in this section attempts to demystify the popular novels that conform to this eminently consumable genre.

Any definition of romantic fiction, Cornish or otherwise, must focus on the textual priority given to 'love', or emotionally heightened heterosexual relationships. The ideology of romantic love rests on an individualist belief in the right to self-fulfilment, but assumes that two can be more fulfilled than one. However, to maintain this pattern, some selves are biologically destined to be more richly fulfilled than others; there is usually an implicit separation of spheres, an acceptance that, for love's sake, the woman willingly gives up more than the man. Much Cornish romantic fiction has a historical (usually nineteenth-century) setting, which helps to sustain this traditional version of the love myth; few novels attempt to modernize the genre by exploring the problems of present-day partnerships within a western culture committed to personal development.[20] The spirited heroine may be centre stage in such fiction, but she is eventually tamed by love. The more shadowy man can be a moody Rochester – no prizes for guessing that the heroine of *Trenhawk* marries 'the stubborn and domineering Rupert Hawksley' – or brave and sensitive, like the soldier and gentleman farmer Julian Polleven in Mary Lide's *The Homecoming*. Together the man and woman form two halves of a whole, without which their lives would lack a vital core of meaning.[21]

Its valorization of a romantic love-match makes Rosamunde Pilcher's best seller, *The Shell Seekers*, a classic of its genre. The novel's unlikely heroine is an elderly lady living quietly in the Cotswolds. But Penelope's heart is elsewhere: in Cornwall, with the memory of her brief affair during the Second World War with a handsome Royal Marine major, both soldier and reader of poetry. The novel takes its title from a picture of children looking for shells on a Cornish beach, painted by Penelope's father. Penelope herself is a seeker not of shells but of true love, awaiting the return of the only man who can make life meaningful for her:

'I only knew that everything changed colour when you walked through the door. It felt as though I'd known you always. Like the best of everything, in the past and the future, all happening at once.'[22]

Such love is forever. Richard is killed on D-Day, but in her last moments Penelope senses his nearness. An old lady dying of a heart attack in her Gloucestershire garden, she is Homer's Penelope reunited with her Ulysses, Catherine with her Heathcliff, Isolde with her Tristan.

What makes this romantic novel Cornish is its assumption of the inestimable value of the landscape, and its expression of love through a plethora of natural images. The couple take a memorable holiday in the mild Roseland region of the south Cornish coast, where their lovemaking mingles with 'The salt smell of a flood tide, rising to fill the creek. The kittiwakes calling' (p.589), sensual images recalled by Penelope as she drifts into death; their first passionate encounter on the stormier north coast finds them 'entwined in each other's arms, watching the clouds tumbling across the sky and listening to the timeless thunder of breakers pounding up onto the empty beach' (p.458), a comforting emblem of transcendence. The imagery of salty tides and rough waves so abundantly offered by Cornwall's landscape expresses the emotional and eternal aspects of true romantic love.

Geographically suited to expressions of passion, Cornwall is equally well-equipped to fulfil another important romantic function of place, its promise of permanence. The reading of a romantic novel offers a sense of security: the repetition of the genre's conventions satisfyingly fulfils our expectations, the hero supplies appropriate emotional and financial support to the heroine, while underlying all are the lasting pleasures of place, guaranteeing a safe harbour away from the flux of life's disappointments. A house can be the casket for a whole collection of powerful feelings; an ancient building, in the apparently immutable setting of Cornwall's granite coast, seems to promise centuries of future security. Heroines frequently aspire to houses rather than heroes: Mary Williams's *Trenhawk* and Victoria Holt's *Menfreya* are books named after vast, castle-like ancestral homes, which the heroines possess through marriage. Qualities are interchanged between heroes and their houses: heroes assume nobility and strength through association with their inheritance, and the houses afford heroines the same kind of security as a loving relationship.

Preferable to a house owned by the hero is a place with ties to the heroine's own past. Inherited mansions, parents' houses, childhood holiday homes: all prove potent sources of inspiration for both fictional characters and their creators. It may be that this charmed circle of passion, permanence and the personal past, is one of the basic attractions that draws writers as well as readers to the genre.

Writers of less formulaic fiction have used Cornwall for similar purposes. Rumer Godden's *China Court* (1961) and Mary Wesley's *The Camomile Lawn* (1984) are centred on a single house; *The Sea Has Many Voices* (1990), Judith Hubback's first novel, takes as its focus for three generations of characters the lovely house, owned by the author's family, on the dramatic cliffs near Dodman Point. The house in Virginia Woolf's *To The Lighthouse* (1927) is the Stephens family's holiday home in St Ives, transposed to a superficially Scottish setting. Woolf's fictional house is a powerful presence, keeping a balance with nature as its family scatters and suffers through the First World War, and drawing the survivors and the mother's spirit back after the fighting has ended. Godrevy lighthouse, in fact a relatively modern addition to the Cornish seascape, works as another powerful symbol of protection and permanence.

Anita Burgh's 'Daughters of a Granite Land' trilogy (1989–92) circles around an imaginary house called Gwenfer, while Burgh's compelling account of her own life centres on a real house, Lanhydrock near Bodmin, where she lived as an evacuee during the Second World War:

> My home was a terraced house in Gillingham, Kent, with an outdoor loo and no bathroom. At the age of two *I was transported to the magical world of Lanhydrock . . . It was such a safe world.* When out in the grounds we were told if we needed help to knock on the door of any house with maroon painted windows and doors as it was an estate house and we would be looked after. *So my world was bounded by its walls and was secure . . .* And so Lanhydrock has always remained with me – *a rootless person it is the closest I have to any roots.* I still love it, deeply. The house always pops up in my books – often unintentionally . . . Although it has changed its face in the trilogy, the soul of Lanhydrock is very much Gwenfer.[23] (my emphasis)

Gwenfer is named by Burgh after a local beach, and built by her imagination in a lovely uninhabited valley close to her present home. She too has formed a circle in her own life, taking herself back to the Cornwall of her happy childhood and perpetually retracing it in her books. It is significant that she describes herself as rootless: possibly it is not people with the experience of roots who need the comforts of romantic fiction, but the deracinated, searching for a place to be.

Rosamunde Pilcher works much of her magic on her readers by manipulating the desire for security. In *Voices in Summer* (1984), Alex suggests to his second wife that she convalesces with his relatives at Tremenheere: ' "Where's Tremenheere?" "Cornwall. The very end of Cornwall. Heaven on earth. An old Elizabethan manor and a view of the bay." '[24] Here the wheel of the generations comes full circle: Alex's pregnant daughter appears, falls in love with the son of the house and decides to stay and have her baby in Cornwall, while Alex's relationships with his daughter and second wife are strengthened before his return to the city. Everyone is made happy and the final chapter is comfortingly entitled 'Homes'. *The Shell Seekers* repeatedly returns to place and past. The reader waits throughout the long book for Penelope to revisit Cornwall, which she does shortly before her death; her father's painting must be bequeathed to a local gallery, returning it to its Cornish origin. In Cornwall, Penelope remembers how she loved drawing perfect circles with a compass on a piece of white paper (p.539); the novel traces its larger circles, bringing them all to a satisfying close.

Sometimes it is the far Celtic past that gives meaning to the unsettled unsatisfactory present. The 'ancient walls' of ruined Castle Chun are the setting in Susan Howatch's *Penmarric* for primitive kinship encounters between members of a modern family.[25] The central scene of *Trenhawk* takes place by night at an Iron Age fort, after the heroine has galloped madly after her husband Rupert:

> Her voice became rhythmic with the soughing sounds of wind and creaking underneath, of thudding hooves and distant screaming of gulls wheeling. Ahead the stark primeval outlines of Castle Tol loomed gradually nearer, tumbled stones and ancient walls lit fitfully by the pale moon against the wild night sky . . . it seemed the spirits of those who'd once lived there moved and spoke again. Castle Tol took shape in her mind as it had been centuries ago – more than three thousand years – a fortress and village armed against invasion by the last Celts and those that followed. Wild broom and heather thrived there now, and only granite monuments remained as guardians of forgotten bones beneath the wild soil. (pp. 232–3).

The sheer nerve of this romantic set-piece can be appreciated only in context: it immediately follows an explosion in the boiler-house of Wheal Tansy, Rupert's mine, with arms and legs blown off and the village in uproar. This scene of working-class horror and tragedy is swept aside by Adelaide's heroic ride and by the spirits of this other Cornish people, conveniently three thousand years distant. Their 'primeval' presence bears witness to the coming together of Adelaide and Rupert, 'his lips savage yet adoring'; they lie together in the snow 'as countless others had lain before in centuries long past and forgotten' (p.235), giving Adelaide strength for the all-engrossing task ahead of counterbalancing 'Rupert's alternating moods of depression and anxiety over the inevitable problems of compensation for the survivors and relations of Wheal Tansy's victims' (p.257). The reader is spared the pain of a specific nineteenth-century mining experience, and seduced into sharing the sham fulfilment of a 'universal' romantic bond.

Crossing the borders

The edges of any genre can never be neatly drawn, and romantic fiction is peculiarly liable to wander off over the boundaries. Local readers did not need an academic to tell them this; many books recommended for my research came with comments on the problems of classification. Romantic fiction was assumed to be enjoyable rubbish, which meant excluding lyrical love stories like Rumer Godden's *China Court* and Helen Dunmore's *Zennor in Darkness* (1993). Interestingly, two famous names popularly associated with romantic writing in Cornwall, E. V. Thompson and Winston Graham, were seen as 'more factual' and placed in a separate category. Similar discriminations appear in Bridget Fowler's interviews with Scottish readers, whose favourable references to Thompson and Graham are based on a qualitative judgement that their writing is more reputable than romance. One reader who singled out a 'marvellous' historical novel by E. V. Thompson for special praise revealingly claimed: 'I'm not very keen on romantic novels, though obviously a wee bit of romance comes into these. Mills and Boon's novels I'd read only occasionally, when I'm not feeling good.'[26] Another woman agreed: 'I tend to look for something that's actually happened. I was never a reader until I read [Winston Graham's] *Poldark* series.'[27] This kind of testimony, which can be heard throughout Cornwall, is not without significance. But closer analysis suggests that, if either writer can be said to subvert the inherently conservative romance, the author of the 'Poldark' novels has the greater claim.

E. V. Thompson's *Chase the Wind*,[28] the first novel in the Retallick series, structurally subordinates romance to realism. The love story between miner's son Josh Retallick and moorland girl Miriam Trago, which frames the plot, gives way to a fascinating account of Methodism, mining, and trade-union militancy on nineteenth-century Bodmin Moor. The plot-line that skilfully and melodramatically shapes each chapter serves to point up the different interests of masters and men, and draws the reader closely into the feelings of the community and the excitement of Josh's rise as a self-made engineer. Although readers of *Chase the Wind* feel they are learning about the history of the Cornish people, the book's popularity does not seem to stem from any desire to identify with the characters – unlike the vogue for working-class historical romance in the north of England, where readers are invited to recognize themselves in novels of strong women surmounting hardship.[29] In the case of the Cornish historical romance, it is wise to bear Bridget Fowler's warning in mind: readers' interest in what they construe as historical realism should probably be interpreted as marking a resistance to contemporary realism, and what looks like a rejection of romance is likely to be merely another conservative impulse away from the problems of the present. Indeed, though the text of *Chase the Wind* does not adopt a conventional romantic focus, the writing is far from radical. In spite of its predominantly working-class cast and strong female characters, the book takes the political stance of a mid-Victorian social novel of self-improvement and class reconciliation, like Dinah Craik's *John Halifax, Gentleman* (1856) or Mrs Gaskell's *Mary Barton* (1848), sympathetic to miners and ministers trying to fight for better social conditions, but traditional in its endorsement of the Victorian work ethic and separate spheres for men and women. The benevolent mine-owner is a *deus ex machina*, who sends Josh away for his training as an engineer, rewards him for his diligence, and steps in at the end to rescue him from the hulks where he is imprisoned for his part in a riot of unionized miners. Miriam Trago, once a *Wuthering Heights*-style heroine 'as wild and untamed as the moor itself' (p.26), leaves for Australia with her childhood sweetheart, now schooled by experience to make him a wise and sweet wife. The love interest is pushed to the edges of the narrative, but the conservative clichés of class and gender politics familiar from the popular romance still control the text.

Long romantic sagas, however, sometimes activate the self-destruct button. Instead of being able to capitalize on brief, intense romances, they are forced to travel beyond the figment of a happy-ever-after ending to record what happens next. The four close-knit volumes of Graham's original 'Poldark' series do much more than chart the courtship of Ross and Demelza. Even in the second book, named after the heroine, our interest is diverted for long periods to the compelling story of Ross's mining and copper-processing ventures, and the novel ends tragically with the death of their first child. The next two volumes trace the shadows over their marriage and the frustrations of Demelza's comparatively privileged wifely existence, which was previously presented as her reward for good behaviour. The fourth book ends happily; Graham has admitted that the 'Poldark' characters are 'a little more in the sun than in the shadows', claiming that this romantic view reflects his own 'truth' that 'Sex is to me one of the best things in life, and love one of the most enduring'.[30] We therefore leave Ross and Demelza in material prosperity and marital harmony. But this is a saga to be continued, and the end of the third volume had its own 'truth' in Ross's philosophy of uncontrollable change as the only sure principle of life:

> Human beings were blind, crazy creatures, he thought, forever walking the tightrope of the present, condemned to ever changing shifts and expedients to maintain the balance of existence, not knowing even as far ahead as to-morrow what the actions of to-day would bring . . . Not by a hairbreadth would a single external circumstance move to accommodate him and his schemes – he knew that.[31]

Romantic novels pretend that love can transcend time, but sagas know that survival means change, that romance is not a real priority, that time transcends love. Big books can also disturb the complacencies of romance-reading in other ways. The Poldark landscape is thickly peopled, obscuring the uninterrupted contemplation of the Cornish landscape, and refusing to exclude the local people who work the mines and inhabit the land between the big houses. Rather than taking up a known place as ruins in a reclaimed and empty moorscape, mines are still under construction, their yield unknown, their work dangerous, and their venture capital precarious.

Christine Bridgwood's analysis of *Penmarric*, the blockbuster by Susan Howatch that is often named as *the* Cornish romantic novel, demonstrates other ways in which a saga can deny its readers the reassurances of romantic writing.[32] Not only does its long view unravel the fiction that true love is forever; it also presents a disturbingly fragmented view of female identity. Janna is the heroine we expect, beautiful and intriguing, the natural subject of the paperback cover illustration. But the plot is unfolded by five narrators, four of whom are male; Janna is allotted one space early in the book in which to tell her own story, and is thereafter the subject of other people's prejudices. In *Penmarric* the present is allowed to unsettle the past, shaking the usual premise of the saga form that family and inheritance establish a chain of continuity in the face of change. Houses are sites of conflict rather than comfort: Penmarric itself is a 'bleak ugly mansion' on 'ugly black cliffs', a place of petty tyranny and division, from which the trapped and estranged Janna (so unlike Swinburne's Isolde at Tintagel) stares out 'at the rain slewing into the stormy sea' (p.214). The novel is punctuated by notes of sour disharmony with the landscape – 'Of course I disliked the Cornish Tin Coast as soon as I set eyes on it' (p.298) – as characters find themselves in places where they do not want to be. In *Penmarric*, the myth of pleasure and permanence in place is severely eroded.

It seems that the terrain of Cornish romantic fiction cannot be more accurately defined by marking off the exceptions; the loves of the Poldarks and the feuds at Penmarric are inside and outside the genre, using and abusing its conventions. The case of Daphne du Maurier, queen of Cornish romantic fiction, is the most unexpectedly problematic of all, for we misremember her novels as more predictable than they really are. As Alison Light has luminously revealed, du Maurier strangely subverts romantic fiction's certainties in her treatment of passion, place and past.[33] Fulfilment in love is repeatedly thwarted, and the codes of heterosexuality are reconfigured; du Maurier creates a hybrid form by crossing women's romantic fiction with the boys' wreckers-and-smugglers adventure novels she read as a child, to create the perfect vehicle for exploring the boundaries of gender and genre. The loveliest places in 'du Maurier country' are not the safest refuges: her books are obsessed with roaming and revisiting rather than settling and putting down roots. And, although several of her Cornish novels are historical, the past is not securely fixed, but is dissolved by time passing and changing, by disturbing tricks of remembering and forgetting.

Yet no woman writer in Cornwall today can escape du Maurier's half century of matriarchal sway over the romance readership. The publishers of the latest romantic paperback in Jamaica Inn's souvenir shop cannot resist making the claim that it 'echoes the best Cornish novels of Daphne du Maurier', and since readers' recollections are likely to be blurred, holidaymakers are probably not disappointed with Mary Lide's *The Homecoming* (1993).[34] Its cover offers 'First Love, A Forbidden Passion amidst the Wilds of Cornwall' with a barefoot long-skirted young woman; this heroine's name turns out to be 'Guinevere', a flashing signal for romance; an early reference to Farmer 'Penwith' brings together the Penwith moors near Penzance and the Bodmin moors where the novel begins. In the middle of the book the scene moves to passion among the pilchard sheds of a coastal village, where Guinevere has to choose between a good-hearted fisherman, who is fortunately (for the narrative) drowned during a heroic sea rescue, and the son of a local landowner who brings her home at the end. This is all very romantic and unmistakably Cornish, but none of it is particularly close to du Maurier. Somewhat more reminiscent is Lide's atmospheric opening, which takes the reader back in time and into the heroine's head with the words: 'My first memory is of rain and storm.' But this is not as haunting as the first words of *Rebecca* (1938),[35] too memorable to require quotation, and not as intriguing as the opening description of *The King's General* (1946),[36] which reflects the process of remembering in the image of a tide falling to reveal buried dreams. The beginning of *My Cousin Rachel* (1951) is backward-looking but far from comforting: 'They used to hang men at Four Turnings in the old days. Not any more, though.'[37] The ensuing scene is shockingly immediate, with a corpse on the gallows described in revolting close-up and the young hero vomiting in the hedgerow.

Du Maurier's endings are no more reassuring than her beginnings. Unlike *The Homecoming*, whose cover slily reveals that love is 'lost and found' and whose title offers an emotional reward for finishing the book, du Maurier's plots are more likely to chart love 'found and lost' and end with a yearning lover. *My Cousin Rachel* finishes with its opening words, not with any effect of complacency and completion, but closing a circle of guilt and doubt that condemns the narrator to eternal repetition of his murderous relationship with his dead cousin. The lovers of *Rebecca* can never go to Manderley again; they are left in limbo, haunted by the first Mrs de Winter, endlessly roaming from one anonymous hotel to another. There is no blissful consummation for du Maurier's own favourite heroine, Honor Harris in *The King's General*, who is crippled before her wedding day and waits all her life in a wheelchair for her lover's infrequent returns. Even in *Frenchman's Creek* (1941),[38] the book du Maurier called her 'romance with a big R',[39] the swashbuckling Dona St Columb turns away from her pirate and the freedom of the seas and goes back to her children and boring husband. Du Maurier is not a writer to end with a happy 'homecoming'.

Although du Maurier's love plots look jagged against the templates of romantic fiction, her Cornish coasts are lavishly romantic. When she first came to Cornwall on a family holiday at the age of nineteen, it was as if she had entered a place of her own imagining. Four years earlier, she had written about a boy who loved to be alone by the sea, running barefoot on the sand and lying for hours listening to the winds which 'whispered of romance and tumultous [*sic*] seas where bleak lands lie'.[40] Her books suggest that, like the boy of her teenage story, she was to the end seeking something that she never found. Throughout her writing life, from *The Loving Spirit* (1931) to *The House on the Strand* (1969), the stormy Cornish coast permeated her work as an expression not of passionate fulfilment but of desire and longing. Yet she also knew that place could offer the greatest compensations of all. Crippled Honor Harris cannot control the movements of Sir Richard Grenvile, her tearaway King's General, or prevent the ravages of the Civil War, but she can inhabit her own territory. Honor is a guest at Menabilly, the same house that du Maurier loved, leased and finally lost to its Rashleigh owners. In *The King's General*, Menabilly is twice sacked by the Roundheads, but chair-bound Honor is allowed to enjoy the unspoilt loveliness of the surrounding landscape:

> The Parliament could strip the place of its possessions, take the sheep and cattle, glean the harvest, but they could not take from me, nor from the Rashleighs, the beauty that we looked on every day . . . Dusk comes slowly to the Gribben hill, the woods turn black, and suddenly, with stealthy pad, a fox creeps from the tree in the thistle park . . . Then his brush twitches and he is gone . . .; and another day is over. Yes, Richard, there is comfort in monotony. (pp.272–3)

These are the daily routines in a familiar place that can be loved like human companions, holding permanent pleasures that the torments of romantic love cannot guarantee. But, even here, all is not stable and secure. The enemy is encroaching on the land. Richard's nickname is the 'red fox', and the brief appearance and disappearance of the wild fox recall his comings and goings. And Honor, with limited power over her own movements, finds herself intermittently threatened with the worst fate conceivable in a du Maurier novel, banishment from Cornwall.

I have made du Maurier out to be different, but this threat of exile and loss forms the subtext for many superficially reassuring romantic novels by other writers. Even in the books that I have cited as offering secure refuges, the hold over property is often precarious. The houses in *Trenhawk* and *Menfreya* appear to the heroines, at times when the hero's fidelity is in doubt, as seats of Gothic nightmare; Janna's tenure of the farmhouse in *Penmarric*, warmly presented as a locus of value in the novel, is cruelly beleaguered by debts and legal claims; at the end of Anita Burgh's 'Daughters of a Granite Land' trilogy, the ageing Alice keeps her beloved Gwenfer from ruin only by bringing paying guests into her precious private domain. Mary Wesley's *Camomile Lawn* (1984)[41] is also about a loved house on the cliffs to which the characters repeatedly return. But outside is the Terror Run, the coast path on which a man plunges to his death after attempting a sexual attack, a representation of what is 'out there' not just for liberated young women but also for the young men who leave the calmness of the camomile lawn for the terrors of the Spanish Civil War and the armed forces. Modern in a way that du Maurier never was, Wesley is here a truer successor to du Maurier than any of the ephemeral writers of Cornish romantic fiction. But even in the ephemera, there are intriguing points where the seamless weave of conventions is curiously snagged.

Roy Phillips is reluctant to give romance writers any credit at all, as his relentless parody of the genre underlines:

' "And the handsome young squire . . . shook his black tousled locks . . . and broke into a canter . . . his dark brooding eyes . . . flashing us a haughty glance . . . as he descended the rugged track . . . past the eerie old tin mine . . . to the dark brooding house on the sea-dashed cliffs." Have you read it?'
'Many times.'
'And under many titles,' I said.[42]

But does that mean throwing 'Cornish' out with 'romantic fiction'? Is the land of Cornish romance merely a cliché, a collective figment of our post-Romantic imaginations? Strangely enough, it is the author of *The Saffron Eaters*, immediately after this caustic dismissal of romantic fiction, who raises unexpected doubts about our new academic confidence that we understand the ideological construction of landscape:

'But how would you describe it? There is a brooding atmosphere, in the sense of waiting, incubating, that I try to capture in my paintings. The landscape seems restless, seems full of suppressed energy, as if it hasn't fully developed. Yet it all looks so old and timeless.' (p.243)

This is Cleo, incomer and artist, speaking. But Roy Phillips, Cornishman and realist, has placed her statement strategically close to the end of his book. Like Alan Kent, the clay country writer whose personal viewpoint follows, he will not let go of some personal faith in the innate power of this terrain. Cornwall can be overrun by emmets, beautified by artists, tidied by the National Trust, packaged by the tourist trade; a 'Poldark mine' can open as South Crofty, the last of the working mines, is threatened by closure; a multi-media 'Cornish experience' can supplant real seagulls at the Land's End with their recorded cries; and romantic novelists can turn the diverse life of coast and moor into formulaic fiction. Is it possible that the people of that place can still lay claim to their natural periphery, and see some underlying beauty with unromantic eyes?

Note

This chapter is for Hazel, reader of romances, who takes such good care of Anna while I work.

I am grateful to Anita Burgh, Judith Hubback and Roy Phillips for their kindness in answering questions.

I would also like to thank the many friends who have generously helped me with their books, ideas and knowledge of Cornwall, especially my supportive and congenial colleagues at Exeter University's Hayne Corfe Centre in Truro: Richard McGrady, John Hurst, Mary Hocking and the irreplaceable Helen Blake.

References

[1] N. R. Phillips, *The Saffron Eaters* (1987: London, Headline,1989).

[2] J. W. von Goethe, *The Sorrows of Young Werther* (1774) trans. Michael Hulse (Harmondsworth, Penguin, 1989), p.125.

[3] Ann Radcliffe, *The Mysteries of Udolpho* (1794: Oxford, OUP [World's Classics paperback], 1980), IV, vii, p.558.

[4] Jane Austen, *Persuasion* (1818: Harmondsworth, Penguin, 1965), pp.116–17.

[5] William Gilpin, *Observations on the Western Parts of England, Relative Chiefly to Picturesque Beauty* (1798: 2nd edn, London, T. Caddell & W. Davies, 1808), pp.189–201.

[6] A. L. Rowse (ed.), *A Cornish Anthology* (London, Macmillan, 1968), p.168.

[7] Richard McGrady, *Music and Musicians in Early Nineteenth-Century Cornwall* (Exeter, University of Exeter Press, 1991), pp.5–9, 63–4; June Palmer *et al.*, *Truro during the Napoleonic Wars* (Truro, June Palmer, Polquick, Nr. Idless, 1992); Philip Payton, *The Making of Modern Cornwall: Historical Experience and the Persistence of 'Difference'* (Redruth, Dyllansow Truran, 1992), chapter 4.

[8] Quoted in McGrady, op. cit., p.6.

[9] Revd Johns, *A Week at the Lizard* (1848: Felinfach, Llanerch, 1992), p.3.

[10] Ibid., pp.22–3.

[11] Dinah Mulock Craik, *An Unsentimental Journey Through Cornwall* (1884: Newmill, Penzance, Jamieson Library, 1988), pp.49–51.

[12] Ibid., p.2.

[13] Ibid., p.18.

[14] A. C. Swinburne, *Tristram of Lyonesse* (1882: Woodbridge, The Boydell Press, 1990), V, p.86.

[15] J. T. Blight, *A Week at the Land's End* (1861: Bosulval, Newmill, Penzance, Alison Hodge, 1989), preface and p.1.

[16] Quoted in *Dictionary of National Biography*, p.437.

[17] Silas Hocking, *Sea-Waif: A Tale of the Cornish Cliffs* (London, Frederick Warne, 1882).

[18] Charles Thomas, 'Hardy and Lyonesse: parallel mythologies', in Melissa Hardie (ed.), *A Mere Interlude* (Newmill, Penzance, Patten Press, 1992), p.16.

[19] R. Colls and P. Dodd (eds.), *Englishness: Politics and Culture 1880–1920* (London, Croom Helm, 1986), p.15.

[20] See Ann Swidler, 'Love and adulthood in American culture', in Neil Smelser and Erik Erikson (eds.), *Themes of Love and Work in Adulthood*

(Cambridge, Mass., Harvard University Press, 1980); C. Lee Harrington and Denise D. Bielby, 'The mythology of modern love: representations of romance in the 1980s', *Journal of Popular Culture*, 24, 4 (Spring 1991), 129–44.

21 See Tania Modleski, *Loving with a Vengeance: Mass-Produced Fantasies for Women* (1982: New York, Methuen, 1984); Jean Radford (ed.), *The Progress of Romance: The Politics of Popular Fiction* (London, Routledge & Kegan Paul, 1986); Janice Radway, *Reading the Romance* (Chapel Hill, University of North Carolina Press, 1984).

22 Rosamunde Pilcher, *The Shell Seekers* (1987: London, Coronet, 1989), p.457.

23 Letter from Anita Burgh, dated 16 February 1993.

24 Rosamunde Pilcher, *Voices in Summer* (1984: London, Sphere, 1986), p.65.

25 Susan Howatch, *Penmarric* (1971: London, Pan, 1972), pp.353–60.

26 Bridget Fowler, *The Alienated Reader: Women and Popular Romantic Literature in the Twentieth Century* (Hemel Hempstead, Harvester Wheatsheaf, 1991), pp.178–9.

27 Ibid., pp.153–4.

28 E. V. Thompson, *Chase the Wind* (1977: London, Pan, 1979).

29 See Roger Bromley, *Lost Narratives: Popular Fictions, Politics and Recent History* (London, Routledge, 1988), chapter 2.

30 Winston Graham, *Poldark's Cornwall* (London, Bodley Head, and Exeter, Webb & Bower, 1983), pp.215–16.

31 Idem, *Jeremy Poldark: A Novel of Cornwall 1790–1791* (1950: London, Fontana, 1968), p.282.

32 Christine Bridgwood, 'Family romances: the contemporary popular saga', in Jean Radford (ed.), ibid.

33 Alison Light, *Forever England: Femininity, Literature and Conservatism Between the Wars* (London, Routledge, 1991).

34 Mary Lide, *The Homecoming* (1992: London, Grafton, 1993).

35 Daphne du Maurier, *Rebecca* (London, Gollancz, 1938).

36 Idem, *The King's General* (London, Gollancz, 1946). In the quotation from *The King's General* on p.169, the page reference given is to the Pan edition (London, 1974).

37 Idem, *My Cousin Rachel* (London, Gollancz, 1951).

38 Idem, *Frenchman's Creek* (London, Gollancz, 1941).

39 Quoted in Margaret Forster, *Daphne du Maurier* (London, Chatto & Windus, 1993), p.162.

40 Quoted in ibid., p.22.

41 Mary Wesley, *The Camomile Lawn* (London, Macmillan, 1984).

42 N. R. Phillips, *The Saffron Eaters*, op. cit., p.243. The ellipses in the quotation are Phillips's.

Smashing the sandcastles:
realism in contemporary Cornish fiction

ALAN M. KENT

When I speak to people from other parts of Britain about Cornwall, they seem to have a quaint and misguided notion that seemingly every third person in the county (or do I really mean country?) is sitting in some tumbledown, cliff-clinging cottage, either painting, or writing. The seagulls are gliding overhead, ancient granite cliffs are being smashed into by breathtaking waves and children are *always* on the beach with red buckets, making glorious sandcastles. It is as if one only has to step outside to feel some mystic Celtic force enter the body, and Lyonesse feels just a sidestep away. Our thoughts are tumbling with Arthurian Romance, *Poldark*, Betjeman's verse and tales of Cornish Smugglers.

There are a lot of clichés about writing in Cornwall, and that was one of them; that the visiting writer who separates him/herself physically and mentally from England can complete whatever masterpiece they are engaged upon, memoirs, fiction or poetry. This is not the indigenous Cornish writer, but just one of the false impressions the rest of Britain receives almost on a day-to-day basis about writing in this part of the disunited kingdom, a complete ideological fabrication. Of course the sheer beauty of Bodmin Moor and Botallack's ruined tin-mines is going to rub off in your work. It's bound to!

Unfortunately, every year a number of these works are published. All too often you've seen them while waiting for a train in Edinburgh: a paperback novel, with some title subverting Frankfort Moore and beginning with either 'Tre', 'Pol' or 'Pen', embossed in flowing golden lettering. On the cover, whilst buying a packet of Polos, you notice the windswept heroine, cliffs (again!), heather (always purple-coloured!), perhaps a seagull or two – oh, and a tin-mine. The blurb on the back runs either, 'A breathtaking saga of family turmoil in eighteenth-century Cornwall' or 'When the Smith Family arrived at St Ives for their summer holidays, right from the time they stepped off the train, things were never going to be quite the same again . . .' Sadly, this is all too often the impression the rest of Britain receives of Cornwall, and the incestuous fiction continues to multiply in bookshelves in railway stations. The sad thing is that they sell in Penzance as well!

It is also the reason why thousands flock to the county each summer, like some huge seasonal migration. The problem is that the very fiction that celebrated the landscape in this way and consolidated the 'world view' of Cornwall, is inevitably causing its destruction.

What I shall be examining in this coda, from an indigenous Cornish writer's point of view is how the much-laboured 'world view' of Cornwall offered by the writers of the passionate periphery is an entirely false representation of Cornwall. The vast sandcastles constructed by these writers take a lot of shifting. The problem in post-war Cornish fiction is that though a siege lay at the battlements, there was never quite a large enough army to ransack the place. In a way, vast Towers of Babel, they have also become as entrenched in the subconscious and as hard to shift as some of the county's granite. Here, albeit briefly, I aim to show with some of my own experiences, and those of other writers in the county, why we must make an effort to knock them down.

Indigenous Cornish writers forming the polemic to the passionate periphery experience many problems in trying to be published through mainstream English companies. There is no doubt that to explore any real 'structures of feeling' about the place, to use Raymond Williams's phrase, you must be prepared to have doors slammed in your face. Firstly, there is the fact that many editors simply do not bother to read novels written about the county because the expectation is of the usual tin-mines and embraces on cliff tops. Secondly – and this has happened to me – should the work be read, then likely it will come back with a note saying that it 'really wasn't Cornish enough for us'; the expectation being that slinging in a few quaint old fisherman and someone making pasties will cure the problem. Thirdly, there is the problem of promotion; how do you market a novel about Cornwall in the rest of the country without destroying all notion that it is about the county, whilst simultaneously trying to progress and develop the fiction? It is a huge problem and one can see why publishers are so reluctant to release realistic Cornish fiction. However, writers in the county have always looked with envious eyes upon other Celtic nations and seen how seemingly well-treated and respected they are. For instance, Ireland appears to them to have a very good crack of the whip with London publishers.

Admittedly, it is a larger country, but the issues being considered – provincialism, paralysis, frustration, change, love – are the same themes as Cornish writers.

There is another factor, however, and one which has worked its way into fiction. I label this the 'dialect' factor. Throughout the media, whereas an Irish accent denotes struggle, origin and status in a U2/Bob Geldof sort of way, why doesn't the Cornish dialect give the same? A contributing reason is that the Cornish never fought hard enough for their rights and consequently paid the price. Unfortunately, in mainstream British culture, such a dialect usually shows stupidity or backwardness. This is unfair and is clearly a misrepresentation. There are plenty of 'Roddy Doyles' in Cornwall, but would Alan Parker make a film about their fiction?

Wales too – of all the regions, the most similar to Cornwall – has always benefited from a much more organized infrastructure which facilitates and develops new writing. Where Cornwall fails is that, unlike Wales, it has no university – no cultural centre or heart – it lacks arts finance and the nationalist movement of Cornwall failed to motivate the working classes. The county remains a Liberal stronghold. The celebration of 'difference' only works in a very limited way (an obvious example being the thousands of Cornish who attend the County Rugby Finals at Twickenham in some mass demonstrations of nationality, but who fail to take that celebration any further either politically or creatively) whereas in Wales it is more organized. Wales has a number of operational small-press magazines to allow new writers a voice. There have been none in Cornwall since *Cornish Review* folded in the mid-1970s. Visiting bookshops like Oriel in Cardiff, I am always impressed with the vast numbers of Welsh-language novels written; whereas owing to the widespread failure of attempts to revive the Cornish language, novel-writing in that field does not happen.

Particularly in the twentieth century, Cornwall has all too easily given up its identity for the official version of British culture, and it is that culture which has all too often dictated what is read and what is not. Sometimes, I think the romantic novels are on sale in Cornwall for those failing to hold onto Cornish culture in their own lives, to be able, albeit in a fantasy way, to step back into it; if the past cannot really be held onto, then some fictional re-creation of it is better than nothing at all. Even the rise of Cornish nationalism into real electoral campaigning from the 1970s onwards failed to release any 'truly' nationalist novel. Wonderful urban legends of Tamar Bridge bomb campaigns and the infamous Stannary parliament's rebellion against the Poll Tax (the Stannaries grew out of a body of ancient customary rights and privileges enjoyed by the tinners, allowing territorial semi-independence) did not generate any fiction. In retrospect we can see the mistake of that.

It would be wrong, though, to say that this is the total picture. In Cornish post-war writing, a number of figures have emerged, who, whilst maintaining their Cornish roots and themes, have managed to operate within the constrictions of mainstream publishing. It is here that Jack Clemo sits. Falling into the so-called 'English Noncon-formist' tradition, Clemo was not consciously taking on the romantic fiction of the county, but his work has helped a great deal in offering readers both internal and external to the county a different vision of it. The setting for much of his work, like my own, is the grim, yet on occasions uniquely beautiful, industrial heartland of Cornwall, which has closer parallels to the Welsh valleys than to the pretty coves of Lamorna and Porthcurno. The only sands here are the vast sand tips, waste from huge-scale opencast quarrying for china clay. The entire mining operation covers the bulk of the mid-Cornwall region; a part of the county bypassed by most tourists. To me, it is perhaps the only part of Cornwall that has managed to retain its indigenous character. Places like St Ives and even Mevagissey are too full of tourism and people from 'up-country'. It is the little-known working-class villages of Cornwall like St Dennis (the largest village in the whole county), Foxhole and Bugle that represent the real Cornwall, places where only over the back garden is a vast man-made crater, a world diametrically opposed to that of the passionate periphery.

Originally intending to be a novelist, until he became blind, it is Clemo's poetry that is now the more famous, with his Calvinist faith imposed onto the stark, quarried landscape. Poems like 'The Excavator' are perfect slices of polemic against the wishy-washy romance of the coast. Here, Clemo writes of a baptism he receives under the machinery of the China Clay Pit:

> I feel exultantly
> The drip of clayey water from the posed
> Still bar above me . . .[1]

This is powerful writing and negates the pulp fiction to nothingness. Clemo's underrated two novels, *Wilding Graft* (1948) and *The Shadowed Bed* (1986), parallel his poetry and demonstrate a similar realism. Of the two, it is perhaps *The Shadowed Bed* which warrants most attention; it is a powerfully symbolic and quasi-magical-realist novel. Over a single weekend the fictional village of Carn Veor is cut off from the outside world by a landslide; therein the industrial scene takes on cosmic significance as the lives of the villagers are changed by warring magnetic forces. It is almost a pity, then, that the work was actually published thirty years later, as an earlier release might have altered conceptions about where writing in the county was progressing. Consider this section from the opening of *The Shadowed Bed*:

> Joe Gool, who was working on the dam early in the afternoon, was not a paid labourer. He had come to the site when these men left it, and yielded to a whim, seeking some exertion before he met Bronwyn Cundy. He was a tall gaunt felloe in his late twenties, obviously a native. The stark grey background suited him; he looked upon the general mess with stolid enjoyment as he added boulders, whitened gorse twigs and frayed clotted hazel boughs to the structure. His pale face had something of the wrenched, warped perversity of the landscape; he seemed to commune with the coldly volcanic clay-world, knowing its vagaries and loving them.[2]

Is language like this synonymous with the usual vision of Cornwall? I think not, yet it is the real Cornwall with which Clemo is dealing here, not that of azure picture postcards. In Clemo then, we have the leader of the campaign against the false vision; one that I was to continue with later.

There are now two problems with such writers as Clemo and others in his generation, such as A. L. Rowse and Charles Causley. Firstly, they are old and their best work has been completed; secondly, all of them failed in constructing enough of a reaction against the pot-boilers. A. L. Rowse, admittedly primarily a historian, has failed to write anything as powerful as *A Cornish Childhood* (1942). Causley seems content enough with whimsical ballads (often for children) about the way things *used* to be, whereas his early verse had bite and fervour; and even Clemo's dramatic early vision has softened to take on broader themes outside of the county. Probably the most prolific Cornish novelist at present is D. M. Thomas. Thomas is a working figure in the Cornish literary scene, but his fiction and poetry have continued to move away from Cornish issues. His 1993 novel *Pictures at an Exhibition* nods more in the direction of *The White Hotel* (1981) than his best novel with a Cornish theme, *Birthstone* (1980), about the strange effects of the Men-an-Tol stone in West Penwith. Perhaps the sad conclusion to be drawn from this is that one of the failures of writing in Cornwall is that writers making a name for themselves in the county have then expanded, to take on wider issues – and so the sandcastles still remain in place.

There is unfortunately, however, a new tide lapping at the castle walls and filling the moat. In the late 1980s, two novels emerged confronting Cornish issues in an altogether different way. *The Saffron Eaters* (1987) by Roy Phillips, discussed by Ella Westland, works almost as a linking device between the romantic fiction of yore and what was to emerge after it. The novel was a timely study of the sentiments of the 'real' Cornish people, resisting – or trying to resist – the erosion of their community and culture. The fiction worked as a cry against the times and, after its serialization on BBC local radio, offered, for the first time in a number of years, a ray of hope to the Cornish literary scene. Phillips, confronting environmental issues head on, has the first page deal with a very real problem, sewage, that which now lies beneath those windswept cliffs:

> 'What's that?' Joe asked. We told him. 'Get on,' he said, 'Nobody has a tuss as big as that.'
> They fished it out with a stick and laid it on the sand, standing in reverence before the great condom before taking it to a tidal pool in the rocks and floating it in the clear salt water.
> 'Must have been made for a bleddy elephant,' said Tim.
> 'See the bleddy g'eat ring on 'n', said Steve.[3]

In those few lines, Cornish fiction had taken an almighty step forward. Phillips has failed as yet to make a second impact: We can however, think of him as the first assault.

Myrna Combellack set herself an enormously difficult task in trying to capture the nuances and dialect of contemporary Cornwall with her novel *The Playing Place* (1989).[4] The Playing Place itself, a site once for the performance in medieval Cornwall of creation drama, acts as a symbol against the development of an estate of bungalows in the fictional parish of St Coen, the sort of impact of new culture upon old that is continually a problem in the county. Combellack is scathing in her attack on those who try to 'develop' Cornwall and each summer, as the county gears itself up for the onslaught of the 'emmets', her voice will continue to be important in the county. Only in such fiction can identity be preserved and the value of the new questioned.

If Jack Clemo's fiction led the way, then, it has been another novel set in the china-clay mining region of Cornwall (as distinct from the centrality, in fiction at least, of Penwith) that has allowed still further dismantling of sandcastles. Both national and regional critics have labelled my novel *Clay* (1991)[5] as the first *real* novel about late twentieth-century Cornwall. Through good reviews, readings, publicity and groundswell opinion on the work, this locally published hardback novel has sold now in excess of 1,500 copies – not a bad figure for a writer in his twenties and one which many London publishers would be proud of. *Clay* is a very different novel from *The Saffron Eaters* and *The Playing Place*. For a start, the novel takes its cues from other post-modernist writing. Thus, no single narrative dominates; there are instead dozens which interlock and weave in and out of the whole.

Secondly, two historically separate time zones are used – one in twentieth-century, the other in seventeenth-century Cornwall. The seventeenth-century sections are written sardonically and the characters are unlikely heroes. Realism prevails; there are no meetings at smugglers' coves, nor heroic duels. I use the fictional device of a journal of a parish clerk of that time to counterpoint the reality of the clay country before the discovery of china clay. Already however, the clerk senses a problem as technology begins to develop. The novel is harsh and brutal; realistic too, I hope. My aim was to construct a miniature cosmography, which appealed both to the native readership and beyond it.

The success of *Clay* proves one thing; that a Cornish readership (and a nation-wide one for that matter) was interested in a new kind of post-modernist fiction about the county. The novel worked because for the first time, it openly challenged so many existing assumptions about what literature set in Cornwall was and could be. A prolific reader of Cornish fiction has since told me that it was the only novel she had ever read about the county where characters do not go for a cliff-top walk. Thinking about it, the bulk of the action actually takes place inside the county, in direct physical contrast to the cliché of the cliff-tops. A new readership is emerging which wants real issues tackled. In the future, it is issues like Cornwall's emerging status within Europe, the threat of Plymouth's expansion into 'Greater Tamarside', environmental concerns, New Age travellers (who, like earlier tourists upon God's Wonderful Railway also seem intent on heading for Lyonesse), 'days at sea' fishing laws and poverty which need confronting against a backdrop of approaching twenty-first century Cornwall, one of carefully cultivated theme parks and surf culture as well as its greater, and conveniently mystical, Celtic heritage.

The other trend with all these three novels is that they were all published locally in high-quality formats. Because of Cornwall's 'difference', there has always been a need for small publishing operations within the county to publish, for instance, specific Cornish language books. For the most part, these have not been expensive editions, but technology is now allowing the same sort of production quality as the larger publishers. Thus, the regional companies are grabbing more of a share of the market, owing to the reluctance of the hegemonic London publishing industry to develop new writers, particularly those in peripheral areas, not writing in the tradition of 'romance'.

The image of Cornish nationhood, as generally represented on our bookshelves, is a sad one, based on outmoded images of life, insulting portraits of local characters and a disengagement with the horrific environmental and serious unemployment problems that areas like Cornwall face. Unfortunately, the days of the pot-boiler saga of *Tre Something or Other* are not over. The success of *Clay* is the reason why I am now writing this coda. What Cornwall needs is some young children to run across the beach wildly kicking down these sandcastles; the castles that have closed and restricted their literary culture for too long.

A few of us have dangerously run across and kicked down some battlements. It won't be easy, but I've a feeling more are just waiting in the shallows.

References

[1] Jack Clemo, *Selected Poems* (Newcastle, Bloodaxe, 1988), p.22.

[2] Idem, *The Shadowed Bed* (Tring, Lion, 1986), p.1.

[3] Roy Phillips, *The Saffron Eaters* (London, Headline, 1989), p.1.

[4] Myrna Combellack, *The Playing Place* (Redruth, Dyllansow Truran, 1989).

[5] Alan M. Kent, *Clay* (Launceston, Amigo Books, 1991).

9

Mother to legend (or going underground): the London novel

KEN WORPOLE

If national identities are among the most persuasive 'grand narratives' of history, so cities are also fictional and cultural constructions. The rise of the city, in Britain, coincides with the rise of the novel itself, and the two have been inextricably linked ever since. As cities develop and mutate in the late twentieth century, subject to national and international population movements and political fissures, multiplying varieties of religion, race, history and politics increasingly contest each other for space and public visibility and legitimacy. New individual and collective identities struggle to emerge; new voices seek to find a hearing above the noisy crowd. Writing and publishing, in all forms, become a central part of this process of establishing a cultural presence in the modern city and the modern world.

The relationship between time and space in modern cities is, therefore, always discontinuous. There was never a single unique moment at which there was a blank sheet of paper to write on, or start again, a *tabula rasa*, neither is there a single moment when geography itself stays fixed. There are parts of London with long-established Irish communities and street cultures, Bengali districts, West Indian quarters, and these are themselves in a process of continual change and reconfiguration. And so the book of the city and its literary representation is always a series of overlapping novels and other writings inscribed over time by diverse hands. This sense of the fictionality of city life – in this case London – is quite explicit in the first of Mike Phillips's contemporary detective novels, *Blood Rights* (1989), for example, featuring black journalist Sam Dean: 'I got off the train with a feeling I always had coming back into the country from abroad. The city was waiting there for me, like a book that hadn't been opened for a long time.'[1] If the city is a book, then the book of the city is also the world. Emanuel Litvinoff called his wonderful evocation of the Jewish district of London in which he grew up in the 1930s *A Journey through a Small Planet* (1972). The planet he described was Whitechapel, a tiny district of London where 'people spoke of Warsaw, Kishinev, Kiev, Kharkov, Odessa as if they were neighbouring suburbs'.[2] The Caribbean writer Samuel Selvon opened his founding novel of post-war black British writing, *The Lonely Londoners* (1956), with a similarly distanced view:

> One grim evening, when it had a kind a unrealness about London, with a fog sleeping restlessly over the city and the lights showing in the blur as if it is not London at all but a strange place on another planet, Moses Aloetta hop on a number 46 bus at the corner of Chepstow Road and Westbourne Grove to go to Waterloo to meet a fellar who was coming from Trinidad on the boat-train.[3]

That estranged, mysterious and often foggy London opening, has become a setpiece of the London novel, from the famous opening lines of Dickens's *Bleak House* to the now well-known opening of Patrick Hamilton's last novel, *Slaves of Solitude* (1947):

> London, the crouching monster, like every other monster has to breathe, and breathe it does in its own obscure, malignant way. Its vital oxygen is composed of suburban working men and women of all kinds, who every morning are sucked up through an infinitely complicated respiratory apparatus of trains and termini into the mighty congested lungs, held there for a number of hours, and then, in the evening, exhaled violently through the same channels.[4]

Already, then, we can see the dangers of trying to conflate into a single construct, the notion of 'the London novel', which in fact is a jigsaw puzzle of pieces that rarely fit, though they may well overlap and produce if not a coherent picture, then at least a chiaroscuro effect. The London novel, or the London constructed over time through published imaginative writing, is characterized by differentiation, antagonistic forms and genres, competing voices, parody, frequent fictional cross-reference, processes of literary accretion but also entropy, and frequent periods of silence, sometimes self-imposed but sometimes blocked.

Dubious origins

The English novel itself can be said to have grown out of the streets, stews and rookeries of outcast proletarian and criminal London, a symbiotic relationship and fascination which continues to this day. The

line which runs from Defoe through Dickens to the 'low-life' novels of
Patrick Hamilton and James Curtis in the 1930s and then through to
the mohair suits, portable phones, cocaine and sawn-off shotguns of
East London's *demi-monde* in Iain Sinclair's recent *Downriver* (1991),
or Victor Headley's contemporary guns and ganja *Yardie* (1992), is at
least one element of continuity in an otherwise broken heritage or
family line. As Lennard J. Davis wrote in his excellent study:

> The frequency with which the early English novel, newspaper and
> ballads focused on the criminal is significant. There seems to have
> been something inherently novelistic about the criminal, or rather
> the form of the novel seems almost to demand a criminal content.
> Indeed, without the appearance of the whore, the rogue, the
> cutpurse, the cheat, the thief or the outsider it would be impossible
> to imagine the genre of the novel.[5]

There was of course another founding fictional line established by
women writers such as Aphra Behn, Mrs Manley and others, which
developed a different trajectory for the novel out of popular romances;
again, that still has resonances in some contemporary fiction, though it
remains less distinct and less directly continuous as far as the London
novel is concerned than the tradition established by Defoe and others
based on the court and prison gazettes, the street-life and *bas-fonds* of
London's urban poor and criminal underworld.

Yet because the rise of the novel in Britain was at times so closely
related to the development of the London novel, there has also arisen
the often spurious or unwarranted correlation between the London
novel and the 'condition of England' novel, so that many novels about
London have also had to bear the weight of being 'read' as national
fictions, iconographies or 'state of the nation' reports. *Bleak House* is
also clearly both London and benighted England, fog-bound, isolated,
a web of litigation between members of a declining *rentier* class, a stew
of poverty, rapaciousness and moral default. But is Martin Amis's
London Fields (1990) really anything more than a rather unpleasant
novel about unpleasant people which simply happens to be set in
1980s Notting Hill – despite the many claims for its metaphorical
stature as a portrait of Thatcherite Britain in terminal decline?

This raises the question as to why some novels transcend their
geographical and temporal settings, and become resonant with wider
allegorical or symbolic meanings and others stay resolutely earthbound
and short-lived? Why, of the many dozens of novels published each
year set in London, do so very few of them qualify even to be
considered as a 'London novel'? The main qualification, surely, is that
the city is not simply a backdrop of the action, but an essential feature
and dominating metaphor throughout. Elizabeth Bowen once said,

'Nothing can happen nowhere', but the relationship between place and action in the novel is not always as successfully achieved as it is in the best of those writings about London, such as in certain novels by Patrick Hamilton, Pamela Hansford Johnson, Graham Greene, Virginia Woolf, Shena MacKay, Iain Sinclair or Michael Moorcock among others. In these the city itself is more than a backdrop, and in fact is part of the very texture of the lives and thoughts of the characters, and constitutes the very air in which they live and breathe. Such novels, which were created out of a London milieu, in turn have created or contributed to the very identity of London itself, so that even today it is impossible not to catch the smell of the Thames mud at low tide at dusk down in Wapping, or to walk through an autumnal London square late at night, or to find oneself in the noise and clamour of a Soho pub at closing time and not see the world filtered through the sensibility of Dickens, Greene or Hamilton. Young black people in London today must feel the same, as they avidly buy and read the new 'rap' novels distributed at the clubs – Headley's *Yardie*, Q's *Deadmeat* – which reflect life on the streets and in the clubs they know at first hand, and realize, as we all do, that the city is written anew every day, and our experience of it is both visual and sensual, but also fashioned in words.

Generic settings

Over time, the London novel – and other realizations of the city through literary forms such as the autobiography, the longer poem, the work of documentary reportage – has developed its own generic traditions and settings. The latter are particularly interesting, for they too represent the key spatial and territorial forms of the city itself, notably in the novel of the street, the novel of the tenement dwelling or rooming-house, and the novel of the bourgeois interior embodying the psycho-drama of familial and sexual relations as lived behind closed doors.

The novel or documentary of the street remains one of the most vivid fictional forms of London writing, deriving its energy and movement from the popular life of the streets, whether in Arthur Morrison's *Tales of Mean Streets* (1894), Katherine Woodward's *Jipping Street* (1928), Nell Dunn's *Up the Junction* (1963), Patrick Hamilton's *Hangover Square* (1941) and *20,000 Streets under the Sky* (1935), Pamela Hansford Johnson's *This Bed Thy Centre* (1936), Samuel Selvon's *The Lonely Londoners* (1956), Colin MacInnes's *Absolute Beginners* (1959), and so on. The very titles of the books themselves signal their preoccupation, and they are often constructed through a

184

multiplicity of minor character studies, infused with a sense of the demotic speech of the streets, largely constructed around a succession of small incidents and contingent happenings, often sentimental, but also mixing both laughter and tears in the tradition of the melodrama or music hall which still haunts the London sensibility, most notably in recent years in Angela Carter's last novel, the engaging mock-theatrical, *Wise Children* (1991). These are novels of public places, of the street, the music hall, the race-track, the pleasure garden, the café or the pub; and the interior lives of the characters are often told directly by the characters themselves, as they are in Carter's exuberant novel, rather than through authorial or third-person narration. Samuel Selvon's *The Lonely Londoners* is directly narrated in the patois and grammar of West Indian speech; Nell Dunn's *Up the Junction*, opens: 'We stand, the three of us, me, Sylvie and Rube, pressed up against the saloon door, brown ales clutched in our hands.'[6] The narrative mode is that of direct storytelling rather than that of explication of events through the workings out of a grand plan.

The tenement novel has also enjoyed a resilient life, represented by, among others, Richard Whiteing's *No. 5 John Street* (1899), Patrick Hamilton's first novel, *Craven House* (1926), Norman Collins's *London Belongs to Me* (1945), Shena MacKay's early and very fine novel, *Music Upstairs* (1965), Lynn Reid Banks's *The L Shaped Room* (1960), Alexander Baron's *The Lowlife* (1963), and the early and powerful novels of Buchi Emecheta such as *In the Ditch* (1972) and *Second Class Citizen* (1977), in which the tenement is replaced by the story of life, racism and hardship on a modern council housing estate. The use of the device of the tenement easily brings together a variety of characters, each with a story to tell, so that London itself is represented by the migrant story. Of course the tenement can also be England, too, as it clearly was in Richard Whiteing's enormously popular novel, *No. 5 John Street*, written out of reforming zeal to show the life of the London poor in the year of Queen Victoria's Diamond Jubilee, reprinted many times in the early part of this century, but now largely and undeservedly forgotten. Whiteing uses the device of a journalist narrator, asked to report on the 'condition of the people' for a foreign ambassador, who acquires a false identity and takes a room in a lodging-house, subsequently telling the story of the people who live there (a device also used in real life by Jack London in *People of the Abyss* and George Orwell in *Down and Out in Paris and London* (1933), and probably still to be used yet again). Luckily for him, No. 5 contains every known working-class stereotype of the period – Low Covey, one of nature's Golden Dustmen, Tilda the Piccadilly flower girl, poor but honest, 'Old 48', an ageing Chartist and republican, together with a self-educated amateur astronomer and a Jewish refugee anarchist who gives lectures in bomb-making to anyone who will listen. What begins as a parody ends as an affectionate portrait of a teeming and resourceful community.

It is not difficult to see how the traditions of the street and tenement novel have now been translated into modern television sitcoms and soap operas, using all the devices of the fictional forms (and earlier melodramatic traditions), in programmes such as *Rising Damp* (the multi-racial tenement), *Only Fools and Horses* or the current soap opera, *EastEnders*, which has all the liveliness, vernacular speech styles and character mix of *Up the Junction* or *City of Spades*, and also is based as much on the life of the street as it is on the domestic interiors.

The psychodrama of the middle-class interior world (both house and inner consciousness) is clearly evident in Graham Green's *End of the Affair* (1951), and in the novels of Elizabeth Brown, Rosamund Lehmann and Iris Murdoch among others. Virginia Woolf's *Mrs Dalloway* (1925), a truly lasting London novel, is *sui generis*, being partly based on the life of the streets and squares, but also mostly based within the mind of the tormented and unhappy narrator. The domestic novel has largely been associated with the 'Hampstead novel', perhaps unfairly, though in the post-war period until well into the 1980s there were an awful lot of not very good novels published about middle-class marriage and betrayal set in north London which rarely looked beyond the lives of the litigants, and which bear some responsibility for atrophying the power of the novel to bear witness to larger issues. The narrowing of the range of the London novel to the confines of a domestic interior left large and important aspects of life in London (notably its rich cosmopolitanism) largely unexamined or even acknowledged.

None of these are watertight compartments, of course, and many novels have moved between locales and genres, yet the nature of the territorial space defined and inhabited by many London novels remains a significant way of defining these historic genres and literary structures.

The cake (and the city) can of course be cut in other ways. Some distinct London districts have over time developed quite strong literary traditions of their own, notably in the literature of the Jewish East End – starting with Israel Zangwill's *Children of the Ghetto* in the 1890s, and moving through the rich tradition of novels and plays by writers such as Alexander Baron, Simon Blumenfield, Willy Goldman, Bernard Kops, Emanuel Litvinoff, Ashley Smith and Arnold Wesker – the topographies, mythologies, tones and cadences of which are still in play in Iain Sinclair's contemporary writings, notably in *Downriver* (1991). I have described this rich East End Jewish fictional tradition at length elsewhere.[7] Soho, not surprisingly, features in many novels, including significant parts of Compton MacKenzie's *Sinister Street*

(1913), through to the novels and documentary reporting of Mark Benney's *Low Company* (1936), and the work of Frank Norman and Colin MacInnes; Soho life and culture is also strongly represented in the writings of Dan Farson, Bernard Kops and others. Only Notting Hill and Hampstead perhaps can claim to have developed strong fictional associations of their own, though in recent years Brixton, in for example David Simon's *Railton Blues* (1983), Geoff Dyer's *The Colour of Memory* (1988), Camden (in the work of Beryl Bainbridge and Alice Thomas Ellis), Stoke Newington and even Wimbledon (in the comic novels of Nigel Williams) have been used and explored as significant locales and distinct psychological territories (as they have equally with television and film). Today visual and literary representations of London life reinforce each other.

In 1988 Michael Moorcock published *Mother London*, a long, labyrinthine novel covering the lives of a group of discharged or voluntary mental patients from 1945 to the present day. It was clearly an attempt to provide a totalizing vision of London's post-war social history, and although unevenly reviewed (and never taken seriously by the dominant metropolitan network of reviewers, publishers, prize panellists and favoured writers), is I believe a serious and important achievement, and will in time be regarded as one of the great novels of London life. The title is taken from a poem by the little known Wheldrake, 'Ode to the Capital':

> LONDON! Mother of Half the Sphere;
> Mother to Commerce: Mother to Ease;
> Parent to Truth; Mistress to Lies;
> Matriarch to Empire's Rule of Peace:
> Mother to Legend: Let Fools despise!

In the novel, David Mummery, one of Moorcock's characters, who earns a living of sorts writing articles on 'Legends of London', is obsessed with London's secret history and 'imagines the city streets to be dry riverbeds ready to be filled from subterranean sources'.[8] Another character, the effusive *boulevardier* Josef Kiss, failed to finish a study on 'London's Hidden Burial Grounds'. Moorcock's small band of penitents, rather like a medieval wandering band of fools, start out in the opening chapter as 'The Patients', and end the novel as 'The Celebrants', seeing signs and portents in every street and change of weather in London that the rest of us fail to see, and embodying a secret knowledge of the city and its endless myths, genealogies and stories. *Mother London* shares with the writings of Iain Sinclair, notably *Scarlett Tracings* (1987) and *Downriver*, Peter Ackroyd's novel *Hawksmoor* (1985), and Barbara Vine's *King Solomon's Carpet* (1991), an obsessive concern with the continuing relationship between past

and present, a sense that history and history's victims leave their scars
and haunting spiritual presences behind them, only adding to the
intensity and distress of subsequent generations. The stones indeed
talk, and the scratchings on the river tunnel walls, in the sewers and
the dungeons, remain unanswered. This is what one might call the
'new cabbalism', a preoccupation with occult presences and
determinations, of irrational correspondences, of hidden rivers and
streams, votaries and gods, of death in life and the nightmare of the
past still weighing down upon the living. Moorcock's great novel
remains essentially humanistic; but there are elements in Sinclair's
writings (which have a brilliant style and a humour of their own) that
are less attractive and rather disturbing. Notable among these is the
obsession with the Jack the Ripper murders and the mythology of the
Krays, both of which have become among some London intellectuals
and booksellers the literary equivalent of collecting Third Reich
militaria or shrunken heads, and equally suspect and distasteful.

King Solomon's Carpet by Barbara Vine (more widely known as
Ruth Rendell), published in 1991 and dedicated 'To the men and
women who work for London Transport Underground', is already
regarded by many as her finest – if her bleakest – novel to date.[9] It
shares with *Mother London* many similar characters and preoccupations. One of her characters, Jarvis, is writing 'a complete
history of the London Underground'; the novel is also based on
another band of lost souls whose lives and relationships make up the
story, though what they share in common is not an outpatients' clinic,
but a large 'squat' in a decaying preparatory school building inherited
by the obsessive chronicler of the underground. Unlike Moorcock's
penitents, Vine's lack almost any kind of self-knowledge or insight into
the city they inhabit: they are broken people, coming from broken
families, and producing in turn unhappy and aimless children. There
is, it has to be said, a very strong sense of original sin in the novel; in
fact the opening epigram is taken from G. K. Chesterton's *The Man
who was Thursday*, written before he finally converted to Catholicism,
in which it is suggested that the victory of the London underground
system is 'the victory of Adam'. There are direct references, too, to
Conrad's fictional portrayal of nihilism in London, *The Secret Agent*,
with Vine's propagandist of the deed, Axel Jonas, looking at himself in
the mirror on the night he sets off to place a bomb in the London
underground and quoting Conrad: 'Mr Verloc, who by a mystic accord
of temperament and necessity, had been set apart to be a secret agent
all his life.' *King Solomon's Carpet* effortlessly transcends the artificial
boundary between 'genre' fiction and 'serious' fiction, but it is actually
a very despairing book, and fails to register any of the positive
attributes of life in the enervating, chaotic, but thronging city.

Other voices, other lives

It was clear by the end of the 1960s that there was a growing discrepancy between British fiction and British fact: notably the enormous social and demographic changes which occurred in the 1960s, including the rise of distinct youth cultures, the displacement of certain kinds of class identities by cultural lifestyles, patterns of immigration and emigration, the impact of feminism, the weakening of religious affiliations, and the growth of an idea (unhappily short-lived) that social change was not only desirable but possible, and that the world was entering a more tolerant and internationally minded era. Popular culture – particularly popular music, film and television – not only was in the forefront of representing these changes but took a leading part in articulating them as well, a claim it would be difficult to make for the novel. The voices of a newly enfranchised and self-confident urban youth began to come through in pop song, in folk music, and in poetry. In Liverpool, Belfast, Newcastle, Glasgow, Manchester, Swansea – in fact many if not all the large cities – local writing and publishing scenes emerged. In London much of this activity was focused on a number of independent bookshops, such as Better Books (where John Lennon met Alan Ginsberg for the first time), Bogle'L'Ouverture (later renamed the Walter Rodney Bookshop in memory of the influential writer they had first published), Central Books, Collet's (whose collection of political magazines and pamphlets from around the world was an international barometer of the politics of the 1960s), Compendium (for many years the only place to buy imported American beat literature and small-press poetry), New Beacon Bookshop, Turret (where Bernard Stone played host to innumerable and important poetry readings), and later on in the 1970s, Grassroots, Centerprise, Sisterwrite, Virago, Silver Moon, Gay's the Word, among others. Anne Walmsley, in her study of the Caribbean Artists' Movement, described how black writers such as E. K. Braithwaite, Andrew Salkey and John La Rose met in and centred their activities on the New Beacon Bookshop in Finsbury Park, which is still trading today.[10] What these bookshops represented was a close and active link between social movements and literary activities, and a continuous and self-reinforcing process of reading, writing, publishing and public debate, which was crucial to the development of new cultural movements.

Linton Kwesi Johnson was originally published by the magazine *Race Today*; Benjamin Zephaniah by Page One Community bookshop in Stratford; Vivian Usherwood, Hugh Boatswain and Sandra Agard by Centerprise. The first fully fledged anthology of Black British Caribbean writing in Britain, *News for Babylon*, edited by James Berry and published by Chatto & Windus in 1984 was largely collected from work originally published in small, community-based presses and magazines. One of the pioneering collections of feminist writing, *Tales I Tell My Mother*, published in 1978 by the tiny London-based radical publishing house, Journeyman Press, contained early work by a collective of women writers made up of Zoe Fairbairns, Sara Maitland, Valerie Miner, Michèle Roberts and Michelene Wandor, all of whom went on to produce important work in a variety of forms, both within radical and mainstream traditions, demonstrating the value of these networks and groups.

Not surprisingly, many of these new voices often emerged in educational (formal and informal) settings, or as part of social and political movements, either as a result of encouragement, or as a compulsion to bear witness. Few were motivated initially by the challenge of literary creativity *per se*, or by the social status or financial gain that might accrue from professional writing or being published commercially. Much of the writing emerged from community-based workshops or collectives (such as the Journeyman anthology mentioned above), inspired often by a culture of public readings and political festivals. The Black and Third World Book Fairs, organized annually in London from the late 1970s onwards, held in various town halls provided by sympathetic local councils (I attended such festivals in Lambeth, Islington, Camden and Ealing town halls in that period, where the atmosphere was often exuberant and even electric with hope and energy) brought writers (and the work of small publishers) from all over the world, and were enormously important in consolidating an indigenous black literary tradition in the UK.

In London, much of the early writing by young black people emerged directly from schools, particularly from Tulse Hill (where Linton Kwesi Johnson began his writing career), from Stepney (where teacher Chris Searle was sacked in 1973 for publishing an anthology of children's poetry, *Stepney Words*), and from various schools in Hackney as a result of the Centerprise community publishing initiative, or from other community presses such as Commonplace Workshop and Black Ink. Also important at this time was the ILEA (Inner London Education Authority) English Centre, and English teachers' resource centre, which produced several very fine anthologies of young people's autobiographical writing – much of it about their experience of London as first-generation British citizens, or as newly arrived migrants. These school writings often represented a great outpouring of frustration, anger and despair. Indeed Chris Searle was sacked as much for the 'pessimistic' tone of the *Stepney Words* anthology as he was for the presumption of publishing it without permission. The autobiographical writings published in the English Centre anthology,

Our Lives, many of which were by recent arrivals to Britain, recounted direct experiences of fleeing from genocide, of witnessing the rape and torture of family and friends, of famine and flood, of separation and the pain of exile, of life in children's homes and in care in ways which made conventional teenage writing and publishing seem not only inappropriate but in bad taste. Yet these were the new Londoners, young people from many countries throughout the world, exploring through writing a new identity in a new city in a new land. London's traditional geographies were configured anew.

Some of the most trenchant writing about the black experience is still emerging from self-published or community-based networks and traditions. Victor Headley's novel, *Yardie,* was published originally by X-Press in 1992, set up by two journalists from the *The Voice,* a long-standing newspaper for Britain's black community, and sold mostly in dance clubs, in hairdressers' shops, and on the streets. The title was republished by Pan in 1993. Headley's novel uses a fast-paced, action-packed narrative to describe with considerable realism the world of Jamaican drug-dealing in London, the club scene and the fragmented relationships of those who get caught up and involved. It is largely based in Harlesden and Stoke Newington, with very little attempt to disguise real streets, clubs or estates. Much of the dialogue is written in a tough patois or slang, and the narrative takes no sides in describing a violent, amoral and ruthless world, one in which women are mostly treated with a callous, bemused contempt. It makes very uncomfortable reading, largely, one assumes, because it rings authentically true. *Deadmeat,* a novel by a young black writer who calls himself Q, was originally written on an Apple Mac at a neighbourhood business resource centre in Notting Hill, and sold outside clubs from a specially painted Ford Escort car. It has sold thousands of copies and, again, has been bought up to be republished by one of the mainstream publishing houses. This relationship echoes, of course, precisely that of the music industry, where the small labels discover and promote the new talent and new ideas, which the 'majors' then buy up once the risk element is absolved.

Many black and feminist writers who started out in the local workshops, in the educational projects or with the community-based presses, have gone on to mainstream success, as the subsequent careers of the original contributors to the *Tales I Tell My Mother* anthology clearly show. Benjamin Zephaniah's second collection of poetry was published by Heinemann; Hanif Kureishi, it should be remembered, began his career attending workshops for aspiring young playwrights at the Royal Court Theatre. A number of writers involved in workshops at Centerprise, and first published there, such as Roger Mills, Lotte Moos, Rebecca O'Rourke and Bridget O'Connor, are now published by mainstream publishing houses. In fact, Rebecca O'Rourke's feminist thriller, *Jumping the Cracks* (1987), is one of the more successful recent attempts to use the thriller form to explore a range of social issues – housing corruption, street crime, sexual identity – whilst attempting to get inside the subculture and topography of a particular part of London, while Bridget O'Connor's first book of short stories, *Here Comes John* (1993), establishes yet another powerful first-person testimony to the febrile post-punk London lifestyles of the 1990s.

What is now clearly evident is that, since the 1960s, some of the most powerful writing about London has emerged in more fragmented forms, and through many different routes and channels. This reflects probably more acutely the creative sources and new solidarities of London's cosmopolitan experience, than the more traditional and conventional mainstream novel. There is still a wide gap between the London represented by what the mainstream publishing houses produce and that evident in the community-based initiatives. Partly this remains a clash of literary form: publishers understand and want to publish novels, yet many emergent voices and experiences come through strongest in the form of oral history, testimony or direct storytelling. Perhaps the greatest lacuna in the continuing London narrative is that of the Irish labourer in London. A long history of male immigration to the capital to work on the building sites or on the great civil engineering projects, establishing tremendous networks based in pubs, dance halls, lodging houses, and with a considerable mythology of its own, is hardly recorded at all either in print, on tape, on the stage or in any other form of cultural representation, including the novel.

The growth of 'alternative comedy' and the rise of performance poetry, has reinstated the importance of the spoken word in the articulation and representation of experience to a wider audience. As James Berry pointed out in his introduction to *News for Babylon*, the importance of a group such as RAPP (Radical Alliance of Poets and Players) in the 1970s to the growth of the performance tradition, mixing music with poems, stories and ballads, was considerable, a tradition strengthened more recently by Apples & Snakes, a very successful promoter of poetry readings in pubs, schools, clubs, and a real forcing house of new literary talent among young people. They judiciously programme an appropriate mix of performance poetry, music and storytelling, using the skills more of a variety promoter than a traditional literary agent or editor. Storytelling in London now has a regular venue in a Camden pub, the Crick-Crack Club, and its organizational and promotional skills are currently in great demand, particularly in schools.

So what is clear is that even if the 'London novel' remains a contested project, the wish to tell stories, to speak to each other, to articulate and sometimes celebrate the life of the city and its cosmopolitan peoples, is as protean and expressive as ever. The novel as a literary form has enjoyed a long life and survived many attempts to supplant, renew or reinvent it. Yet in the life of the modern cosmopolitan city, at times it seems a weak form of representation, particularly in the shape of the short-run hardback novel written and published within a purely 'literary' critical and cultural tradition. The renewed interest in the short story, and of storytelling itself, may tell us something generally about a desire among readers to return fiction to a much closer association with everyday speech, to the rhythms of patois and dialect, to the expressiveness of the vernacular, to the ways in which people every day try in some ways to tell a story – and get heard.

References

1 Mike Phillips, *Blood Rights* (London, Michael Joseph, 1989), p.66.
2 Interview with Emanuel Litvinoff, *Guardian*, 27 March 1993.
3 Samuel Selvon, *The Lonely Londoners* (London, Longman, 1956).
4 Patrick Hamilton, *The Slaves of Solitude* (London, Constable, 1947).
5 Lennard J. Davis, *Factual Fictions: The Origins of the English Novel* (New York, Columbia University Press, 1983), p.125.
6 Nell Dunn, *Up the Junction* (London, McGibbon & Kee, 1963).
7 Ken Worpole, *Dockers and Detectives* (London, Verso, 1983).
8 Michael Moorcock, *Mother London* (London, Secker & Warburg, 1988).
9 Barbara Vine, *King Solomon's Carpet* (London, Viking, 1991).
10 Anne Walmsley, *The Caribbean Artists' Movement* (London, New Beacon Books, 1992).

10

Writing from the margins

GEORGE WOTTON

Commenting on the cultural designation of certain regions as 'subordinate areas', Raymond Williams observed that while the lives of people of particularly favoured regions 'are seen as essentially general, even perhaps normal' the life and people of other regions are seen as, precisely, 'regional' and he asks whether

> a novel, 'set in' or 'about' the Home Counties, or 'set in' or 'about' London or some district of London – Chelsea, Hampstead, or Bloomsbury – would be described as 'regional' in a way comparable to descriptions of similar novels 'set in' or 'about' the Lake District or South Devon or mid-Wales – or, shall we say, Dorset or 'Wessex'?[1]

Williams describes the late-bourgeois prejudice which marginalizes novels 'set in' or 'about' different kinds of social life because the novel is regarded as being essentially about people, individuals 'living sexually, spiritually, and above all privately'. He adds that the 'very idea of a novel which recognizes a wider social life is pushed away',[2] pushed, in other words, to the periphery.

In this ideological structuring of cultural space, the private and spiritual concerns of the metropolitan and international middle class which Doris Lessing described as 'that class of the world's citizens who have the best of everything',[3] are located at the centre. The effect of this ideological centring is the marginalization of the material and social relations which keep the bourgeoisie in power. Although he did not have the novel in mind, Timpanaro's observation that 'every ruling class always needs a discourse on spiritual values suggests the ideological necessity for this emphasis.[4] By placing the private and spiritual life of the individual at the centre and locating social and material life at the periphery, a distorted mirror image of social relations is produced in which the 'spiritual values' of the bourgeoisie appear to sustain the material edifice of society. Any writing which springs out of the social life of a particular group, whether of gender, class or race or any combination of these, is automatically perceived as peripheral.

F. R. Leavis's critical judgements in *The Great Tradition* are notoriously dismissive in this sense. On the one hand there are the 'great' writers such as George Eliot compared by Leavis to Tolstoy 'who, we all know, is pre-eminent in getting "the spirit of life itself"'. Or Henry James whose 'registration of sophisticated human consciousness is one of the classical creative achievements' which '*added* something as only genius can . . . of great human significance. He creates an ideal civilized sensibility'.[5] Thomas Hardy, on the other hand, writing about the life and labour of 'Wessex', reflecting on the economic chaos of the great depression at the end of the nineteenth century which largely destroyed an entire social group, is dismissed as 'a provincial manufacturer of gauche and heavy fictions'.[6] What is central, what is 'of great human significance' is the creation of an ideal civilized sensibility, giving form to the spirit of life itself. What is peripheral is giving form to the material lives of a particular social group. In another context, Virginia Woolf similarly dismissed certain voices to the margins when she wrote:

> In *Middlemarch* and in *Jane Eyre* we are conscious not merely of the writer's character, as we are conscious of the character of Charles Dickens, but we are conscious of a woman's presence – of someone resenting the treatment of her sex and pleading for its rights. This brings into women's writing an element which is entirely absent from a man's, unless, indeed, he happens to be a working man, a Negro, or one who for some other reason is conscious of disability. It introduces a distortion and is frequently the cause of weakness.[7]

To write *as* a worker, or a black person or a woman is to write from the position of one 'conscious of disability'. Dickens, on the other hand, while he writes about any number of 'disabilities' – social, psychological, emotional, spiritual – does not do so as one who feels himself disabled. In other words the major writer's central concern should be 'man' not 'men', and he or she may write about all forms of social injustice as long as they do not write as one of a socially disadvantaged group.

In fact, as Lionel Trilling points out, the great tradition of the European realist novel is based on just the tale of the disadvantaged man but not, clearly, written by men 'resenting their treatment'. Writing of that great line of novels which runs through the nineteenth century, mentioning Stendhal, Balzac, Dickens, Flaubert, Tolstoy,

Dostoevsky and James, Trilling observes of their central characters:

> The defining hero may be known as the Young Man from the Provinces. He may not come from the provinces in literal fact, his social class may constitute his province . . . equipped with poverty, pride, and intelligence, (he) stands outside life and seeks to enter . . . Usually his motive is the legendary one of seeking his fortune, which is what the folktale says when it means that the hero is seeking himself . . . It is (his) fate . . . to move from an obscure position into one of considerable eminence in Paris or London or St Petersburg, to touch the life of the rulers of the earth.[8]

In this fabulous tale of self-discovery the disadvantaged hero moves from the periphery to the centre. The reason for these quests being entirely free from the 'distortion' of special pleading is to be found in the idealist nature of their goal. In a world bereft of inherent meaning, George Lukács observed, the individual's ideas become ideals and individuality becomes 'an aim unto itself'.[9] Reflecting this idealism, the bourgeois novel assumes the form of a journey undertaken by the hero towards self-realization. The journey becomes a flight from the tarnished reality of class society to the illumination of self-recognition which 'irradiates the individual's life as its immanent meaning'. What the hero finds through experience is that a 'mere glimpse of meaning is the highest that life has to offer'.[10] And while the nineteenth-century novel is obsessively concerned with class relations, in what we might call the dominant ideological structure of perceptions, individual, personal and private relationships are seen as central while social, class, economic and political relations are seen as marginal. If we take the term political to mean 'the way we organize our social life together, and the power-relations which this involves'[11] then we might suggest, adapting a phrase of Walter Benjamin, that what we see in the English novel is the progressive privatization of politics. As we move into and through the twentieth century, that 'privatization' becomes progressively concerned with the exploration of sexuality. Without question what Raymond Williams referred to as the late bourgeois prejudice of seeing the novel as being about the sexual, spiritual and private lives of individuals, has meant that while the lives of Isabel Archer or Clarissa Dalloway or Stephen Dedalus or Gerald Crich are deemed to be central to an understanding of the English Novel, the life of Frank Owen (who?) is not. Yet the voice of Frank Owen is one of the most significant in English fiction in that it articulates for the first time a theoretical understanding of the *social* relations upon which our society is founded.

What distinguishes Robert Tressell's *The Ragged Trousered Philanthropists* (first published in 1914, three years after Tressell's death) is that its subject is neither the awful social conditions in which the people he describes lived, nor their personal relationships, but the *relations of production* which produced those conditions and impoverished those individual lives. What Tressell's novel reveals is the naked and unremitting exploitation upon which the capitalist system is built and upon which alone it can survive and flourish. The crucial factor in this perception is the position from which the novel was written, that is, not just working class, but socialist and regional. We may emphasize the point by contrasting Tressell's position with that of Dickens. While no one had greater sympathy than Dickens for the suffering of 'the people', or was more adept at exposing the *effects* of the social relations of capitalist society, the true nature of those relations remains in his work 'a muddle' in that the nature of the system is forever unknowable. This is not the case with Tressell who knew that the system was comprehensible and showed where a true understanding of it was to be located – not in the subjective search for 'authentic values', the idealist quest for the 'meaning of life' but in the material activity of earning a living, the 'Battle for Life'. That is why the novel's dominant motif is not work itself (as it is, for example, in many of Hardy's novels), but driven work, sweated, rushed, pushed, scamped, botched work. For it was Tressell's intention to show how the capitalist system reduced all forms and kinds of productive human activity to the level of an exploitable commodity – labour power. The nature of the whole system is captured in the Bunyanesque/Dickensian names of the Mugsborough building and decorating firms – Makehaste and Slogget, Bluffum and Doemdown, Dodger and Scampit, Pushem and Sloggem, Snatcham and Graball, Smeeriton and Leavit, Dauber and Botchit. These constitute the town's 'ruling class', the Forty Thieves, the Brigands and Bandits headed by Messrs Didlum, Grinder, Rushton and Sweater, the robbers who prey on the inhabitants of Mugsborough. What these names suggest is both the driving exploitation of the workers on the one hand and the rapacious cheating of the customers on the other. Between these two – the producer and the consumer – is realized the true object of the whole system, namely the profit which constitutes the Forty Thieves' plunder.

Remarkably, however, it is not the exploiting class which is the object of Tressell's anger but the working class itself. And this marks the novel off from all those nineteenth-century social problem or 'condition of England' novels which take the bourgeoisie to task for not showing moral, spiritual or cultural leadership. Indeed, part of Tressell's intention is to deride Matthew Arnold's notion that the bourgeoisie are the 'natural leaders' of the working class. This is not a novel 'about' the working class, addressed, over their heads, to middle-class readers. This novel is addressed to the working class and if

Tressell expresses disgust it is not the workers themselves who disgust him but their complacency, their unwillingness to throw off the mind-forged manacles which keep them chained in ignorance of the true causes of their poverty. Tressell wanted to show them how they are deprived of their capacity to think *for themselves*, to realize their proper self-interest as a class. It is their failure to do this which constitutes their philanthropy, working themselves to death not for their own well-being or that of their children, but for the people who exploit them, the Sweaters and the Diddlers, the Grinders and the Slumrents and the Starvems:

> In their infancy they had been taught to distrust their own intelligence and to leave 'thinking' to their 'pastors' and masters and to their 'betters' generally. All their lives they had been true to this teaching, they had always had blind, unreasoning faith in the wisdom and humanity of their pastors and masters. That was the reason why they and their children had been all their lives on the verge of starvation and nakedness, whilst their 'betters' – who did nothing but the thinking – went clothed in purple and fine linen and fared sumptuously every day.[12]

That peculiar 'tone of voice' which is a combination of political debate and popular storytelling is unique to Tressell's novel. At the political level this takes the form of the talks the two radicals, Owen and Barrington, have with Owen's fellow workers to try to explain their real conditions of existence. At the popular level it takes the form of a series of parodies of sermons, after-dinner speeches, council meetings, political party speeches, various public meetings. It is the only novel in English in which this form of address is dominant, radically different from the bourgeois novel with its characteristic mode of private address. That and the anger which comes from Frank Owen's ever present awareness that he is not only up against the system, but up against his fellow workers who refuse to see, who *do not want* to see, that the system which exploits them so ruthlessly can be changed and that they themselves can change it. Two important factors contribute to this refusal. The first has to do with place, for Mugsborough (based on Hastings) is quite unlike those 'self-conscious and confident working-class communities'[13] which were centred on a major industry such as mining, steel-making or ship-building. In Mugsborough with its mixed trades and service industries, small building firms and tradesmen, there is, as Williams points out, 'no common over-riding loyalty proceeding from the conditions of the mining village or dockyard street'.[14] Nor is there the same opportunity for political solidarity and unity of action amongst such a divided and scattered population of workers. The second factor is more complex as it has to do with a perceived identity of interests of the exploited with their exploiters which is mediated through the ideology of 'Englishness' and given ready expression in the pride of being a member of an imperial race and in hatred of the foreigner. Alloyed with chauvinism and even racism, it has to do with that deeply engrained strain of what might be called patriotic anti-socialism which identifies socialism with foreignness, with infernal doctrines born in *continental* back-slums. Significantly, the first chapter of Tressell's novel lays bare the way working-class jingoism is manipulated to transform political action into a racist 'Anti-Foreign Crusade' against 'the bloody foreigner'. The real (class) enemy is embraced in a common hatred of the false: 'The foreigner was the enemy, and the cause of poverty and bad trade.' Joseph Conrad, who would have been amongst the first to denounce Owen's ideas, expressed this rampant anti-socialist chauvinism in language which would be well received in some quarters today:

> The International Socialist Association are triumphant, and every disreputable ragamuffin in Europe feels that the day of universal brotherhood, despoliation and disorder is coming apace, and nurses daydreams of well-plenished pockets amongst the ruin of all that is respectable, venerable and holy . . . Where's the man to stop the rush of social-democratic ideas? The opportunity and the day have come and gone! Believe me: gone for ever! For the sun is set and the last barrier removed. England was the only barrier to the pressure of infernal doctrines born in continental back-slums. Now, there is nothing![15]

A hundred years after Conrad wrote those words many believed that the 'man' had been found and that the tide had, at last, been turned. A grateful nation continues to pay tribute to the avowed enemies of those infernal doctrines no matter what the cost.

Soaked in the imperialist chauvinism and rabid anti-socialist rhetoric of the right-wing press, Tressell's impoverished philanthropists allow their intellectual power to be exploited no less than their labour power. They live in the ideology of 'it can't be helpedism' which they express in the eternal grumbling at 'things as they are', bearing their hardship with the stoic resignation expressed in the old music hall song:

> Its the rich wot gets the money
> Its the poor wot gets the blame
> Its the same the whole world over
> Ain't it all a bleedin shame.

Despite Frank Owen's deep contempt for his fellow workers' abnegation, we must be aware of their vulnerability to the ideological assault constantly being mounted against them. Owen's frustration is caused by a belief, shared by many socialists, that a 'scientific' understanding of social relations *dispels* ideology. This belief is based on the false assumption that what we might call ideology's field of operation is limited to human consciousness and ideology is identified with 'having ideas'. In class terms this means that any member of the working class who identifies with the 'ideas' of the class which exploits her or him is the subject of 'false consciousness'. Socialism endeavours to produce a 'true consciousness' by opening people's eyes to their real conditions of life. In reality, if ideology could be dispersed by science, knowledge or theory, like early morning mist by the warmth of the rising sun, then the revolution would long have been fought and won. It is just because ideology is not solely, or even primarily, a matter of consciousness that it poses such an intractable problem for those who would attack it through reason.

To the dominant class ideology, being working class is indeed a condition. Nobody in their right mind would *want* to be working class any more than they would want rickets or scabies. The people of the abyss, the denizens of the netherworld, the underclass are 'unfortunate', literally without fortune. The only cure for this unfortunate condition is to become middle class. Given an open, democratic society with no barriers to social mobility, those who remain in the working class must self-evidently lack the will to 'get on'. Dickens mercilessly satirized this entrepreneurial ideology in *Hard Times* and, fifty years later, Tressell ruthlessly exposed the relations of production which sustained it. But what is absent from both their texts is any sense of an oppositional working-class ideology. For a sense of what that might be, we have to turn to a novel written almost fifty years after *The Ragged Trousered Philanthropists*, set in the same period although in a very different place.

Kiddar's Luck, first published in 1951, is the story of the first fourteen years in the life of Willie Kiddar, a working-class Geordie. While Frank Owen was struggling to open his fellow workers' eyes to the realities of their oppression in Hastings, at the other end of the country Willie Kiddar was busy exploring the streets of Newcastle upon Tyne. And this is a very different sort of community from Mugsborough. Whereas *The Ragged Trousered Philanthropists* is set largely in the house where the painters and decorators work, aptly named 'The Cave', *Kiddar's Luck* is located in the street. For Jack Common, the street has enormous ideological significance for, as he observed in one of his essays,

> You can usually deduce your fellow-Briton's status from the way he regards the street. To some it is merely a communication between

one spot and another, a channel or runway to guide your feet or your wheels when you are going places. To others it is where you live.[16]

It is where you live, in this kind of working-class community, because it signifies an ideological relationship to your world: while the middle classes live 'privately' in their homes, the working class lives *communally* in the street. Common goes on to write of a characteristic working-class scene:

> crowds of kids flying here and there across the road; boys and youths by the shopwindows and the corner-ends; men strolling the pavements or sitting shirt-sleeved by the doors; and the women in their aprons taking a breather in a bit of gossip with 'next-door'. These people live in the street. But don't think its all a bleedin shame, the way we've got to be thinking about nearly every working-class circumstance. Why, there's such a good communal stir and warmth out on the pavements that it would be a queer kiddy that would sooner sit indoors than mix in it – even if indoors was a palace! From his earliest days he is committed to the communality outside.[17]

That communality, entirely absent in Mugsborough, is the product of a Tyneside where 'almost everyone was working-class':

> Our fathers worked on the railway, in the factory, in the shipyard, most of them, and you get the scale of it for this area if you reflect that a factory or shipyard employing five thousand men would be unlikely to count more than two hundred and fifty middle-class folk among them.[18]

The only time Kiddar moves out of that world is during his brief friendship with the petty-bourgeois Edmund from whose claustrophobic home environment Willie flees. Even before he could properly walk he gains 'the freedom of the streets':

> when you could crawl and totter, you always made for the street whenever the door was open ... [it] was my second home ... I had the freedom of it by right and could come into its full heritage whenever I was able ... I belonged to that street by the same right that I had to belong to a particular family in it, and this social certitude stayed with me as it did with all of us, no matter what contemporary upheaval might be splitting our homes apart.[19]

Willie Kiddar is at home in those streets, partaking of the freedom they bestow on him as a right. Despite poverty, hardship and domestic tragedies the individual shares a sense of security, 'social certitude', which comes of belonging to, and being part of, a community where to be by oneself does not have the sense of being alone.

Here there is none of the 'ontological insecurity' we find expressed in the works of modernist writers who consistently express their sense of essential alienation. It is the very opposite of isolation which Willie Kiddar finds in his journey through the streets because in the working-class crowd 'you got a more vivid sense of your own being'.[20] As 'a member from birth of the community of the streets'[21] the individual is completely integrated into the working-class environment, feels at home in it. We get the full impact of this sense of belonging if we compare it with that more common perception of the city as alien, threatening, inhuman, ugly and above all, alienating. The imprisoning streets of Dickens's London, for example, 'melancholy streets in a penitential garb of soot' which 'steeped the souls of the people . . . in dire despondency'.[22] Or the totally *unknowable* streets of Conrad's London, swarming with its inhuman inhabitants who are 'numerous like locusts, industrious like ants, thoughtless like a natural force . . . impervious to sentiment, to logic, to terror too, perhaps'.[23] Or the ugly streets through which Connie Chatterley passes and from which she feels so alienated, sensing only 'the utter negation of the gladness of life', asking herself 'what could possibly become of such a people . . . in whom the living intuitive faculty was dead as nails, and only queer mechanical yells and uncanny will-power remained?'[24]

The difference between *those* streets and the freedom of the known community of the streets and the 'inner gaiety of the crowds'[25] in *Kiddar's Luck* suggests both the novel's integrity and its limitations. Willie Kiddar's world is, in Raymond Williams's phrase, a knowable community. Knowable, however, in the sense of intimately *experienced*. To know that world in the way Tressell attempts to know it, the relations of the community of the streets have to be placed against the relations of exploitation of the wider world of which the intimate community is only a part. While Tressell endeavours to produce a *knowledge*, in the strict sense of a theoretical understanding, of those relations, what we have in *Kiddar's Luck* is both more limited but also more difficult to articulate because it does not have the coherence of a political or economic theory. For what Common gives us in his novel is a view of what we can only call a working-class ideology, an ideology which is not specifically political let alone socialist.

This historically specific ideology is determined by many factors which are not themselves ideological but, for example, geographical and historical: Northumbria, that ancient border country with its strong regional traditions; economic: the specific nature of the productive activity in which the workers were engaged (heavy industry), which determined a particular form of the division of labour; socio-cultural: the identity drawn from being a Tynesider, a Geordie. While such factors all contribute to the specific form of the ideology, the ultimately determining factor was the relations of production, class relations. For any working-*class* ideology is born of a situation, and *The Ragged Trousered Philanthropists* shows this over and over again, where there is no survival for the individual outside the group. This is not an altruistic ideal but a legitimate self-interest, a materialist strategy for self-defence, a recognition that the individual can survive only through the solidarity of the collectivity. This was the ideology of people who were, in Common's words, 'in terror of being utterly defeated; it belongs to the days when the all-conquering bourgeoisie were so confident of carrying everything before them that all you could hope for was to check their rapacity two or three paces off murder'.[26]

The necessity for political solidarity in face of this constant economic threat finds ideological expression in the unequivocal rejection of what Common frequently refers to as bourgeois individualism. Willie Kiddar soon discovers what the workers in Tressell's novel never do, that 'Our Lord Jesus Christ [is] the traditional patron of individualism'.[27] Those who had taken to Christianity and 'struck out the collective bit, contracted out of comradeship'[28] were not part of the community of the streets. They were the ones who had gone over, ideologically, to the side of the ruling class, deserted the collectivity to embrace individualism and worship, even in the figure of Jesus Christ, the bourgeois hero – the individual. As Common wrote in an early essay:

> The private man, the single individual, has been our hero. For his sake we have made history the record of great individuals, we have made art individual self-expression, as authentic almost as religion in its powers of revelation; we have gained a literature given over to the fond study of the humble individual character; even the Son of God has become for us Jesus the Miraculous Person.[29]

It is against this ruling ideology that the freedom of the streets stands, a necessary survival tactic in face of a rapacious ruling class. But Common shows that it also has a positive side, for if 'I' is indeed only realizable on the basis of 'we', then individuals may achieve their true identity and full potential through the community. What the freedom of the streets bestows on the individual is a true sense of oneself as a member of a class. Being a member of the working class is, or can be, a matter of *choice* and this is what the ruling ideology has always to suppress by representing being working class as a failure: in bourgeois ideology the working class is represented 'not as a separate class of different traditions to the dominant one' but merely as 'a category of the least successful would-be bourgeoisie; men in whom the authentic economic flame burns though dimly'.[30] On the contrary, claims Common:

> many people actually choose to work as proletarians, not because that's the only work they'd ever be able to do but because it actually seems more attractive to them. It comes naturally after the corner-lad stage. In the factories, mines and shipyards, there is the same opportunity for physical hardihood, the same rough equality and unadorned respect for one's essential manhood, the same sense of outlawry and alien oppression formerly represented by the teacher and the constable, now symbolised by the bosses and the managerial staff. If you were happy in the street, you'll be at home in the works.[31]

So the community of the streets turns naturally into the community of the factory, mine or shipyard. Unity, solidarity, community and the sense of personal identity. All these are on the positive side, but their very strength points to the negative side, the limitations and absences.

In *Kiddar's Luck*, class relations are radically simplified because of the nature of the labour process on which the community depended. In Tressell's novel, on the other hand, because that unitary and unifying activity is absent, class relations are much more complex. Again, it is the dominant labour process which points to the other major difficulty: 'if you were happy in the street, you'll be at home in the works'. But who is that 'you'? We are bound to realize that the subjects of this working-class ideology are *masculine*. 'Many people actually choose to work as proletarians', but those people turn out to be the 'fortunates [who] sit round in dirty overalls, proud of their calloused hands, the tang of maleness on them from rubbing against a rough crowd in the local shipyard or factory'.[32] What the life in the streets trains 'people' for is the working life in the factory, mine or shipyard where 'there is the same opportunity for physical hardihood, the same rough equality and unadorned respect for one's essential manhood, the same sense of outlawry and alien oppression'. As soon as the young Kiddar can totter he makes for the street to assume his rightful freedom. But this is also the first step which takes him away from the disorganized, domestic, female world of the 'Ma Gang', his first step into the essentially masculine world of work in the shipyard or the factory.

Louis Althusser defined ideology as an expression of the *lived* relations between people and their world, that is, 'not the relation between them and their conditions of existence, but *the way* they live the relation between them and their conditions of existence'.[33] This gives us an indication of the difference between *The Ragged Trousered*

Philanthropists and *Kiddar's Luck* in that while Tressell's novel is mainly concerned with the relations between people and their conditions of existence (relations of exploitation), *Kiddar's Luck* is concerned predominantly with the way people live the relation between them and their conditions of existence in and through ideology, in this case a defensive, masculinist ideology of rebellious manhood, what we might call the ideology of 'the breadwinner'. *Kiddar's Luck* was produced out of the contradiction between the real fact of exploitation and a specific way of *living* that exploitation, that is, between the real wage slavery of the factory workers and the way those workers *lived* that slavery as an 'imaginary' kind of freedom. To understand which is to understand all those 'restrictive practices' – demarcation disputes, tea-break stoppages, the readiness to strike over apparent 'trivialities', – which grew out of a long struggle in defence of that 'freedom'. All those local actions were the guerrilla tactics of the class struggle. It is for this that the 'Street Warfare' (chapter 7) prepared the new generation of workers, namely the constant 'warfare' against 'alien oppression' represented, for the boy, in the figures of teacher and constable, and for the man by the bosses and the managerial staff.

Again, this emphasizes the major division upon which capitalist society is built as well as the forms of conflict it engenders. This, however, is not only a matter of class but also of gender divisions. In *Kiddar's Luck* there is a radical division between the world of work and the world of home, the one inhabited by men, the other by women, and for this separation the life of the streets is also a preparation. When the boys and girls come out to play on Third Avenue their games are quite different. In the separate activities of the boys' gangs and the girls' gangs the division of labour in the adult world is reflected. It produces antagonism and conflict which runs through the novel in the form of domestic quarrels between Willie's parents and is more sharply depicted in the domestic chaos of the swarming life of Oystershell Lane. Between the order of the 'productive' world of work (represented by Mr Kiddar's clocks and timetables) and the chaos of the 'reproductive' world of home (represented by Mrs Kiddar's lameness, untidiness and insobriety) there is perpetual friction. It is caused by the lack of understanding each has of the other's experience of exploitation and the resentment this radical separation produces. Neither can escape from their respective forms of exploitation and yet they cannot share their experience so that there is less solidarity between husband and wife who are separated by their different activities than there is between workmates or the housewife members of the Ma Gang.

Willie Kiddar was eleven in 1914 and perpetual president of The Sons of the Battle Axe. Far from being the idealized period of boyhood innocence before the onset of adulthood, the play at being outlaws was an ideological apprenticeship for life as an industrial worker. Over half a century later another child roams the streets of a working-class quarter of a city in the north-east of England, the eleven-year-old Kelly Brown. She, too, is 'at home' in the streets:

> The street was her home now . . . She moved through the empty streets with unnamed purposes at work inside her, and her body, inside its boy's clothing, was as cold and inviolate as ice . . . she seemed to be drying up, to be turning into a machine. Her legs, pumping up and down the cold street, had the regularity and power of pistons. And her hands . . . were as heavy and lifeless as tools.[34]

How are we to account for this remarkable difference? Sixty years of 'progress' separate Kelly Brown from Willie Kiddar. How is it that the member from birth of the community of the streets turns into a machine-like marauder haunting a decaying community of derelicts? In the twenty years between the publication of *Kiddar's Luck* (1951) and the time in which *Union Street* is set (1971–2) profound changes had taken place in British society, the most far-reaching being the change from a mass-production to a mass-consumption society. Although this had been a developing trend since Britain ceased to be the primary 'workshop of the world' in the last quarter of the nineteenth century, it was only in the decades after the end of the Second World War that it became the dominant fact of economic life. This radical change had profound consequences for the patterns of British working-class life, eroding, as Eric Hobsbawm has pointed out, 'the very foundations of the working class as traditionally understood, that is the men and women who got their hands dirty at work, mainly in mines, factories, or working with, or around, some kind of engines'.[35] The effect of this relentless transformation was the destruction of the working-class community as Jack Common had known it, based as it had been on specific productive processes.

Union Street gives us a detailed view of the effects of this accelerating process of deindustrialization on the 'traditional' working-class community. But the novel focuses on a critical moment in this development, a winter of particular discontent. Unemployment had risen to a post-war peak and the TUC was in conflict with the Heath government over its legislation on industrial relations. It was a period which culminated, in the words of one historian, 'in the most bitter class conflict the country had witnessed since the General Strike of 1926'.[36] Of those months, a senior advisor to the Heath government later wrote:

> At the time many of those in positions of influence looked into the abyss and saw only a few days away the possibility of the country

being plunged into a state of chaos not so very far removed from that which might prevail after a minor nuclear attack. If that sounds melodramatic I need only say that – with the prospect of the breakdown of power supplies, sewerage, communications, effective government and law and order – it was an analogy that was being used at the time.[37]

That sense of social crisis is echoed in the acute crisis in the lives of the inhabitants of Union Street. But the novel was written and published a decade after those events, a decade which had seen only the rapid worsening of the situation to a point where mass unemployment was four times the level it had been in 1972 due, in large measure, to the wholesale dismantling of those industries which had sustained the 'traditional' working-class communities. Suddenly the rhetoric of the 'hungry forties' – the 1840s – returned, the rhetoric of social anarchy, of the two nations, of North and South. But whereas the novelists of the 1840s and 1850s – Dickens, Disraeli, Gaskell, Kingsley – had been visitors to the terrible birth struggles of those communities, Barker writes about their equally terrible death, not from the perspective of a visitor to the deathbed but rather from that of the dying. In a sense it is a return to Mugsborough, to a working class scattered and divided, bamboozled by propaganda and terrorized by unemployment, but with one major and defining difference: it is a world in which men have no place. As the 'productive' world of *The Ragged Trousered Philanthropists* and *Kiddar's Luck* was a world of men without women, so the 'consumerist' world of *Union Street* is one of women without men, a world in which men are redundant – unemployed, retired, absent, dying or dead.

If the location of *The Ragged Trousered Philanthropists* is the workplace and *Kiddar's Luck* is located in the 'traditional' masculine communality of the streets, then the location of *Union Street* is the home, signifying 'family' rather than 'work'. It is essential to understand this distinction correctly in order that women's labour in the home is seen neither as 'natural' to them, nor as being of lesser importance than labour performed outside it. Indeed, were it not for the (unpaid) labour performed in the home the capitalist system would grind to a halt, for the 'family' is the very source and fount of the commodity from which surplus value is extracted, namely labour power. However, because the working-class novel has tended to be concerned only with the world of 'work', where the productive exchange between wage labour and capital takes place, it has 'overlooked' the reproductive world of the 'family'.

What Pat Barker's novel shows with great clarity is the home as the reproductive centre of the capitalist system, the place where labour power is reproduced both in terms of its daily renewal and in terms of the reproduction of future generations of workers, and that this reproductive process is no less of a struggle against exploitation than the productive. Indeed, doubly so because 'reproductive' workers have to contend not only with the exploitative relations of capitalism but also with those of patriarchy. The women in Union Street live so defensively for their lives are a constant struggle against economic exploitation which keeps them perpetually 'short' – of money, food, clothing, heating and adequate housing – as well as against the, often violent, exploitation of men. And it is through the use of 'bad' language that they express their situation and at the same time relieve the tensions and unresolved conflicts of the family environment. There is no tenderness in the tone of these utterances. When Kelly calls her mother's latest boyfriend a 'wooly-faced bugger' we know it is said in a different tone of voice from that in which one might call someone 'a poor old bugger'. For this is the language of people who always have their guard up, vulnerable people afraid of showing weakness, of being alone, of being loveless, above all of being hurt emotionally and physically. That is what produces the characteristic intonation of the women's speech, that characteristic tone of voice which bespeaks their awareness of their common situation. It is not that the 'bad' language *reflects* the violence of the situation, but that it expresses a definite attitude towards it which goes beyond mere description being, in effect, an *evaluation* of the situation.

The use of 'bad' language is not simply a reflexive technique for producing an illusion of verisimilitude, a device used by the author to show, through the frequent use of 'swear words' how 'real' or 'authentic' are her working-class characters or situations. Traditionally, certain linguistic devices such as dialect words, malapropisms, misspellings and so on have been used to *signify* the working class through dialogue. Barker does not use 'bad' language in this way. 'Bugger off' in *Union Street* is not equatable with 'gorn orf' as a device to signify that the speaker is working class. Indeed, we should not think of Barker's use of 'bad' language as 'signifying' meanings or states of mind or 'things' but as language which is productive of a genuine difference. In this she achieves what neither Tressell nor Common were able to achieve, a genuine working-class voice without recourse to what Common called 'the traditional outbreaks of funny spelling':[38]

> finally there it was: a smooth, gleaming, satiny turd. She picked it up and raised it to her face, smelling her own hot, animal stink. It reminded her of The Man's cock, its shape, its weight. She clenched her fist.[39]

There is a nakedness about this language and what might almost be called a fearlessness which prevents us from playing the old game of identification, the fusing of consciousnesses and ideal civilized sensibilities. I do not recognize in this girl who, as she watches the shit squeeze through her fingers, is reminded of the cock of the man who raped her, my Self. I am forced to recognize in the mirror of this work that the face which stares back at me is not my own – but another's.

When Kelly breaks into and vandalizes her school she tries to revenge herself against The Man and the impersonal system which will continue to exploit her throughout her life. In the place where she is being educated to assume her (reproductive) role in life Kelly daubs her excrement over the headmaster's office and writes the 'bad' words on the blackboard of her classroom: 'PISS, SHIT, FUCK. Then, scoring the board so hard that the chalk screamed, the worst word she knew: CUNT.'[40] In writing the worst word she knows, Kelly names the 'thing' she is to become and the functions being that 'thing' impose on her. For just as productive workers become reified into bearers of labour power who were interpellated accordingly as 'hands' – factory hands, mill hands – so reproductive workers become reified into bearers of children and are interpellated as 'housewives'. What the 'bad' language of the women of Union Street exposes is the reality behind that euphemism. In a world where productive workers are reduced to hands, reproductive workers are reduced to the worst work Kelly knew, to that *thing* at which George Harrison gazes, actually seeing it for the first time in his life: 'A gash? A wound? Red fruit bitten to the core?'; or up which Joanne Wilson's boyfriend thrusts himself, 'grinding and screwing and banging'; or through which Alice Bell's mother's womb would fall 'till the doctor came to put it in again'; or into which the doctor who examines Liza Goddard inserts his gloved and creamed fingers: or out of which Brenda King's aborted baby comes to die 'on the floor of the lavatory with the *News of the World* spread over him'. It is the worst word because it signifies subjection, that life sentence to which being a 'housewife' condemns a woman. As Iris King forewarns her daughters, 'a man can put his cap on, you can't, you're stuck with it. And it isn't months, it's years. Sixteen years. They don't do so much as that for murder.'[41]

Through the historical trajectory of the novel Barker suggests that there has been little change in the condition of the English working-class woman from the nineteenth century to the present. Although Alice Bell was born in the year in which *Jude the Obscure* was published, her last years have been devoted to saving enough out of her meagre social security money to avoid the two dreads of her life, the workhouse and a pauper's funeral. To pay for her funeral she deprives herself of heating and food, lying in bed in the bitter January days and nights wrapped in old newspapers haunted by the old rhyme she had chanted as a child:

> Rattle his bones
> Over the stones,
> He's only a pauper
> Whom nobody owns.

The class memory of the 'Bastilles of the poor', of which the name of the street in which the women live is a constant reminder, takes us back 140 years to the world of Oliver Twist. But it is not only the memory of the past but also present experience which forges links with the nineteenth century. To the leering, form-filling social security official who tries to get her to go into a 'home' Alice is just another 'case'. 'It's not a workhouse now', he says. 'In your day it was. But it's all changed now.' But, of course it has not changed from Alice Bell's perspective. Strip lighting, central heating and 'your meat and two veg' do nothing to change the underlying social relations. And that is what the workhouse means to Mrs Bell, the system of exploitation for which she is now, in her words, 'Rubbish. Ready for the tip'.

But this old campaigner for whom socialism was a way of life does not give in. She fights, literally, to the death 'to keep for herself the conditions of a human life'. That she feels she has to do this by freezing to death alone on a park bench is both a tribute to her indomitable spirit and a terrible indictment of a society in which, at least for those like Mrs Bell, there is no alternative. Her experience had been of a life of struggle, both personal and political, which had brought little change for the better – rather, indeed, to the contrary for, remembering her youth, she finds that 'she was poorer now than she'd been then. And worse housed'. Yet despite the woeful inadequacy of Alice's present house it is her *home* and that is what they threaten to take away from her. To 'them' it means only dirt and disorder while to her it means independence and the last vestiges of human dignity. In perhaps nothing so much as in Alice's last struggle to cling to her reduced and squalid house do we see what the word 'home' signifies in *Union Street*. For working-class women like Alice Bell and Iris King home does not mean *property*, ownership, possessions; it means a space of their own. It is that space, inadequate, cramped and often dreadfully overcrowded though it might be, which assumes an enormous importance in Iris King's life.

For Alice Bell the dread of pauperism becomes, at the end, a struggle to avoid that awful place of final abandonment, the workhouse. The terror against which Iris King struggles is homelessness. Just as for the older woman the workhouse is more than a building, so for the younger, Wharf Street is more than a row of houses. To Iris King it means the abandonment, poverty, hunger, beatings and above all homelessness of her childhood during the

1930s. 'She was no longer in Wharf Street, but Wharf Street was still in her. She remembered it. Knew it. Knew every brick of it.' And just as Alice's £100 is not only funeral expenses but a kind of talisman against the final indignity of a pauper's funeral, so Iris's 'nice house' is a talisman against Wharf Street. She takes a pleasure in housework because it is a way of controlling the chaos which Wharf Street represents and her beloved china cabinet is a polished and gleaming altar to order, stability, permanence. Her life is a constant battle against 'the blackness that came from her past', that chaos of 'men in prison, women spending the social security money on the prize Bingo, kids dragged up anyhow'. It was into that blackness that Iris felt her daughter's pregnancy would plunge her. Again, Barker makes us feel the iniquity of a society which forces people to make the kinds of choices Iris King has to make in order to survive. This woman, who mothers half the street, ends by burying her daughter's aborted baby in the rubble of a waste site of derelict houses.

What impresses about these intensely felt, intensely suffered experiences is their *materiality*. There is a complete absence of 'spiritual' or psychological introspection, a fact which emphasizes the distance between Barker's writing and that which articulates the middle-class obsession with the 'inner life', the self-reflexive discourse of subjective individuality. But they also point to another of the novel's characteristics, namely the tension which exists between the peculiar intimacy of domestic life and the isolation which the women experience in their daily lives, which is much more akin to Tressell's workers than the inhabitants of Common's community of the streets. And this raises the question as to the nature of the relation between the individual and the community in *Union Street*. There are passages in the novel which seem to suggest, at first glance, an unbridgeable separateness between people. But the recurring images of isolation – Kelly trapped in the blind alley by the rapist, Alice Bell lying in her frozen yard, the isolation of birth and death in a hospital ward – are not images of the ontological solitariness which characterizes the human condition, but images of social failure. Loneliness there is certainly, as there · is individual human weakness, but it is not *inescapable*. Muriel Scaife's sense of desolation after the death of her husband is not all there is, for the experience is balanced by her continuing involvement in the lives of her children. And Liza Goddard's acceptance of her daughter forges a bond which is more than maternal. She experiences joyful solidarity in the recognition of the woman in the child, and draws strength from that. Above all there is the unity between the two most lonely figures, Kelly and Alice, in the park. There are two versions of this final meeting, first the young girl's, second the old woman's. In the first, Kelly gets an intimation of her own mortality and stares at the dying Alice 'as if she held, and might communicate, the secret of life'.[42] In Alice Bell's last moments the two hold hands:

> The girl held out her hand. The withered hand and the strong young hand met and joined. There was silence. Then it was time for them both to go. So that in the end there were only the birds, soaring, swooping, gliding, moving in a never-ending spiral about the withered and unwithering tree.[43]

And so they take their separate ways, the young girl to go home, the old woman to die. But those ways are, in the end, one. As Kelly leaves, her attention is attracted by a sound like the chirping of the starlings gathering in the park trees to roost for the night. It was the chatter of the women coming out of the bakery. Most began to run 'anxious to get home, to cook the dinner, to make a start on the housework'. Some stay to chat awhile, one, probably Joanne Wilson, is met by her boyfriend. 'Kelly stared after them, hungrily. Then she bent her head and followed in their footsteps. She was going home.' There was no need for Alice Bell to communicate the secret of life, for as Kelly watched it opened out before her: the bakery, courtship, marriage, children, housework, old age, death. As a working-class girl Kelly was going home to begin the life to which history had destined her.

Kelly Brown's tale is the first episode in a story which operates at both historical and symbolic levels. While the novel is located at a particular historical moment it also moves progressively back in time through the remembered life experiences of the characters to the 1890s. But because of its cyclic structure it also looks forward to its future and our present. Thus implicit in the novel are the various 'ages' of capital from its 'imperial' stage at the turn of the century to its present 'post-industrial' stage. But this historical time span is mirrored in the three score years and ten of a single symbolic life for each chapter bears the name of a progressively older woman which, taken together, cover the first seven decades of the twentieth century. Thus the novel can be read as a cyclic tale dramatizing the seven ages of woman in industrialized Britain from childhood to old age. Against the historical experiences of the individual women, experiences of poverty and hardship, cruelty and loneliness, is set the final image of 'the withered and unwithering tree', the symbol of womanhood. While the individual woman, Alice Bell, 'the tree in winter' withers, the life bearing goes on and her final vision is of the tree of life singing in a blaze of light.

Like Tressell's and Common's novels, Barker's is written from a particular location on the 'periphery'. It is a position which is determined by a number of diverse co-ordinates – political, ideo-logical, geographical, historical, economic as well as class and gender. What we get in *Union Street* is a specific view of the situation of working-class women in 'post-industrial' Britain. And while this view is inevitably partial it is one which links a historically specific situation to a more general life experience of women in urban patriarchal societies. While this is no more 'the whole story' than that told by other writers on the periphery, it enables us to see in new, or at least different, ways. For these novels are like fractured mirrors located on the borders of a mythical united kingdom which reflect back the cohering images beamed out from the centre but now fractured, fragmented, splintered. And in those refracted images the unifying myths of nationhood are revealed as the ideological forms of a rapacious class exploitation.

This essay has been largely concerned with the absence of certain writing from the canon of English literature. The construction of that canon played an important role in the forging of the ideological hegemony of the English ruling class contributing to the development of a nationalist ideology of a United Kingdom, a *Great* Britain ruling over an even greater British Empire. The establishment of a national culture was, as Matthew Arnold perceived, a priority for a class which was claiming the role of world leadership for itself. Hegemonic ideology gave the appearance of a united nation to a society resting upon a foundation of smouldering class conflict which periodically flared into open class struggle. What better bearer of a common cultural heritage in which all could feel pride, which excluded no one and which bore witness to a common and unifying human nature than English Literature?

What is absent from this account, however, is English literature's imperial role. The ideology of British imperialism was largely based on the assumption of a 'natural' superiority. It was a superiority, however, which carried with it a heavy moral duty. The white man's burden was to carry civilization to the lesser breeds of the earth. In point of fact, this civilizing mission had quite limited utilitarian aims, namely to educate a native subaltern class of junior officials and administrators. Whatever the intention, the implanting of English in those colonial regions has born a fruit undreamed of by the lesser breed's pastors and masters. And it is, arguably, in post-colonial writing that we find the most acute perceptions of the centre, for these peripheral visions see metropolitan culture in all its shabby duplicity, exposing it precisely as a *dominating* culture. Taken together, these peripheral visions, these fractured images of class and gender and race, begin to form a new perception of society as a decentred totality. Against the spurious unity which ruling ideologies attempt to impose on class societies the writing from the margins emphasizes the real complexity of social life. It recomplicates what ideology strives to simplify and fragments the unifying myths of national unity.

References

[1] Raymond Williams, 'Region and class in the novel', *Writing in Society* (London, Verso, n.d.), p.230.

[2] Ibid., p.232.

[3] Doris Lessing, *The Summer Before the Dark* (Harmondsworth, Penguin, 1979), p.69.

[4] Sebastiano Timpanaro, *On Materialism* (London, NLB, 1980), p.31.

[5] F. R. Leavis, *The Great Tradition* (Harmondsworth, Penguin, 1974), p.27.

[6] Ibid., p.146.

[7] Virginia Woolf, 'Women and fiction', in *Women and Writing*, ed. Michele Barrett (London, The Women's Press, 1979), pp.44–52.

[8] Lionel Trilling, *The Liberal Imagination* (London, The Women's Press, 1954), pp.59–60.

[9] Georg Lukács, *The Theory of the Novel*, trans. Anna Bostock (London, Merlin Press, 1971), p.78.

[10] Ibid., p.80.

[11] Terry Eagleton, *Literary Theory* (Oxford, Blackwell, 1983), p.194.

[12] Robert Tressell, *The Ragged Trousered Philanthropists* (London, Lawrence & Wishart, 1984), p.278.

[13] Raymond Williams, 'The Ragged-*arsed* Philanthropists', *Writing in Society*, op. cit., p.246.

[14] Ibid., p.247.

[15] Joseph Conrad, in Paul O'Flinn, *Them and Us in Literature* (London, Pluto Press, 1975), p.40.

[16] Jack Common, 'The freedom of the street', *The Freedom of the Streets* (London, 1938), p.55.

[17] Ibid., pp.55–6.

[18] Jack Common, *Kiddar's Luck* (Newcastle upon Tyne, Frank Graham, 1975), p.111.

[19] Ibid., p.20–4.

[20] Ibid., p.164.

[21] Ibid., p.184.

[22] Charles Dickens, *Little Dorrit* (London, Collins, 1964), p.40.

[23] Joseph Conrad, *The Secret Agent* (Harmondsworth, Penguin, 1971), p.74.

[24] D. H. Lawrence, *Lady Chatterley's Lover* (Harmondsworth, Penguin, 1960), p.158.

[25] *Kiddar's Luck*, p.166.

[26] Jack Common, 'The right to get drunk', *The Freedom of the Streets*, op. cit., p.96.

[27] Ibid., p.80.

28 Jack Common, *Kiddar's Luck*, op. cit., p.102.
29 Idem, 'The eclipse of the person', *The Freedom of the Streets*, op. cit., pp.24–5.
30 Idem, 'The freedom of the street', *The Freedom of the Streets*, op. cit., p.72.
31 Ibid., p.75.
32 Ibid.
33 Louis Althusser, 'Marxism and Humanism', *For Marx*, trans. Ben Brewster (Harmondsworth, Penguin, 1969), p.233.
34 Pat Barker, *Union Street* (London, Virago, 1982), pp. 48, 58, 64.
35 See E. J. Hobsbawm, op. cit., pp.283–6.
36 David Thomson, *England in the Twentieth Century* (Harmondsworth, Penguin, 1981), p.321.
37 Brendon Sewill, quoted in David Thompson, op. cit., p.317.
38 Jack Common, *The Ampersand* (London, Frank Graham, 1954), Author's Introduction.
39 Pat Barker, *Union Street*, op. cit., pp.55–6.
40 Ibid., p.56.
41 Ibid., p.201.
42 Ibid., p.67.
43 Ibid., p.265.

Index